WITHDRAWN

THE
RELEVANCE
OF
CULTURE

WITHDRAWN

Many, many years ago I flirted with
the notion of ecological determinism. A
teacher and friend took me aside and fed
me a quick dose of wisdom. This book owes
its origin to Charles Wagley's statement:
Morris, *culture* really does exist!

THE
RELEVANCE
OF
CULTURE

EDITED BY
MORRIS FREILICH

CARL A. RUDISILL LIBRARY
LENOIR-RHYNE COLLEGE

Bergin & Garvey Publishers
New York • Westport, Connecticut • London

GN
357
.R45
1989
150276
Nov.1990

Library of Congress Cataloging-in-Publication Data

The Relevance of culture / Morris Freilich.
      p. cm.
    Includes bibliographical references.
    ISBN 0–89789–181–3 (alk. paper)
    ISBN 0–89789–180–5 (pbk. : alk. paper)
    1. Culture. 2. Anthropology—Philosophy. I. Freilich, Morris.
GN357.R45   1989
306—dc20   89–17729

Copyright © 1989 by Bergin & Garvey Publishers

All rights reserved. No portion of this book may be
reproduced, by any process or technique, without the
express written consent of the publisher.

Library of Congress Catalog Card Number: 89–17729
ISBN: 0–89789–181–3
ISBN: 0–89789–180–5 (pbk.)

First published in 1989

Bergin & Garvey Publishers, One Madison Avenue, New York, NY 10010
A division of Greenwood Press, Inc.

Printed in the United States of America

The paper used in this book complies with the
Permanent Paper Standard issued by the National
Information Standards Organization (Z39.48–1984).

10 9 8 7 6 5 4 3 2 1

CONTENTS

Introduction

IS CULTURE STILL RELEVANT?

Morris Freilich

Every decade or so it is necessary to retool.[1] Old concepts which have died must be buried. New concepts which are vibrant must be mastered. The question is: Which of the old have actually died, and which of the new are actually vibrant? I limit my remarks to one old concept: culture. Is culture dead, as some say? Most scholars find culture very much alive. To them, I hasten to say: I come to praise culture, not to bury it. But critics of culture must be answered, and their ancestry revealed. Culture, just recently, was the central, integrating idea in anthropology, a construct which gave anthropology a distinctive personality within the social sciences. But as more and more disciplines were sold on the value of culture, the sellers broke rank. Let me begin with a few examples.

Chapple and Coon (1942) wrote a sophisticated text book in which "even the word 'culture' was expunged except for a few oversights" (Kroeber 1952: 34). Hallpike (1971) claimed that society rather than culture was the central concept in anthropology. Murdock (1972), at a Huxley Memorial Lecture, proposed that ideas such as culture were "illusory conceptual abstractions." Laughlin (1972) proclaimed that culture was dead. Moore argued (1974) that culture was an ideological position, not a scientific concept. And Wolf, in a Distinguished Lecture in America (1982), presented culture as more of a problem than a panacea. What happened to culture, triggering responses such as these? What is happening to culture, giving it the vigor of a young concept?

The historical question "What happened to culture?" will be given two different answers. The first is based on a structural equation: concepts grab meanings the way endomorphs grab food. Both concepts and endomorphs, it is suggested, tend to grab indiscriminately. Therefore, for both these systems, size is a function of age: the older the system, the larger it tends to be. Culture is an old concept. Necessarily then, it must be big or overflowing with meaning. Such a fat concept impedes rather than aids the development of a human science. In short, the "old concepts get fat" thesis concludes that culture is no longer relevant as a scientific concept.

The second answer is based on a quite different interpretation of culture history. It posits that complexities — many meanings, various formulations, different research strategies — are natural for concepts that are basic. Over time, much superfluous information is weeded out, so that the concept's essence is able to shine forth. History is now seen as a process which includes *progressive simplification and clarification*. These two interpretation of culture's history focus on different aspects of that history. Both interpretations make sense, but the latter, I believe, makes better sense.[2]

OLD CONCEPTS GET FAT

Professional anthropology found rather than invented culture. The culture captured by anthropologists was already heavy. Coming from the Latin *cultura* and *cultus*, culture originally designated cultivation, as in *agri cultura*, the cultivation of the soil. Later culture grabbed a set of related meanings: training, adornment, fostering, worship, and cult. From its root meaning as an activity, culture became transformed into a condition, a state of being cultivated. In the Roman Empire, culture became synonymous with *humanitas*, the human against the animal state; with *urbanitas*, the superior condition of the city dweller and citizen; and with *civilitas*, the cultivation of those with civility and good manners. For the Germans such notions as humanitas, urbanitas, civilitas represented superficial ways of being cultivated. For them, *Kultur* was tied to *Bildung*, the cultivation of a complex inner life. A person who had *Kultur* had education — transmitted knowledge — and profound mental and spiritual capacities.

Montesquieu (in *l'Ésprit des lois*, 1784) and Voltaire (in *Essai sur les moeurs*, 1757) anticipated modern anthropological interpretations of culture. They wrote of the *genius of the people*, the *general spirit* and *style* of life. Between Montesquieu and Voltaire, on the one hand, and the developers of a science of culture on the other, stands a host of scholars; far too many for full treatment in a short essay. Among the more notable are the English critic, essayist, and poet Matthew Arnold (1822–1888), the Swiss historian Jacob Burckhardt (1818–1897), and the German writer Johann Gottfried Herder (1744–1803). The great variety of ideas woven around culture left its mark on early anthropological writings and understandably so, for old conceptualizations tend to fade away rather than disappear. And in this fading process strange mixtures of ideas cling together and creep into the work of many scholars.

Sir Edward Tylor inherited just such a strange mixture of ideas. He clung to notions of superior (*civilized*) societies, when such ideas contradicted some of his other ideas. And he held on to beliefs about *savage* and *barbaric* societies when such beliefs similarly fuzzied up aspects of his conceptual framework. Such incongruities, I suggest, led to a definition which was either strategically or accidentally ambiguous. In Tylor's words:

> Culture, or civilization, taken in its wide ethnographic sense, is that complex whole which includes knowledge, belief, art, morals, law, custom, and any other capabilities and habits acquired by man as a member of society. (1871: 1)

"Culture or civilization," when taken in the context of Tylor's evolutionary views, could have two interpretations. First, culture is synonymous with civilization, and therefore only the civilized have culture. This interpretation conflicts with other writings by Tylor and makes the title of his book *Primitive Culture* (1871) into nonsense. Second, the terms culture and civilization describe a limited number of shared characteristics: knowledge, belief, art, morals. This interpretation gives culture to the noncivilized and weakens Tylor's arguments for distinguishing people into savages, barbarians, and civilized. After all, even the lowly savage has knowledge, art, morals, and law.

Tylor's fuzziness on culture makes sense when considered from the dual perspectives of fashion and conceptual problems. In the nineteenth century, culture was often discussed as synonymous with civilization (Leopold 1980). By writing "culture or civilization," Tylor kept his work in the mainstream of social thought, thus maximizing chances for its acceptability. Conceptually, Tylor struggled with a puzzle which can be presented as two related problems: (1) *The animal problem*. Humans belong to the animal kingdom. Why then do human societies differ dramatically from animal societies? (2) *The human problem*. *Homo sapiens* is a distinct species with many common biopsychical characteristics. Why then do human cultures differ so drastically?[3]

Tylor's attempts to solve this two-problem puzzle included a juggling of three concepts: *evolution*, *psychic unity*, and *culture*. To keep things moving smoothly, culture had to be given two faces: a rational, problem-solving mask and a mysterious, self-regulating mask. To maintain logically sound arguments, humans, similarly, had to be presented in dualistic fashion: as creative manufacturers of culture and as passive receivers of culture. Let me explain.

To solve the animal problem, humans had to be distinguished from other animals and presented as special animals. These different animals were special because they had culture — a system of knowledge and beliefs — which everywhere was essentially similar. Humans had similar culture because they shared a biopsychic unity, similar environments, and similar challenges. As Opler summarized Tylor's views:

> Everywhere there was need for protection against the elements and foes, human and nonhuman. Throughout most of the world, nature provided materials to be utilized for shelter, dress, and artifacts, and in nearly all regions, sufficient animal and vegetable food existed to support human groups. The world and its people appeared to Tylor to be a vast laboratory in which uniform causes operating in similar settings might be expected to yield comparable results. (1964: 125)

Wielding Ockham's razor ferociously, Tylor attacked the animal problem and came up with a simple formula: Similar systems, encountering similar problems, developed similar solutions called "cultures." In solving the animal problem, Tylor presented humans as creative animals who creatively manufacture culture. This *creativity focus* can be summarized by three propositions: (1) Humans are actively involved in the creation of culture; (2) Culture is a problem-solving system; and (3) Culture, essentially, is the same everywhere.

To solve the human problem, humans had to be distinguished from each other. Given a psychic unity of mankind, and given similar environments and similar problems of survival, how can cultural differences be explained? Tylor's simple answer was evolution — not biological evolution, but cultural evolution. Again let us turn to Opler for a summary of Tylor's position:

> In successive evolutionary stages family life becomes more secure, thinking more logical, knowledge more detailed, artifacts more efficient, religion more firmly wedded to morality, and abundance more general. Tylor applied this conception of evolutionary progress through stages of Savagery, Barbarism, and Civilization. . . . (1964: 130)

Culture, like man, evolves, and cultural evolution, like biological evolution, is progressive. Hence, inferior forms regularly give way to superior forms. Just as humans are superior to nonhuman animals, so civilization is superior to barbaric and savage culture. Within this evolutionary frame, culture invariably moves along a path whose endpoint is civilization. Individuals, moreover, inevitably ride on a cultural elevator whose directions read "Up only!"

When tied to inevitable, unilinear evolution, psychic unity has a changed meaning. Now psychic unity means that all humans can accept progress. And progress, the way Tylor understood it, includes radical changes in the human mind. For example, beliefs and practices subsumed under magic came from "a condition of mind which we of the advanced races have almost outgrown." In the lowly state of culture, humans have a primitive mentality. They believe "that between the object and the image of it there is a real connection. . .and that it is accordingly possible to communicate an impression of the original through the copy" (Tylor 1865: 3, 120).

Note that Tylor's explanation of cultural differences, with the aid of cultural evolution, transforms the human animal from a creative being who creates culture to a passive receptacle into which culture is poured. Tylor's *passivity focus* includes three propositions: (1) Humans passively accept culture; (2) Culture is mysteriously programmed for progress; and (3) Various cultures represent different stages in cultural evolution. By presenting what I call a creativity focus and a passivity focus, Tylor was promoting inconsistent views of culture and humans. This "sin" committed by the father of cultural anthropology, consistent with Old Testament teachings, was visited upon his children for several generations.

While Tylor was unable to resolve this dualistic view of humans, his definition of culture broadcasts a partiality towards passivity. This is more obvious when his definition is translated into more modern language: Culture is a system of information *acquired by* humans as members of society.

Tylor's vision of culture influenced anthropological thinking for at least fifty years. Particularly influential was his passivity focus, with its stress on cultural evolution, mysteriously self-regulated for progress. Franz Boas strongly disagreed with a mysterious culture directing passive humans. In his words:

> It is hardly necessary to consider culture a mystic entity that exists outside the society and of its individual carriers, and that moves mysteriously by its own force. The life of society is carried on by individuals who act singly and jointly under the stress of their own activities. (1928: 235–36)

Boas's great concern with empirical research, according to some scholars, hindered the development of culture theory (Wax 1972). Kroeber went so far as to say that Boas was not interested in discussing a distinct cultural level.

> Tylor defined culture, Boas estimated very justly many of its properties and influences, but the thesis of a distinct cultural level interested neither of them. Indeed it has been left largely to myself and then to Leslie White to propound it explicitly. (1952: 15)

Whatever Boas did, for or against culture (cf. Stocking 1968, 1974), his emphasis on empirical research changed the meaning of what could be considered as valid data. With Boas came the end of the rubber-data stage of Tylorian anthropology. Data were no longer stretchable to fit the models of armchair theorists. With the coming of a holy-data era, anthropologists defined their labors as including fieldwork: collecting data firsthand. With the zeal and dedication of missionaries, anthropologists combed the globe in search of interesting tribes to study.

Fieldwork gave anthropology a special personality in the social sciences. And frequent trips to "the field" transformed anthropologists into professional wanderers, marginal natives abroad and marginal academics at home (cf. Freilich 1970). These interesting roles had some important influences on culture. In the service of science, anthropologists wandered from tribe to tribe and whatever they brought home was defined as culture. Culture had to find a place for life histories, settlement-pattern charts, data on curing ceremonies, and, among a host of other phenomena, axes, drums, and masks. In the service of personal survival, anthropologists wandered from academic department to academic department. Alliances were formed with, among others, law professors, sociologists, psychologists, ecologists, economists, psychiatrists, and historians. Soon joint projects were being developed, and allies quickly got sold on culture.[4] Put otherwise, wherever anthropologists went and whatever anthropologists did, culture was always an intimate companion. Culture became a concept for all seasons, an idea for all scholarship, and a perspective for all problems. To meet the requirements of a great variety of data, collected in a great variety of contexts, it was necessary to develop a great variety of explanations of culture. Anthropologists did not retreat from this challenge. In bold and insightful works, culture was linked to almost everything that could be imagined: for example, to migration of peoples and diffusion of ideas (Schmidt 1939), to basic needs (Malinowski 1931, 1944), to geography, ecology, and modes of production (Wissler 1917; Steward 1955), to child-rearing practices (Whiting & Child 1953), to national character (Gorer 1950), to patterns and configurations (Benedict 1934), and (among other connections) to themes in music (Opler 1945).

Linton's belief that culture actually was a twin, ideal culture and real culture (1936), was hailed as a significant contribution to cultural theory—a strange evaluation which merits some analysis. The ideal, surely, means rules, guides which ought to be followed. The real, clearly, means behavior, concrete, observable acts. But behavior comes in at least two different types: behavior consistent with the ideal (proper) and behavior inconsistent with the ideal (deviant). Linton's ideal/real, therefore, was a triad — rules, proper behavior, and deviant behavior — masquerading as a dichotomy. Linton deserves credit for pulling off a neat trick. He took a puzzling concept, made it enigmatic, and earned public applause.

Along with explanations — perspectives, models, and theories — came definitions of culture, dozens of them. Definers differentially focused on history, on normativeness, on values, on adjustment and human psychology, on learning, on sharedness, on habit, on sublimation, on structure, on ideas, on symbols, and on human association (Kroeber & Kluckhohn 1952). Consistent with the law of supply and demand, as the number of definitions increased, their price (read "value") decreased.

The minimal utility of most of the definitions of culture cannot be fully explained by the law of supply and demand. Additionally, those who worked on new definitions of culture seemed magnetically drawn to Tylor and his classical definition of culture. Put otherwise, many of the new definitions borrowed notions from Tylor, including ideas which made culture fuzzy (Pierce 1977). Thus some new definitions hovered between a humanistic conceptualization and an anthropological, relativistic conceptualization (Bidney 1953). Others lumped guides-to-action (rules, norms, values) with action and with the results of actions (material culture). Few scholars bothered to distinguish society from culture (Kroeber 1952) or tried to make cultural processes less mysterious. Culture, too many agreed, was a "vague abstraction" (Radcliffe-Brown 1949) which lacked "ontological reality" (Spiro 1951).

Four score or so years after Tylor's classic definition was published, a Harvard group counted and categorized definitions of culture. Their labors (Kroeber & Kluckhohn 1952) enabled anthropologists to discover quickly whose definition was being used. Still unclear was whose definition was useful. White's (1954) review of the Kroeber and Kluckhohn volume was a mixture of nostalgia and scientific concern. White lamented the disagreements that existed over the meanings of culture and attacked those who claimed that culture should be limited to *ideas*. To follow them, White argued, would be rather awkward, given the "long established tradition among ethnographers, archaeologists and museum curators of calling tools, masks, fetishes and so on, 'material culture'."[5]

Sciences advance by rejecting long-established traditions and by embracing rather awkward ideas. Galileo, for example, found it rather awkward to reject the long-established Ptolemaic system and to embrace the Copernican system. This does not mean that ideas should be promoted because they are rather awkward. For example, few conceptualizations can compete in awkwardness with Harris's definition of culture. Culture, he wrote,

> is actones, episodes, nodes, nodal chains, scenes, serials, nomoclones, permaclones, paragroups, nomoclonic types, permaclonic types, permaclonic systems and permaclonic supersystems. Culture is also phonemes, morphemes, words, semantically equivalent utterances, behavior plans, and many other emic things. Culture is any and all of the nomothetic nonverbal and verbal data language units previously defined. (1964: 168)

Murphy's view of Harris's metataxonomic approach to cultural things has become the accepted viewpoint. Here was a curiosity plagued by a "methodology that was so laborious that if pursued it would instantly end research" (Murphy 1975: 37).

It should be clear why, for some, culture is an unmanageable concept, useful primarily as a means of proving one's tribal identification. For these scholars, talk which uses culture becomes ritual: important for group solidarity, but irrelevant in so far as scientific work is concerned (cf. Moore 1974). My vote for the best ritual definition of culture is that presented by Kaplan and Manners. Culture, they write, is "a class of phenomena conceptualized by anthropologists in order to deal with questions they are trying to answer" (1972: 3).

CULTURE AND HUMAN UNIQUENESS

Culture's history can be interpreted as a development of an ever fuzzier concept. However, a different reading appears more convincing. A history which focuses on concept clarification gets its inspiration from the notion that humans are uniquely different animals. Wescott nicely captured the many facets of human uniqueness:

> [M]an is quite literally the only "divine"—that is, the only priest or spiritual practitioner in the animal world. Second, man is, literally again a "diviner"—a prophet or foreteller of the future. . . [Third, only man] can picture deity and communicate this picture to his fellows. . . . [Fourth,] man's prowess as a pyrotechnician, or wielder of fire, makes him a master of light and, to the extent of that mastery, an exponent of divinity. And finally, man's very anatomy endows him with divine dispositions. For his large brain and discerning eye are palpable organs of intelligence, and his behavior manifests powers of abstractions and insight unique among his congeners. Together they spell enlightenment. . . the very substance of divinity. (1969: 9–10)

The work of many scholars stimulated the continued clarification of the formula: *culture explains human uniqueness.* Two pioneers who deserve special mention are Adolph Bastian (1826–1905) and Clark Wissler (1870–1947). Bastian was impressed with the similarities which existed between different peoples. To help explain these similarities, he spoke of *Elementargedanken* (elementary ideas) which found specific expression as *Völkergedanken* (folk ideas) in different environments. His folk ideas were the demonstrable elements of culture (cf. Opler 1962). Wissler considered reflective thinking as lying at the base of culture. His definition of culture as a "complex of ideas" (1916: 197) provided a valuable base for some later developments.

In "The Superorganic," Kroeber (1917) kept culture theory on the human-uniqueness track. Culture, he wrote,

> rests in the past. . . [and] exists only in the mind. Gunpowder, textile arts. . . are not themselves transmitted from man to man or from generation to generation, at least not permanently. It is the perception, knowledge, and understanding of them, their *ideas* in the Platonic sense, that are passed along.

Like many works that dig for essences before the critical data are available, this one too was sharply attacked. Its critics, including such renowned scholars as Sapir (1917) and Goldenweiser (1917), argued that humans were not as unique as Kroeber believed. Culture, for them, was an intensification of elements which existed in elementary form among nonhuman primates: communication, play, learning, tool making, and social organization. Moreover, Kroeber downplayed human creativity. In its place, he put a mysterious superorganic process. Goldenweiser found this cavalier treatment of the "biographical individual" of dubious value. And Sapir similarly believed that the person could not be disregarded in the formulation of culture.

Kroeber's critics, by and large, focused on weaknesses in his superorganic approach.[6] They seemed to miss the fact that he had correctly identified three basic aspects of culture. Irrespective of culture's origin in evolutionary perspective, and irrespective of the manner in which it was passed on from generation to generation, as a *system*: (1) culture is a uniquely human phenomenon; (2) culture's essence is ideas; and (3) culture is old — it "rests in the past."

Inspired, perhaps, by the critics of "The Superorganic," Boas tried to include the biographical individual in his conceptualization. Culture, he wrote, "embraces all the manifestations of social habits of a community, the reactions of the individual as affected by the habits of a community, the reactions of the individual as affected by the habits of the group in which he lives, and the products of human activities as determined by the habits" (1930: 75). With Boas, the individual sits at the center of culture, but ideas lose out to vague notions of "social habits."

In two co-authored papers, Clyde Kluckhohn set the scene for modern developments in cultural theory. Writing with Mowrer (1944), Kluckhohn tried to free culture from its image of an all-powerful dictator. Culture, anthropologists were told, is but one among many determinants of human action. Writing with Kelly (1945), Kluckhohn tried to free culture from its utilitarian image. Culture is not necessarily functional and rational. Culture is presented as "all those historically created designs for living, explicit and implicit, rational, irrational and nonrational, which existed in any given time as potential guides for action." While Kluckhohn was a much respected anthropologist and while he regularly interacted with some of the major scientists of the day, his definition of culture never received the wide popularity of Linton's unfortunate dichotomy. Hocart explains this puzzle in a most convincing manner. Ideas, like clothes, are the slaves of fashion. Fashionable ideas, in the 1940s, were those linked to utilitarianism. Hence, for Hocart, popular theories of culture are "based on utilitarianism and not on facts" (1970: 129).

By linking culture to action, Kluckhohn could have been read as downplaying the role of culture in cognition. Such a criticism cannot be levied against Leslie White. For White, culture consists of things and events dependent on symboling: phenomena which have their existence "(1) within the human organisms. . . ; (2) within processes of social interaction among human beings; and (3) within material objects (axes, factories, railroads, pottery bowls) lying outside human organisms but within the patterns of social interaction among them"(1959: 235). White brought the individual into culture, albeit in a rather complex and a somewhat confusing manner. He then made the individual irrelevant by treating culture as if it were a process *sui generis,* moving mysteriously under its own steam. Tylor's ghost still haunted culture.

The individual was placed squarely and convincingly on center stage in Wallace's important book, *Culture and Personality.* For Wallace, all members of a social system do not have precisely the same knowledge of the social system. Moreover, all who do "business" with each other do not have the same motives. Given such differences, one wonders how order is created and maintained. While Wallace does not fully answer this gargantuan question, he does show how culture contributes to social order. Those who share a culture share general *policy* and make *contracts* with each other. As Wallace puts it, culture is

> policy, tacitly and gradually concocted by groups of people for the furtherance of their interests, and contracts, established by practice, between and among individuals to organize their strivings into mutually facilitating equivalence structures. (1970: 24)

"Cognitive nonuniformity" helps to explain how the participants of a sociocultural system are liberated "from the heavy burden of learning and knowing each other's motivations and cognitions" (1970: 35). Culture was being dragged away from being everything an ethnographer encounters in the field. A "dragger" of great distinction will speak for himself in the heart of this volume (ch. 5). Here I would but present his ideas in a brief quotation:

> Culture. . . consists in standards for deciding what is. . . what can be. . . what one feels about it, and for deciding how to go about doing it. (Goodenough 1961: 522)

"Standards" comes close to a definition with a very modern ring, a definition presented by Geertz in 1965:

> Culture is best seen not as complexes of concrete behavior patterns—customs, usages, traditions, habit cluster—as has, by and large, been the case up to now, but as a set of control mechanisms—plans, recipes, rules, instructions (what computer engineers call programs) for governing behavior. (p. 57)

CULTURE TODAY

Currently, the essential elements of culture appear to be known. However, they have yet to be pulled together artfully, presented operationally, and formulated in ways likely to stimulate new and productive research. Culture is old, parts of the past which have been reincarnated and given a halo. This treasure is daily given new form and new purposes as humans use culture in ever new contexts. Culture, then, is tradition (Shanklin 1981; Shils 1981), but it is also more than tradition. Culture, additionally, is ideas, what Kluckhohn and Kelly called "designs for living" and what, even more usefully, might be called a set of plans or a guidance system (cf. Randall 1987). Culture, as a guidance system, leads us to notice important differences between humans and other phenomena that get directed. When a guidance system directs missiles to a destination, generally that is where the missiles go. However, when humans are directed by culture, it is never certain what is likely to happen. Missiles and their guides have (so to speak) a harmonious relationship. Humans and their guides are often in conflict. Humans, or peculiar primates, create a peculiar guidance system, one that is praised, died for, evaded, avoided, and taught to young children. Intuitively, all we know about culture makes sense. But we must move from intuitive sense to a model which has predictive power and which generates exciting hypotheses.

Given that we have only reached the stage of intuitive sense with culture, in what ways is this concept relevant? This question is fully answered in the body of this volume. Here, and first, I wish to present relevance as excitement. Then I will attempt to show how relevance as excitement is actually part of a more complete model of relevance.

An exciting concept generates productive conflict. It attracts proponents and critics, and it triggers encounters between opponents which find an attentive audience. Such conflicts generally create camps, and fights between members of different camps tend to go far beyond the rules of scientific debate. Some scholars laments this type of catch-as-catch-can conflict. Such disagreements, they say, are not constructive; they create winners and losers rather than pathways to truth. I believe otherwise. As the erudite sociologist, Alvin Gouldner, somewhere wrote: In the primitive state of social science, the relevant question is not "Is X true?" Rather, the relevant question is "Is X interesting?" Put otherwise, social science, yet in its infancy, needs to generate ever more excitement among its practicing scholars. If a concept keeps us fighting, it keeps us thinking. Culture, currently, is generating conflict and excitement. The major debate is between the members of two camps: ideationalists and adaptationalists. Cultural ideationalists, including Claude Lévi-Strauss, David Schneider, Ward Goodenough, and Clifford Geertz, agree that essentially culture is ideas. Cultural adaptationalists, including A. P. Vayda, R. A. Rappaport, and M. Harris, agree that essentially culture is an adaptive mechanism. That is, most members of this camp believe that

> Cultures are systems (of socially transmitted behavior patterns) that serve to relate human communities to their ecological settings. . . . Culture change is primarily a process of adaptation and what amounts to natural selection. . . . Technology, subsistence economy and elements of social organizations directly tied to production are the most adaptively central realms of culture. . . . The ideational components of cultural systems may have adaptive consequences. . . . (Keesing 1974: 75–76)

Cultural ideationalists and cultural adaptationalists throw intellectual punches at whoever disagrees with them — be that rogue a member of their camp or a member of the enemy camp. To present an overview of these fights and the excitement they generate, I will summarize the positions of two members of the more popular camp (the cultural ideationalists) and one member of the minority camp (cultural adaptationalists). These summaries will include some of the attacks made by critics.

GEERTZ: THE GENRE IS FOR BLURRING

Interpretive anthropology, perhaps the most popular school in the ideational camp, deserves considerable attention. Under the leadership of Clifford Geertz, culture generates considerable excitement as a semiotic concept. Digging deeply into the work of Gilbert Ryle and translating his philosophical ideas into notions usable by anthropologists, Geertz is revitalizing an old link with philosophy. This revitalization movement has its own vision of culture. Culture is no longer a map lodged in human minds; it is no longer plans, recipes, and rules. Culture, now, is traffic in things which impose meaning. More completely, and in Geertz's words, culture is traffic in anything "that is disengaged from its mere actuality and used to impose meaning upon experience" (1973: 45). Within this context, human activity is well described as a "text," and a culture as an assemblage of texts.

In presenting texts to interested publics and in interpreting their meanings, anthropologists assume old roles with some new labels—observers, scribes, translators, and interpreters. The documents anthropologists present must be deeply embedded in the contextual richness of social life; a text, that is, must be a "thick" description. The problem is, it is quite easy to write a text that is thick, but it is very difficult to write a text that is valid. The problem has not escaped Geertz. He admits that it is difficult to fathom "what our informants are up to and what it all means." Curiously, he settles rather cheaply for "doing the best we can" and using a lot of guessing. In his words:

> Cultural analysis is (or should be) guessing at meaning, assessing the guesses, and drawing explanatory conclusions from the better guesses, not discovering the Continent of Meaning and mapping out its bodiless landscape. (1973: 15)

Guessing, a fundamental strategy in science, generally passes under the more prestigious name of hypothesizing. And hypothesizing, in traditional science, is but part of the opening moves. In the middle game and the end game scientists (1) build and use models and (2) utilize verification procedures. Instead of formal models, Geertz provides two general and rather strange images. Humans, for Geertz, are like spiders "suspended in webs of significance" (1965: 66) they themselves have spun. And culture can be considered as these self-spun webs. Put otherwise, spiders spin webs and catch prey; humans spin culture and catch themselves. Culture, beyond its thick content, also has organization. For Geertz, a useful image for organization are the tentacles of the octopus (1965: 66).

Having provided two images, Geertz tells interpretive anthropologists to do nook-and-cranny anthropology, to descend into detail and stare at the truth directly,

> past the misleading tags, past the metaphysical types, past the empty similarities to grasp firmly the essential character of not only the various cultures but the various sorts of individuals within each culture if we wish to encounter humanity face to face. (1973: 53)

Those who survive a face-to-face encounter with truth—very few, if we are to take Plato's image of the cave seriously—must then go on to make interpretations. And their interpretations can come from the free rein of the imagination, since verification procedures are nonexistent. Science's traditional end game here becomes "My intuition is better." As Charles Taylor has explained it, there are "no verification procedures we can fall back on. . . . We can only continue to offer interpretations." Ultimately, there is a reliance on deeper insight and superior intuitions. "Hence, if you don't understand it, then your intuitions are at fault, are blind or inadequate"(1979: 66–67).

Proponents describe the thick fruits of interpretive anthropology as rich in humanistic insights, as stimulating, as entertaining. Moreover, some anticipate a closer relationship with traditional science, a hope of finding "ways of moving back and forth between an actor's subjective interpretation and a set of objective determinants" (Rosaldo 1982: 198). While some, like Rosaldo, descend into detail and ascend to debate critics, Geertz keeps his nose to the ground. This strategy of flight from intellectual conflict, rather than fight against detractors, is strange (cf. Shankman 1984). For Geertz has praised interpretive anthropology as providing "a refinement of debate"(1973: 29).

Opponents of interpretive anthropology have presented strong arguments, a few of which will here be considered. Howe suggested that thick description is but detailed documentation of events and circumstances (1984: 274–75). As such it is, and for long has been, "the cornerstone of much anthropology whatever its theoretical framework." And, Howe continues, "to set up interpretive theory with its semiotic bent as the only alternative to comparative, so-called scientific explanation is spurious and tendentious."

Connor demonstrated that "nook-and-cranny" anthropology can lead to weighty errors. To present just a few, trance states in Bali are not what Geertz claims — they are not a crucial part of every ceremony — and they include a much wider range of emotions than those which Geertz describes (cf. Belo 1960: 219–25). Further, and still contrary to Geertz's writings, *nadi* is neither the only nor the main term associated with trance. As Connor writes, "It is difficult to understand how this obscure word could be rendered as the Balinese word for trance. . . . There are dozens more terms recorded that describe the phenomena associated with trance" (1984: 271). Connor concluded:

> Geertz shows that he is not aware of the single most important fact a phenomenological study of Balinese trance can produce: *that there is no generic term for "trance" in Balinese.* [italics mine]

Descent into detail seems to provide no insurance against grabbing faulty data. Clearly so, since some who stoop to conquer data arise truthless.

A puzzle remains: erudite and sensitive scholars see themselves as creating a necessary revolution in anthropological thinking. These genre-breaking professionals are attracting many bright and energetic students. How can so many, who are so gifted, be so deceived? I have three answers that probably make most sense when woven into each other. I will leave the weaving to the reader and present the answers separately. First, interpretive anthropology provides an enormous intellectual challenge. To mix knowledge from fieldwork with knowledge "from theater, painting, grammar, literature, law, play" (Geertz

1980: 178) is to participate in the "biggest game" in town. Who can resist a big game in which everybody wins? Every interpretation can be defined as a good interpretation!

A second answer comes from a provocative paper by Paul Friedrich. After identifying some weaknesses in interpretive anthropology, Friedrich points out its fascination for some, "comparing anthropologists with *ad hominen* intensity. Anthropologist-watching, like poet-watching, has come to sell better than ethnography and verse" (1985: 6). Interpretive anthropology, interpreting Friedrich, has all the allure of gossip about members of the family.

The final answer comes from a splendid 1986 paper by Melford Spiro. Interpretive anthropology, following Spiro, is locked into a flawed paradigm called "epistemological relativism" (ER). Looking at reality through flawed lenses, the interpretive anthropologists are forced into false analogies and unpromising strategies. Burdened by epistemological relativism, the brightest minds must falter. Let us consider the ER paradigm, concentrating on its cracks.

ER postulates that "virtually all human and social psychological charac-teristics are culturally determined." This "wholesale cultural determinism" is linked to "an all but limitless view of cultural diversity" (Spiro 1986: 261). Since cultures differ radically from each other, cultural comparisons are impossible. How can the radically different be compared? What standards could be used with which to compare? Generalizations across cultures become, essentially, meaningless. Hence, *a science of culture* becomes impossible. If native watchers are no longer scientists, what are they? And, what is their purpose? Here hermeneutics enters as a savior of an established but floundering profession. Anthropology is redefined as an interpretive or hermeneutic discipline. As such it can join forces with other interpretive enterprises: theater, painting, literature. Where, then, are the cracks in the foundations?

Following ER, humans raised in different cultures are so different that it makes no sense to speak of the psychic unity of mankind. But, as Spiro argues (1986: 259–86), if no psychic unity exists, how is it possible to interpret meanings from cultures which are not our own? Interpretive anthropologists, in a hunt to kill scientific anthropology, fall into a dilemma. If interpretation is possible, then so is comparative anthropology, with its valuable fruits called cross-cultural generalizations. However, if comparative anthropology is really impossible, then so is interpretive anthropology. Interpretive anthropology can cast a blind eye to this dilemma and try to keep moving straight ahead. Or, interpretive anthropology can make a sharp right turn. "Straight ahead" will continue to provide all the excitement of a big game where everyone is a winner. A sharp move to the right will require a scientific commitment to methodology and theory. Interpretive anthropologists prepared to move to the right have valuable allies close at hand. I will briefly discuss two sources of assistance.

Ricoeur and his followers consider ethnographic accounts as texts. Ricoeur, however, has developed a text model (1971) which generates meanings linked to culturally specific assumptions. Using Ricoeur's text model, Bentley (1984: 642–65) was able to present a convincing interpretation of Morano disputing.

There is no reason to suppose that Ricoeur's text model would not be equally useful for work in many other cultures on many other topics.

Ethnomethodologists view human reality in much the same way as interpretive anthropologists do. Here in ethnomethodology lies a goldmine of information "wherein the constants [read "culture"] are neither in the individual nor in the world, but rather in the relation between the two" (Rawls 1985: 132). These words, coming from an ethnomethodologist, could easily have been written by a Geertzian interpretive anthropologist (cf. Garfinkel 1967; Sacks 1979; Jefferson & Lee 1981).[7]

Schneider: Culture and Norms as Siamese Twins

David Schneider's theory of culture is one of very few which seriously considers the difference between culture and social norms. Culture, Schneider writes, "concerns the stage, the stage setting and the cast of characters" (1972: 38). Norms are guides to action, "detailed and specific instructions for how the culturally significant parts of the act are to be performed, as well as the contexts in which they are proper" (1976: 200).

Schneider goes on to specify how culture and norms function in our lives and how these two subsystems of sociocultural existence interact. For Schneider, the essence of culture is a system of symbols and meanings:

> By symbols and meanings I mean the basic premises which a culture posits for life: what its units consist in; how these units are defined and differentiated; how they form an integrated order or classification; how the world is structured; in what parts it consists and on what premises it is conceived to exist, the categories and classifications of the various domains of the world of man and how they relate to one another and the world that man sees himself living in. (1972: 38)

Schneider's image of the order created by culture and norms and the internal order of, respectively, culture and norms is quite complex. Culture is made up of a number of "galaxies," and norms come in interrelated sets called "institutions." Each galaxy consists of a set of interrelated symbols and meanings, unified by one dominant or epitomizing symbol. And a total culture can be characterized by a small number of epitomizing symbols.

It might be thought that institutions are isomorphic with galaxies. Following Schneider, this is not so. Given cultural galaxies crosscut and intersect different institutional structures. This dispersal of sets of symbols and meanings (i.e., galaxies) over various institutions differs from one society to another. How it works in a given system therefore becomes a problem to be researched. Indeed, as Schneider explained, studying the dispersal of symbols and meanings is critical to understanding their relative importance in different contexts:

> It is in the way in which symbols and meanings are dispersed throughout the normative system that defines the meanings of a symbol, that demonstrates which symbols are clustered into galaxies, and that reveals how meanings are ordered and recorded in relation to each other. (1976: 205)

In short, to understand culture well we must study norms. Moreover, the study of norms, by themselves, keeps us far away from symbols and meanings, the fundamental stuff which distinguishes human from animal society. Hence, initially culture and norms must be studied together. They must be treated as if they were Siamese twins. This togetherness of culture and norms is presented by Schneider in various ways:

> Norms are patterns for action which apply to some culturally defined unit. . . . [C]ertain bundles of norms make a distinct culturally designated entity. . . . Every norm has cultural aspects embedded in it. . . . The study of culture is concerned . . . with the question of "meaning-in-action." (1976: 199–201)

Yet for certain purposes, it is necessary to dissect the twins in order to ask some critical questions: How are norms structured? How are they organized as patterns for action? How are symbols and meanings of a culture structured? How do the symbols and meanings of a culture relate to its patterns for action, from the point of view of the normative system? How do the patterns of action of a culture relate to its symbols and meanings, from the point of view of the cultural system?

Schneider has thoughtfully and usefully distinguished a social system ("norms") from a cultural system ("culture"). This sophisticated theory of a sociocultural system — its elements, its interrelationships, and its key questions — needs to be tested. One hopes some members of the ideationalist camp will take Schneider's Siamese twins into many diverse field settings.

Harris: Culture Is Smart

The prolific productivity of Marvin Harris continues to enliven discussions of culture and cultures. Wisely abandoning his earlier metataxonomic approach to culture, Harris now focuses on the nature of the individual as a strategy to think about culture. Using a mixture of Skinnerian psychology and materialist philosophy, Harris presents a curious picture of what makes *Homo sapiens* tick. The typical human, in any culture, can best be understood as a system which needs to eat, which needs love and affection, which has a powerful sex drive, and which desires to expend minimal energy in the pursuance of goals (1979: 63). Of critical importance is the human need to eat, with a special hunger for protein. From this perspective, society is a business organized to satisfy human needs and desires. Culture is a clever set of institutions designed to create the means and mechanisms for providing food, love, affection, and sex. Culture's cleverness lies in its highly rational approach in reaching goals and especially in the use of economizing techniques: costs are minimized and benefits maximized. Harris's theory of humans, society, and culture is presented to professional anthropologists and to the public at large in a varied assortment of publications. Here I can but sample bits and pieces of a few of his works.

In *Cultural Materialism: The Struggle for a Science of Culture* (1979), Harris speaks to his peers in neo-Marxian language. A science of culture can be developed because human life is determined. In simplest terms infrastructure (I) determines superstructure (S), or I→S. More completely presented, I—*the mode of production* (subsistence technology, technoenvironmental relationships, ecosystems, and work patterns) and the mode of reproduction (demography, mating patterns, infant care, and population control mechanisms) – creates or determines S – *the behavioral superstructure* (the arts, ritual, advertisement, recreational activities, and science) and the *emic and mental superstructure* (knowledge, thoughts, and ideology). Although Harris postulates that feedback operates from the mental superstructure to the rest of the system, this process is never elaborated theoretically. Nor is feedback explicitly utilized in the analysis of specific cases. Essentially, this neo-Marxian model is presented as if feedback, a fundamental process for all human systems, was relatively unimportant on the human scene (cf. Harris 1979: 52–56).

As Westen (1984: 642) argues pointedly, science is part of superstructure. Superstructure is determined by infrastructure. Hence Harris's science of culture is determined by the infrastructure within which Harris lives: American subsistence technology, technoenvironmental relationships, work patterns. Harris's model appears to sit on a curious dilemma. If the model is correct, Harris's analyses are suspect, because they are predetermined by his infrastructure. If the model is incorrect, then the analyses are equally suspect.

In works written for popular consumption, Harris presents lively accounts punctuated by materialistic reasoning. His fundamental thesis – "Nothing is present to the mind that does not first appeal to the stomach" (Sahlins 1978: 49) – is eloquently developed in *Cannibals and Kings* (1978). The thesis permits a simple explanation of male supremacy, capitalism, and the Eucharist. War becomes quickly understood, as do the logic of Jewish dietary laws, the reason why Hindus make cows sacred, the causes of matrilineal descent, and, among other strange phenomena, how to make sense of Aztec sacrifices. Nothing is strange or bizarre. Strangeness, like beauty, sits in the eye of the beholder; seen through lenses provided by Harris, everything makes good, materialistic sense, even Aztec sacrifices. Harris describes Aztec priests as "ritual slaughterers" and cannibalism as a "system geared to the production of substantial amounts of animal protein in the form of human flesh." Unfortunately for Harris, a convincing essay exists (Sahlins 1978) which makes the cannibalism-for-protein thesis quite implausible.

Sahlins argues first that the Aztecs were not short of protein:

> Indeed, of all peoples of the Hemisphere who practiced intensive agriculture, the Aztecs probably had the greatest natural protein resources: the lakes of the Valley of Mexico, teeming with *animalitos* and algae processed for food, as well as fish, and in the winter, millions of ducks. (1978: 48)

Second, given that culture is clever, how do we explain the fact that the Aztecs pursued a very inefficient means for getting extra, unneeded protein? Put another way, from a costs-and-benefits perspective, it is clear from historical accounts that "the sacrifice business was running at a loss, owing to the high costs of upkeep of the stock and low yields in arm and thigh cuts" (p. 48).

Sahlins's analysis of Aztec sacrifices fits in well with general, anthropological views of sacrifice. Moreover, unlike Harris's materialistic theory, Sahlins's account provides considerable insight into the *content* of Aztec sacrifice. Following French sociological theory on sacrifice, Sahlins suggested that "the victim takes on the nature of a god. . . . As enemies are thus assimilated to gods, so the high Aztec god Tezcatlipoca had as another name 'Enemy' (Yaoti)" (pp. 46–47).

Victims were "helped" towards their transformation to gods. Before sacrifice, they were often dressed and painted as idols and sometimes were given "divine wine." Finally, they were ritually killed, "usually on the pyramid, their hearts held up to the sun and their blood smeared about the god's sanctuary. But there remained the body, now also sacred matter and capable of useful effects." To firm up the notion of sacrifice as a religious ritual, Sahlins continued, the victim's body was

> rolled down the western steps of the temple, in a descent that at once paralleled the course of the sun and the Aztec metaphor of birth. [The body was then] received and shared by the owners of the death. . . . In the last moment, victims, gods, and communicants became one. The consumption of human flesh was thus deifying, not degrading. (p. 47)

Sahlins's case against so-called cannibalism among the Aztecs, and against cultural materialism in general, is much stronger than I have space to present. His point, and one which all members of the ideationalist camp accept, is: each culture develops meaningful forms which demand careful study. To try to explain them simplistically is but to explain them away.

Harris, like Geertz, has provided culture with the relevance of excitement, triggering conflict, and debate. Following a path cut out by such great communicators as Ruth Benedict and Margaret Mead, Harris has placed culture prominently in the marketplace of ideas. In the American marketplace simple, instantly understood theory does well. While such theory does little for anthropology as science, it continues to generate much interest in anthropology as a discipline. Harris has provided more than instant understandings. Additionally, he has always presented good reading—works loaded with spicy argumentation and fascinating examples. Finally, although his text trivializes human existence, his subtext rings true. Human life does make sense.

CULTURE AND RELEVANCE

In every language, words exist which function as mood transformers and spirit energizers. In the United States, words which have this magic quality include "money," "success," "instant," "research," "fun," "therapy," and "science." In East Asian societies, a set of magical words exist which deal with "face," with maintaining a certain level of dignity. In Trinidad, "fete"—a party which includes food, music, drinking, dance, and sexual adventure—has a powerful magic attached to it. In anthropology, "culture" enjoyed this magical quality for several decades. The concept of culture took an infant discipline and gave it respectability, stature, and scientific legitimacy. Understandably, culture picked up much magic. Understandably, some of this magic evaporated as anthropologists discovered that their respectability no longer rested on their identification as culture promoters. There is more to culture than magic. And the more includes relevance.

In presenting culture as relevant, I have a model in mind. I assume that relevant is governed by two criteria captured, respectively, by the terms *environment* and *science*. Culture is environmentally relevant to the extent it makes some contributions to issues important in our environment, issues pertaining to suicide, crime, health care, and, among others, policing. Culture is scientifically relevant to the extent it makes contributions to issues pertaining to the nature and methodology of science. When environmental and scientific relevance are considered together, we get a 2 x 2 model I call SPAB: Science, Play, and Bleeding. SPAB has four cells, about which a few words are in order (see Figure 1).

Figure 1.   SPAB: Relevance as Science, Play, and Bleeding

Scientific Relevance

	(+)	(–)
Environmental Relevance	Monastic Science 1	Linguistic Play 3
	Involved Science 2	Sympathetic Bleeding 4

(+)=relevant   (–)=not relevant

Monastic science, anthropological work which is *only* relevant to science, presents all the attractions that monasteries have over marketplaces. Here truth is pursued slowly and serenely, but spiced with the excitement of intellectual conflict. Only rarely is there direct reference to environmental issues. Monastic scientists working with culture attempt to develop models which more completely capture and interrelate its various aspects. The goal is to make culture a more scientifically useful concept.

Involved science, anthropological work which is relevant to both science and environmental issues, is an attempt to use what we know to try to solve environmental problems. Such work is both a type of experiment (and thus aids the development of science) and a commitment to involvement. As a "natural experiment," it lacks the precision of laboratory experiments, but it has other benefits (cf. Freilich 1963). As a commitment to involvement the argument is: If the world were calmer; if the race toward destruction of the earth were slower; if our destructive technology were weaker; then arguments against involvement by a primitive science might be more persuasive.

Linguistic play, anthropological work which essentially is relevant neither to science nor to environmental issues, is fun. It pursues questions such as "Is Claude Lévi-Strauss a Marxist?" "What did Marx really mean when he wrote '…'?" "Did Boasian empiricism really hurt the development of cultural theory?"

This interest in personalities – this attempt to make gods or demons out of our intellectual forefathers and foremothers – can only be a game leading to trivial results.[8]

Finally we have *sympathetic bleeding*, the discussion of environmental problems and their "research," with a minimal concern for methodology and theory. Sympathy, like measles, is contagious, so this work is not a total loss. But what else can be said in its favor?

The chapters in this volume, all examples of either monastic science or involved science, should contribute to a yet greater revitalization of culture. Culture is much like electricity: both generate power; neither can be seen directly; and both, under given conditions, provide shocks. Many experience electric shock and understand the cause of their discomfort. Many experience culture shock and (probably) are mystified as to the cause of their discomfort. In this age of instant communication between cultures, with the possibility of instant destruction of all cultures, ever more people can expect ever more culture shocks. We need to understand culture better so that little culture shocks can be understood and big culture shocks can be avoided. We need to understand culture better so that those with different cultures are not necessarily defined as enemies whose life-styles are a threat to our way of life. We need to understand culture better to know better how to live with modern technology – so that cultures will still be around to be studied in the twenty-first century and beyond.

NOTES

1. This essay has profited from critical comments by Steve Rayner, Miles Richardson, Sandra Burkhardt, Karin Andriolo, and Mirjana Freilich.
2. More extensive historical accounts are found in Harris (1968), Stocking (1968, 1974), Freilich (1972), Diamond (1980), Ortner (1984), and Shweder (1984).
3. Charles Hockett presents the anthropological puzzle quite similarly:

> What are we? How did we come to be? . . . What are those features, if any, shared necessarily by all human communities? Which of these are uniquely human? (1979: 641)

4. An early (1941) and very fruitful collaboration was between anthropologist E. A. Hoebel and law professor K. N. Llewellyn. For additional important collaborations, see Bateson et al. (1956); Benjamin (1955); Kluckhohn and Murray (1961); Parsons and Shils (1951); and Spicer (1952). See also John Bennett's valuable 1954 article, "Interdisciplinary Research and the Concept of Culture."
5. Worries concerning so-called material culture continue to burden anthropological minds. Those who dare dismiss material culture as a contradiction in terms are now attacked as producing "the crassest form of idealism as the reigning philosophy in anthropology" (Weiss 1973: 1377).
6. Criticisms of the superorganic approach to culture parallel criticisms made of a Saussurian approach to language. If we replace "linguistic" with "cultural" and "language" with "culture" in the following quotation we get an apt summary of arguments such as Sapir's (1917) and Goldenweiser's (1917):

Linguistic theory is led by an inner necessity to recognize not merely the linguistic system ... but also man and human society behind language, and all of man's sphere of knowledge through language. (Hjelmslev 1963: 127)

7. Jeffrey Alexander has recently published a marvelous overview of Geertzian anthropology. Among his conclusions is that we are being presented with "an indeterminancy within an indeterminancy"; scientifically speaking, a dead end. (1987: 302–29)

8. That linguistic play is still part of critical anthropology is very clear from the following passage, found in Boon's review of two edited books by Ino Rossi:

Is Lévi-Strauss a roundabout logician of totalized order, or is he a dialectician (Hegelian or otherwise) tracing pervasive codes of contrast to arenas less melodramatic than antagonistic class interest? (1984: 809)

Linguistic play, I suggest, is more relevant (and appropriate) to "put down" journalism than to scientific anthropology. For example, although many of us will find Hilarion Henares's statements (below) misguided, we will probably agree that this type of linguistic play is fitting for a column in a daily newspaper. Writing in a Manila newspaper, in a column called "Make My Day," Henares continued his frequent attacks on American "colonialism" by putting Tylor on his head: "America is the only country on earth that's gone from barbarism to decadence without passing through civilization." For a different but useful approach to relevance, see James B. Rule (1978).

REFERENCES

Alexander, Jeffrey C.
  1987   *Twenty Lectures: Sociological Theory Since World War II.* New York: Columbia University Press.

Bateson, Gregory, Don D. Jackson, Jay Haley, and John Weakland
  1956   "Toward a Theory of Schizophrenia." *Behavioral Science* 1: 251–64.

Belo, Jane
  1960   *Trance in Bali.* New York: Columbia University Press.

Benedict, Ruth
  1934   *Patterns of Culture.* New York: Houghton Mifflin.

Benjamin, Paul D.
  1955   *Health, Culture and Community: Case Studies of Public Reactions to Health Programs.* New York: Russell Sage Foundation.

Bennett, John
  1954   "Interdisciplinary Research and the Concept of Culture." *American Anthropologist* 56: 169–79.

Bentley, G. Carter
  1984   "Hermeneutics and World Construction in Morano Disputing." *American Ethnologist* 11(4): 642–55.

Bidney, David
  1953   *Theoretical Anthropology.* New York: Columbia University Press.

Boas, Franz
  1930   "Anthropology." *Encyclopedia of the Social Sciences* 2: 73–110.

  1928   *Anthropology and Modern Life.* New York: Norton.

Boon, James
   1984   "Structuralism Routinized, Structuralism Fractured." Review essay. *American Ethnologist* 11(4): 807–12.

Chapple, E. D., and C. S. Coon
   1942   *Principles of Anthropology*. New York: Holt, Rinehart & Winston.

Connor, Linda
   1984   Comment on "The Thick and the Thin," by Paul Shankman. *Current Anthropology* 25(3): 271.

Diamond, Stanley, ed.
   1980   *Anthropology: Ancestors and Heirs*. The Hague: Mouton.

Freilich, Morris
   1980   "Smart Sex and Proper Sex: A Paradigm Found." *Central Issues in Anthropology* 2: 37–51.

   1978   "The Meaning of 'Sociocultural'." In *The Concept and Dynamics of Culture*, Bernardo Bernardi, ed. The Hague: Mouton, pp. 89–101.

   1976   "Myth, Method and Madness." *Current Anthropology* 16(2): 207–26.

   1963   "The Natural Experiment, Ecology and Culture." *Southwestern Journal of Anthropology* 19: 21–39.

Freilich, Morris, ed.
   1983   *The Pleasures of Anthropology*. New York: New American Library.

   1972   *The Meaning of Culture*. Lexington, Mass.: Xerox College Publishers.

   1970   *Marginal Natives: Anthropologists at Work*. New York: Harper & Row.

Friedrich, Paul
   1985   "Interpretation and Vision." Paper presented at the annual meeting of the *American Anthropological Association*. Washington, D. C.

Garfinkel, Harold
   1967   *Studies in Ethnomethodology*. Englewood Cliffs, N. J.: Prentice Hall.

Geertz, Clifford
   1973   The Interpretation of Culture. New York: Basic.

   1965   "The Impact of the Concept of Culture on the Concept of Man." In *New Views on the Nature of Man*. J. R. Platt, ed. Chicago: University of Chicago Press.

Goldenweiser, A. A.
   1917   "The Autonomy of the Social." *American Anthropologist* 19(3): 447–49.

Goodenough, Ward H.
   1961   "Comment on Cultural Evolution." *Daedalus* 90: 521–28.

Gorer, G.
   1950   "The Concept of National Character." *Science News*, No. 18: 105–22.

Gouldner, Alvin W.
   1970   The Coming Crisis in Western Sociology. New York: Basic.

Hallpike, C. R.
   1971   "Some Problems in Cross-Cultural Comparison." In *The Translation of Culture*. T. O. Beidelman, ed. London: Tavistock.

Harris, Marvin
   1979   *Cultural Materialism: The Struggle for a Science of Culture*. New York: Random House.

1978   *Cannibals and Kings: The Origins of Cultures*. New York: Random House.

1968   *The Rise of Anthropological Theory*. New York: Thomas Y. Crowell.

1964   *The Nature of Cultural Things*. New York: Random House.

Hjemlev, Louis
1963   *Prolegomena to a Theory of Language*. Madison, Wis.: University of Wisconsin Press. (First pub. 1943)

Hocart, A. M.
1970   *The Life Giving Myth and Other Essays*. Ed., with Foreword, by Rodney Needham. London: Methuen.

Hockett, Charles F.
1979   "Forgotten Goals and Unfinished Business in Anthropology." *American Anthropologist* 81: 641.

Howe, L. E. A.
1984   Comment on "The Thick and the Thin," by Paul Shankman. *Current Anthropology* 25(3): 274–75.

Jefferson, Gail, and John Lee
1981   "The Rejection of Advice: Managing the Problematic Convergence of a 'Trouble-Telling' and a 'Service Encounter'." *Journal of Pragmatics* 5: 339–422.

Kaplan, David
1965   "The Superorganic: Science or Metaphysics." *American Anthropologist* 67(4): 958–76.

Kaplan, David, and Robert Manners
1972   *Cultural Theory*. Englewood Cliffs, N. J.: Prentice Hall.

Keesing, Roger M.
1974   "Theories of Culture." In *Annual Review of Anthropology*, vol. 3. B. J. Siegal, A. R. Beals, and Stephen A. Tyler, eds. Palo Alto, Calif.: Annual Reviews.

Kluckhohn, Clyde, and W. H. Kelly
1945   "The Concept of Culture." In *The Science of Man in the World of Crisis*. Ralph Linton, ed. New York: Columbia University Press.

Kluckhohn, Clyde, and O. H. Mowrer
1944   "Culture and Personality: A Conceptual Scheme." *American Anthropologist* 46: 1–29.

Kluckhohn, Clyde, and Henry A. Murray
1961   *Personality in Nature, Society and Culture*. New York: Knopf.

Kroeber, Alfred L.
1952   *The Nature of Culture*. Chicago: University of Chicago Press.

1917   "The Superorganic." *American Anthropologist* 19: 163–213.

Kroeber, Alfred L., and Clyde Kluckhohn
1952   *Culture: A Critical Review of Concepts and Definitions*. Papers of the Peabody Museum (Cambridge, Mass.), vol. 47.

Laughlin, Charles D.
1972   "The Demise of Culture: A Post Mortem." Paper presented at the annual meeting of the *American Anthropological Association*. Toronto, Canada.

Leopold, Joan
1980   *Culture in Comparative and Evolutionary Perspective: E. B. Tylor and the Making of Primitive Culture*. Berlin: Dietrich Reimer Verlag.

Lévi-Strauss, Claude
    1963   *Structural Anthropology*. Clare Jacobson, trans. New York: Basic.
Levy, Robert I.
    1984   "Emotion, Knowing and Culture." In *Culture Theory*, Richard A. Schweder
            and Robert Levine, eds. Cambridge: Cambridge University Press.
Linnekin, Jocelyn S.
    1983   "Defining Tradition: Variations on the Hawaiian Identity." *American Eth-
            nologist* 10(2): 241–52.
Linton, Ralph
    1936   *The Study of Man.* New York: Appleton-Century.
Llewellyn, K. N., and E. A. Hoebel
    1941   *The Cheyenne Way: Conflict and Case Law in Primitive Jurisprudence*. Nor-
            man: University of Oklahoma Press.
Malinowski, Bronislaw
    1966   *Crime and Custom in Savage Society*. London: Routledge & Kegan Paul.
            (First pub. 1926)
    1944   *A Scientific Theory of Culture*. Chapel Hill: University of North Carolina
            Press.
    1931   "Culture." *Encyclopedia of the Social Sciences*, 62–46.
Mead, Margaret
    1961   *Cooperation and Competition Among Primitive Peoples*. Boston: Beacon
            Press.
Moore, John H.
    1974   "The Culture Concept as Ideology." *American Ethnologist* 1: 537–49.
Murdock, George Peter
    1972   "Anthropology's Mythology." *Proceedings of the Royal Anthropological In-
            stitute of Great Britain and Ireland for 1971*, pp. 17–24.
Murphy, R. F.
    1975   *The Dialectics of Social Life: Alarms and Excursions in Anthropological
            Theory*. New York: Basic.
Opler, Morris
    1964   "The Human Being in Culture Theory." *American Anthropologist* 66: 507–
            28.
    1962   "Cultural Anthropology." In *A New Survey of the Social Sciences*, B. N.
            Varma, ed. Asia Publishing.
    1945   "Themes as Dynamic Forces in Culture." *American Journal of Sociology* 51:
            198–206.
Ortner, S.
    1984   "Theory in Anthropology Since the Sixties." *Comparative Studies in Society
            and History* 26: 126–66.
Parsons, Talcott, and Edward Shils, eds.
    1955   *Toward a General Theory of Action.* Cambridge, Mass.: Harvard University Press.
Pierce, Joe E.
    1977   "Culture: A Collection of Fuzzy Sets." *Human Organization* 36: 197–200.
Radcliffe-Brown, A. R.
    1949   "White's View of Culture." *American Anthropologist* 51: 503–12.

Randall, Robert A.
1987   "Plans and Planning in Cross-Cultural Settings." In *Blueprints for Thinking: The Role of Planning in Psychological Development*. S. L. Friedman, E. K. Skolnick, and R. R. Cockings, eds. New York: Cambridge University Press.

Rappaport, R.
1979   *Ecology, Meaning and Religion*. Richmond, Cal.: North Atlantic Books.

Rawls, Anne Warfield
1985   "Reply to Gallant and Kleinman on Symbolic Interactionism *vs.* Ethnomethodology." *Symbolic Interaction* 8(1): 121–40.

Ricoeur, Paul
1971   "The Model of the Text: Meaningful Action Considered as Text. *Social Research* 38: 529–62.

Rosaldo, Renato
1982   Review of "Geertz and Culture," by Kenneth A. Rice. *American Ethnologist* 9: 197–98.

Rule, James B.
1978   "Models of Relevance: The Social Effects of Sociology." *American Journal of Sociology* 84: 78–98.

Sacks, Harvey
1979   "Hotrodder: A Revolutionary Category." In *Everyday Language*. George Psathas, ed. New York: Irvington.

Sahlins, Marshall
1978   "Culture as Protein and Profit." *New York Review of Books* 25(18).

Sapir, Edward
1917   "Do We Need a Superorganic?" *American Anthropologist* 19(3): 441–47.

Schmidt, W.
1939   *The Culture Historical Method of Ethnology*. S. A. Sieber, trans. New York: Fortuny's.

Schneider, David M.
1976   "Notes Toward a Theory of Culture." In *Meaning in Anthropology*, K. Basso and H. Selby, eds. Albuquerque: University of New Mexico Press.

1972   "What Is Kinship All About?" In *Kinship Studies in the Morgan Memorial Year*. P. Reining, ed. Washington, D. C.: Anthropological Society of Washington.

Shanklin, Eugenia
1981   "Two Meanings and Uses of Tradition." *Journal of Anthropological Research* 37: 71–89.

Shankman, Paul
1984   "The Thick and the Thin: On the Interpretive Theoretical Program of Clifford Geertz." *Current Anthropology* 25(3): 261–80.

Shils, Edward
1981   *Tradition*. Chicago: University of Chicago Press.

Shweder, Richard A.
1984   "Anthropology's Romantic Rebellion Against the Enlightenment, or There's More to Thinking than Reason and Evidence." In *Culture Theory*, Richard A. Shweder and Robert A. Levine, eds. Cambridge: Cambridge University Press.

Shweder, Richard A., and Robert A. Levine, eds.
1984   *Culture Theory: Essays on Mind, Self and Emotion*. Cambridge: Cambridge University Press.

Spicer, Edward H.
1952   *Human Problems in Technological Change*. New York: Russell Sage Foundation.

Spiro, M. E.
1986   "The Future of Anthropology." *Cultural Anthropology* 1(3): 259–86.

1951   "Culture and Personality: The Natural History of a False Dichotomy." *Psychiatry* 14: 19–46.

Steward, Julian
1955   *Theory of Culture Change*. Urbana: University of Illinois Press.

Stocking, George W.
1974   *The Shaping of American Anthropology 1883–1911: A Franz Boas Reader*. New York: Basic.

1968   *Race, Culture and Evolution: Essays in the History of Anthropology*. New York: Free Press.

Taylor, Charles
1979   "Interpretation and the Science of Man." In *Interpretive Social Science: A Reader*, P. Rabinow and W. M. Sullivan, eds. Berkeley: University of Califoria Press.

Tylor, E. B.
1871   *Primitive Culture*. London: J. Murray.

1865   *Researches into the Early History of Mankind and the Development of Civilization*. London: J. Murray.

Vayda, Andrew P.
1983   "Progressive Contextualization: Methods of Research in Human Ecology." *Human Ecology* 11: 265–81.

Wallace, Anthony F. C.
1970   *Culture and Personality*. New York: Random House.

Washburn, Sherwood L.
1960   "Tools and Human Evolution." *Scientific American* 203(3): 1–15.

Wax, Murray
1972   "The Anthropology of Boas." In *The Meaning of Culture*. Morris Freilich, ed. Lexington, Mass.: Xerox College Publishers.

Weiss, Gerald
1973   "A Scientific Concept of Culture" *American Anthropologist* 74: 1376–1413.

Wescott, Roger W.
1969   *The Divine Animal*. New York: Funk & Wagnalls.

Westen, Drew
1984   "Cultural Materialism: Food for Thought or Bum Steer?" *Current Anthropology* 25(5): 639–54.

White, Leslie A.
1959   "The Concept of Culture." *American Anthropologist* 61: 227–51.

1954   Review of *Culture: A Critical Review of Concepts and Definitions*, Alfred L. Kroeber and Clyde Kluckhohn. *American Anthropologist* 56: 461–86.

Whiting, John, and I. Child
   1953   *Child Training and Personality: A Cross-Cultural Study.* New Haven: Yale University Press.

Wissler, Clark
   1917   *The American Indian: An Introduction to the Anthropology of the New World.* New York: McMurtril.

   1916   "Psychological and Historical Interpretations for Culture." *Science* 43: 193–201.

Wolf, Eric
   1982   "Culture: Panacea or Problem." Distinguished Lecture, Annual Meeting of the Northeastern Anthropological Association. Princeton University. March.

PART I

CULTURE: A REAL BASE FOR A HARD SOCIAL SCIENCE

Culture, as anthropologists see it, gives meaning, logic, and importance to many discrete and seemingly unconnected facts about human life. Anthony Wallace tackles the important problem of sharing. In general we can say, along with Peter Gardner:

> Actual informants do not know everything; they manifest cognitive variability in many ways. Actual informants also appear to share concepts and propositions about a great deal. (1976: 464)

But this generalization indicates the wide gap between what we know about sharing and what we need to know. We need to know, very precisely, who shares what, with whom, when. Wallace suggests that we add the notion of "plot" in culture, the better to understand sharing and nonsharing. Plot, "in the sense of an evolving structure of conflict," can help us understand how members of the "same" culture can yet have sharply opposing views in fundamental areas of human social life. Wallace's chapter will stimulate many to work toward a better understanding of "the division of labor in who knows what" (D'Andrade 1981: 180). Work in this area will also profit from the idea that we "need to make a provision for the possibly unequal distribution of knowledge among 'experts' or specialists and nonspecialists in a society" (Romney, Weller, and Batchelder 1986: 314).

Economics, considered by many as the hardest of the soft sciences, provides a curious picture of human behavior. Little "capitalists" somehow develop stable preferences and somehow live peacefully with their neighbors. The latter somehow is most problematic since, as Mary Douglas tells us, their theory has "no way of allowing for moral feelings such as altruism or commitment." Clearly, the individual belongs to some larger system, and this belonging provides a "Cultural Bias" (Douglas 1982). In chapter 2, Douglas provides a very detailed discussion of three forms of society, each form having its own special cultural bias. These forms are based, respectively, on (1) the logical principle of inclusion—the distinction between insider and outsider—(2) exchange, and (3) hierarchy. Each of these forms has its own distinct theory of human nature, of human purpose, of goodness, and of evil.

Douglas's typology of cultural forms is actually a two-by-two matrix, providing four cultural types: hierarchy, individualism, egalitarianism, and fatalism. These types, Aaron Wildavsky argues very persuasively, provide frames of reference for individual behavior. Not only does an individual know how to react properly in given situations and in particular interactions, but here there are built-in integration and built-in solidarity. Put otherwise, individuals who belong to the same cultural type have similar ideas as to the meaning of envy, blame, inequality, fairness, growth, scarcity, leadership, uncertainty, and apathy. Wildavsky summarizes this approach very neatly: "Culture is the organization of social life. Organization is bias."

These writers have provided a large number of sources which offer useful information for the creation of a real social science. Miles Richardson and Robert Dunton push us to incorporate some ideas developed by George Herbert Mead. A Meadian perspective asks us to think about humans on a lower level of analysis. Each level, it must be emphasized, provides its own special insights. Each is a searchlight which illuminates one area and thus, necessarily, puts other areas into darkness. What kind of light does Mead produce?

> Mead—in accordance with the humanistic insistence on the centrality of human action—stresses behavior. . . . For Mead, the past, evoked by the objects about us, is not a dead weight that condemns us to eternal repetition, but a creative act of becoming. Freed from the past and directed forward, the Meadian perspective is, nonetheless, dominated by the present. The future of the farseeing eye is shaped by the reality of the formative hand.

These morsels from the chapter by Richardson and Dunton should whet the appetite for a greater understanding of Mead's contribution to a theory of culture. And these authors provide such. With their help, the concept place takes on new and richer meaning.

The chapters in Part I demonstrate the continued relevance of culture. Beyond that, they show that culture is usefully considered as a base for hard social science. In using culture for such a goal, would-be synthesists are encouraged to go out of their specialized fields and buy concepts from whomsoever appears to have goods worth having. Yet some caution is advisable; remember the economic dictum, *caveat emptor* (let the buyer beware). All concepts which appear useful may not be so. Consider Werner Heisenberg's words:

> The concepts initially formed by abstraction from particular situations or experimental complexes acquire a life of their own. (1975: 72)

In their own, acquired lives some concepts go astray and develop meanings which make "reality" more fuzzy (Kempton 1984). So I repeat, *caveat emptor*.

REFERENCES

D'Andrade, R. G.
  1981   "The Cultural Part of Cognition." *Cognitive Science* 5: 179–95.

Douglas, Mary
  1982   "Cultural Bias." In Mary Douglas, *In the Active Voice*. London: Routledge & Kegan Paul.

Gardner, Peter M.
  1976   "Birds, Words and a Requiem for the Omniscient Informant." *American Ethnologist* 3: 446–48.

Giddens, Anthony
  1979   *Central Problems in Sociological Theory. Action, Structure and Contradiction in Social Analysis*. Berkeley: University of California Press.

Heisenberg, Werner
  1975   *Across the Boundaries*. New York: Harper & Row.

Kempton, Willet
  1984   "Interview Methods for Eliciting Fuzzy Categories." *Fuzzy Sets and Systems* 14: 43–64.

Romney, A. K., Susan C. Weller, and William H. Batchelder
  1986   "Culture as Consensus: A Theory of Culture and Informant Accuracy." *American Anthropologist* 88 (2): 313–38.

1

"PLOT" AND THE CONCEPT
OF CULTURE IN HISTORIOGRAPHY

Anthony F. C. Wallace

One of the issues that must be addressed in any conception of culture is the matter of sharing. Whether one speaks of culture as information, symbols, webs of meaning, proprieties, rights and duties, cognitive maps, infra- and suprastructures, or just plain customary behavior and artifacts, one always implies that the thing, whatever it is, is shared. But two questions must immediately be asked: Shared by whom? When? To say that an element of culture – let alone a whole culture – is shared by all the members of a society, even a small one, is to use a figure of speech that can be supported only by disqualifying from membership all those who do not share – infants, the senile, and "deviants" in general. In actual practice, most anthropologists readily accept as parts of a culture many features that are clearly the special property, sometimes the secrets, of special subgroups – men, women, children, adults, hunters, shamans, carpenters, bakers, soldiers, peasants, priests, kings, and whoever. When one adds the various other kinds of cultural pluralism to be found in almost every nation-state – which means all societies that have left written records for the historian – clearly the conception of culture must allow for considerable diversity. No real culture that is knowable to the historian is one giant harmonious pattern felt, understood, and practiced by all members of a society. It is, rather, a structure of diversity, separate parts of it maintained, developed, and changed by different groups, and in many of its aspects experienced in a slightly different way by every individual.

I have discussed individual variability in other publications.[1] Here I wish to deal with cultural differences between groups within society. How these groups, and the parts of the structure that appertain to them, are related to one another, and how the structure changes, are questions that interest all of us. There are several structural principles and several processes of change that are commonly recognized, and I shall not take time to discuss them; they are analyzed at length in various functionalist formulations and are implicit in such formulations of culture change as revitalization movements and paradigmatic processes.[2] What I want to emphasize here are a type of structure and a related process of change that are perhaps easier to recognize in the historical record than in ordinary ethnographic fieldwork because of the length of time involved in the evolution of the structure itself. I am referring to what I shall call "plot" in culture, i.e., plot in the sense of an evolving structure of conflict between parties at interest, a struggle that moves, over decades or generations, toward resolution by means of important cultural change.[3] These structures of conflict may include opposing views of human nature, of the existing culture, and of the desirable society of the future, and they generate what might be called tactical structures of myth and ritual that do not so much express a general societywide consensus as articulate the cultural strategies of their proponents. Thus a myth, or a ritual, that in cross-section may resemble those strain-reducing mechanisms familiar in functional analysis, may in longitudinal perspective appear as one party's persistent proposal of a formula for resolving an unresolved conflict. How the conflict will, ultimately, be resolved may of course be prefigured in neither strategy.

To illustrate the point, let us turn our attention to the coal regions of Pennsylvania, and in particular to the small mining town of St. Clair and the county seat of Pottsville two miles away. The visitor to Pottsville today is confronted by a spectacular public symbol: a white-painted, cast-iron statue of the nineteenth-century statesman Henry Clay, standing fifteen feet tall upon a cast-iron column some fifty feet high, gazing benevolently over the town from a hillside above the extreme southern edge of the coal field. The particular incident which I want to consider is the Fourth of July celebration at which this statue was dedicated, over a hundred years ago, when Pottsville and St. Clair were busy mining communities. On the Fourth of July of 1856, the Henry Clay statue was officially "inaugurated"; the parade and speech-making ceremonies celebrating the inauguration constituted the principal public event of the day.[4] Henry Clay (1772–1852), although a Kentuckian, had been a political hero to many Pennsylvanians throughout his long senatorial career because he consistently supported the protective tariff on coal, iron, and cotton products. It was believed by many that such a tariff was necessary to the economic health of Pennsylvania's industries. The coal regions were doubly indebted to his services because English coal and English iron were both excluded, thus providing a market for anthracite not only in household stoves but also in blast furnaces and foundries. Anthracite was peculiarly well adapted to smelting iron because its high carbon content made coking unnecessary. The economic historian Alfred Chandler has argued persuasively that the energy source for the industrial revolution in America in the nineteenth century was very largely the anthracite produced in Schuylkill and two other Pennsylvania counties.[5]

The Fourth of July has since the early nineteenth century, at least, been a secular ritual of patriotism that celebrates national solidarity, honors national heroes, and symbolically unites all social groups in opposition to domination – or loyalty to – a foreign power, by encouraging participation in flag raising, picnics, parades, and displays of fireworks. Its text is the Declaration of Independence, with its praise of political freedom and equality of opportunity in the pursuit of happiness. Nothing would seem more suitable to such an occasion than to organize the festivities around the dedication of an iron statue to Henry Clay, the Great Protectionist, whose advocacy of a protective tariff nourished American manufactures (particularly of the military hardware that guarded the nation's independence and thereby supported the miners of Schuylkill County). The parade in Pottsville was a patriotic extravaganza. A grand procession moved to the grounds of the statue. Let us read some of the words of the town's historian describing this parade:

> Foremost came the staff officers, clad in gay trappings, the panoply of war, on their prancing steeds; these were followed by the cavalry and other military companies, many of them in new and rich uniforms, bearing their polished arms like soldiers trained for battle. They were the pride of the citizens, the delight of the ladies, and the glory of the small boys, who did not fail to show their enthusiasm by incessant volleys of firecrackers.

> In the vast procession, the Middleport Lodge of Odd Fellows and the Masons attracted much attention; and the old soldiers of the Mexican War, though few in number, were objects of peculiar interest. The children representing the different States and Territories were loudly applauded, and conspicuous in the entire procession moved a beautiful Goddess of Liberty. Much praise was accorded Colonel Hobart and his aides, for the active manner in which they discharged their duties, for when the heavy fall of rain threatened an almost general stampede, they were everywhere present, directing, conducting and giving life to the whole.

> On arriving at the monument grounds, where a dense crowd had collected, the orator of the occasion, the committee, invited guests and other gentlemen present, among whom were the Honorable H. K. Strong, Honorable James H. Campbell, Honorable Joseph Casey, Honorable C. W. Pitman, General George M. Keim, Reverend Daniel Washburn, and Mr. Porter, were conducted to the platform, from whence the throng of spectators were to be addressed.

> Captain Frank Pott opened the meeting, and it was formally organized by the election of the following named gentlemen as officers:

> President:—John Bannan, Esq.

> Vice President:—Honorable Strange N. Palmer, Christopher Loeser, Daniel Hill, William Mortimer, Sr., Benjamin Pott, Andrew Russel, Burd Patterson, John Shippen, Jeremiah Boone, Dr. R. H. Coryell, Colonel J. J. Conner, William De Haven, Daniel R. Bennett, Lewis Royer, Jacob Hammer, Rowland Jones, David Hunter, George Reifsnyder, Charles W. Taylor, William Graeff.

> Secretaries:—Eli Bowen, John B. McCreary, George Spenser, Doctor Robbins, Alexander Sillyman, Daniel Koch, Adam Etien.

> After a few pertinent remarks, in which Mr. Bannan expressed his acknowledgments for the honor which had been conferred upon him in selecting him as the presiding officer of the meeting, the Reverend Daniel Washburn delivered a few remarks, and then offered prayer.

At the conclusion of the prayer, Mr. Bannan introduced the Honorable Charles Gibbons, the orator of the occasion, whose address was brilliant, teeming with great thoughts, and delivered in the happiest manner.

Letters from distinguished invited guests, who were not present, were ordered to be published.

Eli Bowen, Esq., then read the Declaration of Independence, after which the Honorable James H. Campbell was loudly called for. After Mr. Campbell had concluded the meeting was adjourned, with loud cheering for Mr. Gibbons, the gentleman connected with the work, etc.

In commenting upon the occasion, Mr. Bannan remarked, "As a general thing, the day passed pleasantly; if liquor could be exiled from Pottsville, it would be one of the most delightful places in the world."

This indigenous account would seem to emphasize the universal acceptability of the ceremonies, but if one examines the event more closely, one finds that the Fourth of July, 1856, in Pottsville, was not simply a drunken and joyous celebration of patriotic values to which all Americans subscribed. The "great thoughts" expressed by the orator concerned what might be called a second American Revolution. The first, launched in 1776, delivered the country from *political* colonial subordination to Britain. The second, begun in 1812, freed the United States from *economic* subordination (or what might today be called a neocolonial dependency). In that process, Henry Clay is depicted as playing a dual role: the patriotic Congressman who urged the nation to enter the War of 1812 and the architect of the so-called American System that combined self-sufficiency in agriculture with independence in manufacturing, particularly by means of the protective tariffs of 1824 and later, which Clay supported despite the growing opposition of the agricultural South. That tariff, of course, supported the American iron industry, which in turn was fueled by anthracite.[6]

The ceremony itself, and the statue that towered (and still towers) over the town, also made a tactical statement. In a purely political sense, the statue was an advertisement for the newly formed Republican Party, whose first national convention had been held in Philadelphia one month before and whose candidates would take the campaign trail in their first presidential election a few weeks later. Henry Clay, a proto-Republican Whig, had been and was still, even in 1856, the target of much political invective from Democrats. The agricultural part of Schuylkill County, populated largely by Pennsylvania Germans, had been a Democratic stronghold for a generation, and the Democrats won in Schuylkill County in 1856. Nevertheless, the statue remained as a permanent rebuke to those Americans (and there were many, both North and South) who opposed the protective tariff for American industry on the grounds that it resulted in higher prices for manufactured goods and reduced the foreign market for American agricultural products.[7]

Raising a statue of Henry Clay that looked remarkably like the statue of Admiral Nelson in Trafalgar Square also consolidated the image of the economic and the military hero at precisely the time when a cadre of writers and lecturers, led by the Englishman Samuel Smiles, were raising up engineers, industrialists, and promoters of commerce and manufacturing generally as the heroes of the Industrial Revolution.[8] And in the organization of the parade itself, this consolidation of the military and the economic was conspicuous. The order of parade was as follows:

Military

(1) Major General of the 6th Division, and Staff,
(2) Brigadier General of the 1st Brigade, and Staff
(3) 1st Regiment of the 1st Brigade, 9th Division
(4) Other Military of Pennsylvania, and other States
(5) 2nd Regiment of the 1st Brigade, 6th Division (6) Mahantongo Battalion

Civic

(1) Chief Marshall and Aides
(2) Invited Guests
(3) Orator of the Day
(4) Committee of Invitation
(5) Building Committee
(6) Committee of Arrangements
(7) Assistant Marshal and Aides
(8) Brass Band
(9) Masonic Fraternity
(10) Brass Band
(11) Workmen engaged in the Erection of the Clay Monument: (a) Robert Wood, Moulder of Iron Statue, and workmen (b) George B. Fissler, Moulder of Iron Column, and workmen (c) Wrenn Bros., Moulders of Iron Capital, and workmen (d) Jacob and Charles Madara, stone masons, builders of stone pedestal, and workmen (e) Waters S. Chillson, engaged in erecting Monument, and workmen
(12) Children representing different States and Territories
(13) Judges of the Courts of the 21st Judicial District, Members of the Bar, and other professions
(14) County Officers
(15) Chief Burgess and Town Council of the Borough of Pottsville, and School Directors of the Borough
(16) Chief Burgesses and Councils of surrounding Boroughs
(17) Soldiers of the Revolutionary War, of the War of 1812 and of the Mexican War
(18) Officers of the Army and Navy of the United States
(19) Assistant Marshal and Aides
(20) Brass Band
(21) Independent Order of Odd Fellows
(22) United Order of Odd Fellows

(23) Schuylkill County Agricultural Society
(24) Brass Band
(25) Sons of Temperance
(26) Order of United American Mechanics
(27) Germania Benevolent Societies
(28) Hibernian Benevolent Societies
(29) Brass Band
(30) Citizens on Foot
(31) Citizens in Carriages
(32) Citizens Mounted

Thus it was the militia regiments who led the line of march and Citizens Mounted who brought up the rear, with industrious civilians and old veterans on foot marching in between, convoyed, as it were, through the crowd of cheering women and children.

Analysis of the members of organizing committees and officers of the inauguration meeting tells us more. It reveals who were the local party at interest in raising the Henry Clay monument and who were the local opponents. The idea of a Henry Clay monument was first proposed by Samuel Sillyman, a wealthy owner of coal lands, and John Bannan, a Pottsville attorney (a large proportion of whose work involved coal properties), a hero of the War of 1812, and brother of Benjamin Bannan, editor of the principal local newspaper, *The Miners' Journal*, which was the voice of the coal trade. John Bannan donated the land for the monument; Benjamin Bannan advertised the ceremony. Benjamin Bannan was also the close associate of Henry Carey, who owned the entire town of St. Clair nearby and leased the mines under it to various operators. Henry Carey had retired wealthy from managing the principal publishing house in the United States, founded by his father Mathew Carey, and now devoted himself to writings in economics and sociology. He was, indeed, America's foremost economic philosopher of the time. His brand of economics touted the merits of the protective tariff, criticized the emergence of great corporations, and opposed Adam Smith's notions on the importance of international trade in promoting the wealth of nations; his was one of the more important voices in the new Republican Party. Bannan used *The Miners' Journal* to promulgate Carey's economic and political philosophy. Henry Carey's business agent was included, and so also was militia Colonel John M. Wetherill, who acted as agent of the Wetherill clan of Philadelphia, who owned all of the land surrounding St. Clair that Carey did not own. The list could go on; suffice it to say that, of the forty-odd organizers of the occasion, a large proportion was connected with the coal trade either as landowners, or landowners' business agents, or landowners' attorneys. Not represented in any explicit way in the organization of the festivities and not recognized in the order of march were two groups of men who also had an interest in the coal trade, the mine operators and the underground miners themselves. The mine operators were underfinanced small capitalists who were chronically pinched between the wage and safety demands of their miners and the demands for royalties on coal by the landowners. Within twenty years the independent mine operators would all be wiped out by bankruptcy or absorbed into the growing bureaucracy of the Reading Railroad's vast Coal and Iron Company, which purchased 80 percent of the coal land in Schuylkill County between 1868 and 1874. The miners, however, remained as a party who increasingly saw their interests as opposed, first to those of both the independent operators and the absentee landowners, and later to those of the Reading Coal and Iron Company. When the Workingmen's Benevolent Association of St. Clair — the first effective miners union — was formed in 1868, there was already considerable unrest in the coalfields over mine safety and wages: for instance, ten years after the Henry Clay monument was raised, the Pottsville militia which had marched in the parade was called out to suppress a strike among the miners at St. Clair.[9]

Thus the raising of the monument took place in the context of developing conflict between miners, on the one hand, and mine operators and landowners on the other, over two major issues — wages and mine safety. Each side saw itself as having legitimate interests incompatible with the claims of the other. It can be no accident, therefore, that the choice of Henry Clay honored a man who represented the art of compromise, who was credited with devising an American System that promoted both manufacturing and agriculture. Nor is it an accident that Henry Carey, the economic philosopher of the American system, had just published (in 1852) a volume of essays under the title *The Harmony of Interests, Agricultural, Manufacturing, and Commercial*. This work, and others of the genre, argued among other things that the workers shared with their capitalist employers a common interest in the financial prosperity of the enterprise that supported them both. The tactical proposition was plain: if only you workers would cooperate with us by restraining your demands for higher wages and more expensive safety procedures, we would all profit more in the long run.

There is no opportunity here to describe the evolution of the opposing cultural strategies of labor and capital in the coalfields or its interim denouement in a new synthesis that pitted permanent industrywide labor unions against great corporations, under the intermittently watchful eye of a legislatively established state mine safety bureau. But I think the point stands out clearly even from this brief recitation of meanings surrounding the Henry Clay monument: far from a ritual that effectively bound social conflict by invoking a harmony of interests, the movement was essentially a tactical construction advanced as a ploy in a prolonged social conflict between mine owners and miners.

Clearly the kind of culture that appears in analyses of such events as the dedication of the Henry Clay monument is not what Edward Sapir has in mind when he describes "genuine" (as opposed to "spurious") culture. Genuine culture is "inherently harmonious, balanced, self-satisfactory," and he goes on to assert that industrial society in America, both before and after the Civil War, did not have a genuine culture.[10] But a concept of culture useful in the analysis of the societies revealed in the actual historical record (not idealized reconstructions of egalitarian communities or homogeneous states) must include plot as one of the essential structures of diversity. And the opposed cultural strategies of groups in conflict should be regarded not as a confusion of tongues but as the matrix of culture change.[11]

Notes

1. See, for example, *Culture and Personality*, 2nd ed. (New York: Random House, 1970).

2. For my views on these processes, see *Religion: An Anthropological View* (New York: Random House, 1966), and *Rockdale: An American Village in the Early Industrial Revolution* (New York: Knopf, 1978).

3. This use of the term "plot" differs from Margaret Mead's usage in her early paper, "On the Concept of Plot in Culture," *Transactions of the New York Academy of Sciences*, Series II, 2 (1939): 24–27. Mead used the term to refer to the parallel between the dramatic plot of a particular Balinese ceremony and the actual course of relations between the Balinese mother and her child. I am indebted to the member of the audience in Washington who drew my attention to Mead's paper and the ethnohistory seminar member Samuel Schreger who tracked it down for me.

4. The following account of the Henry Clay monument is drawn from Ermina Elssler, "The History of the Henry Clay Monument," *Publications of the Historical Society of Schuylkill County* 2 (1910): 405–17.

5. Alfred Chandler, "Anthracite Coal and the Beginnings of the Industrial Revolution in the United States," *Business History Review* 46 (1972): 141–81.

6. *Miner's Journal*, July 7, 1855.

7. For a careful study of Pennsylvania politics in this period, see John F. Coleman, *The Disruption of the Pennsylvania Democracy 1848–1860* (Harrisburg: Pennsylvania Historical and Museum Commission, 1975).

8. See Thomas Parke Hughes's edition of Samuel Smiles, *Lives of the Engineers* (Cambridge: MIT Press, 1966).

9. An excellent general history of the early coal trade in Schuylkill County is Clifton K. Yearley, *Enterprise and Anthracite* (Baltimore: Johns Hopkins University Press, 1961).

10. Edward Sapir, "Culture, Genuine and Spurious," in David G. Mandelbaum, ed., *Selected Writings of Edward Sapir* (Berkeley: University of California Press, 1949).

11. For an extended treatment of the anthracite industry, see the writer's *St. Clair: A Nineteenth-Century Coal Town's Experience with a Disaster-Prone Industry* (New York: Knopf, 1987; Ithaca: Cornell University Press, 1988 [paperback]).

2

CULTURE AND COLLECTIVE ACTION

Mary Douglas

Culture is nothing if not a collective product. The very idea of collective action bristles with difficulties in economics. This chapter is an attempt to have a theory of culture that complements the theory of rational choice. There is no intention of supplanting the latter – indeed, some sort of rational choice should enter cultural analysis. The concept of culture is here developed to illuminate some of the dark areas in economics concerning the idea of the individual.

Economic theory does not pretend to offer an account of the place of the individual in society. Yet nowhere else in social theory is there anything like such a rigorous or elaborately developed account of interaction between individuals. Even psychology is not a close runner-up because its argument is so dispersed; it has too little disciplinary cohesion for formal axioms to be generally accepted. Economic theory can be as cohesive as it is because of the professional intensity of its discourse and because Western thought is impregnated with the Western experience of market. Louis Dumont has aptly said, "The economic mode of thought naturally enjoys an ideological supremacy over the political in the liberal or capitalist world thanks to its embodying a purer or more perfect form of individualism" (Dumont 1985: 259 – 60). In the market the focus is upon individuals exchanging privately owned goods; the individual and the rights that accrue to him from ownership are the given of the economic mode of thought, the rarely questioned starting point of the analysis. As Armen Alchian (1967) puts it, "the question of economics, or of how prices should be determined, is the question of how property rights should be defined and exchanged and on what terms."

Economic theory, like most disciplines, comes in a variety of forms. The form with which I am here concerned has as its basic assumption that individual behavior is motivated entirely by self-regarding preferences. There is a certain implausibility about this, in that we know from experience that individuals often do not even try to pursue their self-interest consistently. Moreover, this assumption makes it difficult for economics to allow for moral feelings such as altruism or commitment. As a result economists from the earliest times have sought means of extending their field to encompass other motivations. Adam Smith, for example, used material gain as the basis for his theory of economic behavior and sympathy as the basis for his theory of moral behavior.

It is, of course, possible to extend the notion of self-interest to include "sympathy," "psychic reward," "social approval," or virtually any kind of emotion or moral sentiment which may be supposed to influence behavior. Some economists have indeed endeavored to do just this. The trouble is that by doing so we lose much of the predictive power of economics, and economics becomes what Amartya Sen calls "a remarkably mute theory. Behavior, it appears, is to be explained in terms of preferences, which are in turn defined by behavior" (Sen 1977: 325).

The technique which Steven Jones (1984) has called "calculating avarice" is an extremely powerful methodology which has provided economics with many of its classic findings. When an economist "proves," for example, that under conditions of perfect competition, prices will equal marginal costs, he is not making an empirical observation; he is, in effect, deducing this proposition from the assumption that each individual supplier in the market will seek the maximum material return for his effort. Any solution other than the equation of price with marginal cost can be shown to lead to lesser material reward for every individual under conditions of perfect competition. A market in which the supplier were motivated by some other passion than the pursuit of "his own gain" would have a different equilibrium point. Amartya Sen argues that it would be possible to develop a range of "meta-economics" assuming different dominant motivations.

Gary Becker is one economist who finds the economic approach not at all constraining. He claims that the three assumptions — maximizing behavior, stable preferences, and equilibrium — which are used for understanding markets, also illuminate all types of decisions. Even within the family, usually regarded as a stronghold impregnable to economic analysis, he shows that allocations of time and money income can be interpreted on economic principles, although preference schedules may sometimes need to be enlarged to include more than conventionally defined material gain. For example, he claims that he can "justify the popular belief that more beautiful, charming, and talented women tend to marry wealthier and more successful men" (1981: 75). Any woman who has ever felt that she could be much more beautiful and more charming if she could only first marry a really successful man will resent the circularity here. His account of altruism in the family has the quality of total irrefutability: either the utility function of a person, say the husband, depends positively on the well-being of his spouse or children, so what passes as altruism is included in self-interest, or else the effects of envy within the family constrain what the egoist would like to do. After the event, apparently altruistic behavior turns out to be in the narrower rational interests of the so-called altruist (1981: 178–201). Thus he falls into the trap of circularity, explaining behavior in terms of preferences.

A market presupposes a society of people with preferences, and how there can be a society at all is the question that economists cannot broach from their chosen platform. In analyzing the market for private goods, classical economics jumps from individual self-interest to community interest, the interest of the society, by invoking the magic of an invisible hand. It is not difficult to see through something invisible. Behind it lies the community engaged in its normative debate and the laws, conventions, and social values to which the normative debate gives rise. Humans speak, they use rhetoric and scrutinize one another's speech. Their individual conflicts of interest surface and are overruled as they try to persuade one another to compromise or to stand firm. Faced with conflict, contestants have to resort to the rhetoric of the common good to support their private claims. Tocqueville, writing of public associations, identified the basic mechanism of the normative debate that sets the ground rules for any form of social structure, whether that of a market, the state, or the voluntary associations with which he was primarily concerned. Citizens, he argued, "converse, they listen to one another and they are mutually stimulated to all sorts of undertakings" (1966: 124). As a result they may even "learn to surrender their own will to that of all the rest and to make their exertions subordinate to the common impulse" (p. 127). Once engaged, the normative debate about how the common good should be achieved puts the rhetoric through local tests of noncontradiction. Anthropologists find that certain priorities, once agreed, rule out others. Listening to the debate is their way to approach the nonmarket behavior which is so difficult to make sense of within economic theory.

MARKET FAILURE

Economists recognize that market transactions do not include all rational transactions concerning goods. They have developed various ways of thinking about rational nonmarket transactions, generally designated by the term "market failure." Measuring the spillover to the community from individual market transactions is one approach to the nonmarket used by economists. Externalities are a powerful tool for analyzing certain problems in a market society (for example, the damage done by pollution, a "negative externality," or the benefits of an educated citizenry, a "positive externality"). To the anthropologist's eye the theory of externalities (and market failure generally) seems an elaborately backhanded way of studying the collective interest. Moreover the concept of externalities can both include too much and, at the same time, fail to explain some quite common forms of nonmarket behavior.

Almost any action can be shown to have some externalities (whether positive or negative) and, as Richard Nelson points out, literally everything has externalities once we grant that one individual derives satisfaction from the happiness of another. (Or, indeed, contrariwise! We are all members one of another, whether the bonds that link us are mutual envy or mutual charity.)

At the same time, the concept of externalities has little if any explanatory power in the case of several common forms of nonmarket society, those in which production is not for market and in which almost all legitimate transfers of property are made on grounds of kinship or friendship, as war booty, or as feudal dues. At first sight, another concept, that of public goods, seems more promising than externalities. It does not treat the collective good as a side-effect of individual market transactions, and it clearly distinguishes the private goods of market from the public goods of the community.

PUBLIC GOODS

Public goods are defined by Samuelson (1954) as goods which are freely available and from the enjoyment of which no one can be excluded. The first characteristic, joint supply, postulates a good the consumption of which by one consumer does not reduce the amount available for others: if I consume a loaf of bread that same loaf is not thereafter available for anybody else; if I watch a circus or theatrical production, my enjoyment of that performance does not eliminate the possibility of someone else enjoying the same performance at the same time. Clearly the consumption of bread-eaters and the consumption of theatre-goers differ — indeed it is difficult to think of a theatrical performance being "consumed" by the audience even though the demand for theatre clearly comes within the consumption pattern of the audience. Even so, the number of "consumers" who can enjoy a theatrical performance is not literally infinite. Crowding soon introduces similarities between the two forms of "supply" — the theatre has a limited capacity, and too large an audience will reduce the enjoyment of all (Buchanan 1965). Markets, as the circus and theatre examples show, can cope with joint supply so long as access to the good can be controlled.

The second characteristic, nonexcludability, is necessary to put the good into the public category. However, it is as rare to find goods that are necessarily nonexcludable as it is to find goods that are in absolutely joint supply. In its origin the idea of public goods assumed superabundant supply, such as air or land in a sparsely populated country. But we have less and less reason to think of these as being in plentiful supply. Moreover, as Russell Hardin says, it is "not easy to think of pure cases of goods characterized by the impossibility of exclusion . . . large bodies of law have as their purpose to erect exclusionary barriers where the naive might have thought exclusion impossible" (1982: 18).

Olson's 1965 analysis of collective goods does not emphasize free availability so much as nonexcludability. He seems to be right in avoiding, despite its obvious attraction, a definition that rests on the technical or material properties of the thing itself. National defense is a favorite example of a nonexcludable public good: whether you pay your taxes or not, the defensive arm of the nation will cover you as well as your tax-paying neighbor. But even in this often cited case, military history records protection being withdrawn from border regions, according to the exigencies of defense. Samuelson (1955) admitted that public education, defense and highway programs, the courts, police, and fire services do not fit well into the rigid category of public goods available to all. He defended his theoretical model of pure public goods as a polar extreme to contrast with the competitive equilibrium model of the pure private economy, each on an equally high level of abstraction. Essentially his concept of public goods divides individual transactions in the market which depend on private property from some polar opposite which depends on public or no ownership. Between pure public goods and purely private goods lies a whole spectrum of intermediate positions to which the very concept of ownership is ill adapted. Where the market is not highly developed most resources are not claimed by individuals, and so, by default, they are assumed to be held in common. As Richard Nelson (1986) says, "it is a commonplace . . . to remark that pure public goods are rare. That is true but so also are pure private goods." This is enough to show that the economist's conception of the nonmarket bristles with difficulties.

We can face this issue much more directly when positions on the scale between private and public goods are seen to rest on a collective decision. Public availability is conferred by the collectivity itself. What enters the list of public goods and the list of private goods and positions in between depends on community fiat and varies from one community to another. In England postwar governments tried to treat health care as essentially a nonexcludable public good (although obviously not in joint supply) while in America it is largely treated as a private good. In many societies food and water are treated as nonexcludable.

Recent developments in England give point to Peter Steiner's emphasis on "nonexcludability" as the main criterion, at the expense of "joint supply." Unlike Samuelson's definition, Steiner's says that "any publicly induced or provided collective good is a public good" (1974: 247). As Steiner points out, under this definition, a public good is not necessarily in joint supply (a collective consumption good). Instead, it is a good that differs "appreciably in either quantity or quality [from] the alternative the private market would produce and [there is] a viable demand for the difference" (ibid.). Steiner's definition allows for health care to be provided simultaneously in the same community as a collective good and also as a good provided by the private market, with some differences of quantity or quality. Under Samuelson's definition, the fact that health care is clearly not in joint supply would, strictly speaking, preclude its ever being treated as a public good. Unlike Samuelson, Steiner fastens not on some inherent characteristic of the good itself but on the public's reaction to the good. For him, clearly, "demand" has a political even more than an economic connotation. The economist is, to some extent, passing the buck to the politician; as the doctor said to the priest on the patient's deathbed: "*À votre tour, cher collègue* [It's your turn, my friend]."

Absolutely anything can be a public good in this sense. The concept can break out of the ethnocentric bounds to which contrast with markets had confined it. Three conditions need to hold: one is the decision to make something freely available; another is the will to make the public decision effective. The third is for the anthropologist or economist to set the analysis sufficiently far back from the individual transfer. For example, at too close range a transfer seen in isolation may appear to be a purely private benefit. When a trade union has negotiated a higher wage for a particular kind of job, each worker who takes his share has evidently a private benefit. But at the level of the ruling that all workers in that category now receive the higher wage, the ruling has made a true collective good — obviously nonexcludable and, in some sense, in joint supply in that no one worker's receipt of the higher wage reduces the rate available to the others. Of course, the total number of workers in receipt of a wage may be reduced in consequence but this is not essentially different to the crowding that limits the applicability of the concept of joint supply in other cases.

Among many people who live by hunting, complex rules ensure that meat is distributed through the whole camp. Sometimes the rule is negative in form, such as that no one should go without. In this case, the product of the hunt is treated as a collective good very much in the way Olson suggests. In other cases, the rules prescribe the precise categories entitled to a particular cut, as for example, a haunch for the father of the hunter, one for the village chief, another part for the mother, another for the paternal aunt, and so on. In addition to observing distributive rules of this kind, the Lele hunter was also required to give a generous piece to anyone who saw him kill or bring home the game, "because of the eyes." This referred to the practical infeasibility of excluding anyone who had seen the meat. The effect is to make the whole kill into common property, out of which the hunter himself gets a modest allocation.

In constructing such distributive patterns all the various beneficiaries seem to have colluded. Such patterns are not merely the result of a number of individual voluntary transactions. The individual has no choice in the matter. It is true that if the rules have proved viable, in some statistical sense most individuals on balance are likely to benefit more than they lose from the maintenance of the rules, but the individual is entirely bound by the rule. A collective effort has established and sanctioned the rules of distribution. The result is a social order in which nearly every transfer lies in the domain defined as public. (Anthropologists somewhat confusingly term this a "gift economy.")

Putting gift economies into the theory of public goods does not help us to go much further, because economic theory is not very well developed on the subject. Another route is to go back to the idea of the normative debate and trace the institutional options confronting individuals deciding what shall be put into the public domain. For this we need to revise the economist's concept of the rational individual.

THE NORMATIVE DEBATE

The rational individual is not a solipsist, but rather a *zoon politikon*: a being whose needs are not determined in isolation, but only in society. Accountability is written into his makeup. The rational individual has to be conceived as one who expects to be held accountable, who therefore seeks approval, and who gives out praise and blame to others. This individual has to be redefined as incorporated in a community of one sort or another. The change is not to deny the individual self-regarding preference but to point out that it can operate only within a context of accountability determined by the community. Capitalism is the system which probably gives the most scope for the exercise of the self-regarding preference (except, perhaps, for Hobbes's "state of nature"). Yet even within capitalist society, the way the individual can pursue his own gain is determined by the society, its laws and conventions.

As to collective action, we can assume either that it is fraught with difficulty or that there is no problem about it. We can assume that the social bond is inherently fragile or inherently tough. The choice depends on the model of the individual with which we start. If we take the benign view, there is no need for a theory to explain collective action; the initial assumption about human nature does duty in place of inquiry. Economists do not take that line; their initial assumption that self-regarding motives are dominant implies that the social fabric is vulnerable to private depredations. Experience backs the economists' assumption. When keeping the streets clear of litter is left to individual householders, some sweep their doorsteps, and some do not. In social theory inertia is still a power to be reckoned with, whatever reservations may be held about the concept of the individual fired only by self-regarding passions.

There may be a misleading natural bias towards thinking that the norm is that collectivities are viable. To justify that bias we would need to ignore all the attempts at organizing that we ourselves have made and been forced to abandon for lack of sustained support. Our eyes get drawn to the enduring institutions, and we tend to forget the attempts at revolution or reform that have failed. The records of anthropologists, on the other hand, keep track of communities that have split in acrimony or died out. An interest in failed collectivities, without being cynical, sharpens the spirit of inquiry. So the first assumption is that collective action is difficult.

The next assumption for cultural analysis is that in the course of judging one another's accountability individuals use their reasoning powers to scrutinize their social arrangements. They need to do so as they excuse themselves and monitor each other. From the first they involve one another in a primitive form of constitution making. Each individual who enters a social relation is drawn at the same time into a debate about what the relation is and how it ought to be conducted. This is the normative debate on which cultural analysis fastens attention.

At any time individuals may be heard reasoning with one another about how to achieve the goals they share. In the course of the debate they construct conceptual categories appropriate for their exchanges. Their shared experience, shaped in metaphor and fixed in ritual and history, is a collective good that they have made together. The object of their debate is to legitimize the form of their society.

One practitioner of cultural analysis addresses the point of interchange at which the individual choice distinguishes itself from the cultural pattern. Morris Freilich uses the term "proper" to indicate the outcome of the public debate on what ought to be. Proper are shared techniques, agreed standards, stereotyped modes of behavior, all that is recognized as correct and formal. In contrast, he uses "smart" for individual skills, private ends, unpredicted and ingenious solutions (Freilich 1980). This usefully captures the difference between the idea of culture and the concept of the individual exercising his rational choice within cultural constraints. Freilich then proceeds to concentrate on their point of convergence, as he does in chapter 12 of this volume. In contrast, I want to consider in detail how the proper category gets its content and the main varieties of proper ways of doing things.

Pierre Bourdieu practices another form of cultural analysis using the concept of Habitus. This describes the social field in which individuals compete for legitimacy. The struggle is waged largely in the form of contested aesthetic and moral judgments (1977: 171–83). This analysis illuminates the form that the contest takes and the strategies open to the contenders. It is not concerned with the form given to the society itself nor with how the social structure guides the progress of the debates. The cultural analysis I will present is like a prolegomenon to Bourdieu's analysis of Habitus. The typology of cultural forms displays the internal debates between members of different kinds of social unit. It reveals the attitude to authority and the concept of the individual that make sense to those who have combined to form a social group of a particular type. It is an account of the prior debate that individuals will be having among themselves, whether they ever enter the larger political scene or not.

In the public debate the future form of the society is at stake; the contenders define the options. This is where individuals are heard threatening to defect, threatening to coerce or promising to bribe, promising to resist coercion or bribery, and mobilizing support for the common good. Their dilemma of whether to cooperate or to defect is very much on the surface of their talk. Even if individual self-interest were their only motivation, the debate must necessarily be conducted in terms of the collective interest, since the forum in which collective support is mustered is public.

CULTURAL THEORY

From these preliminary assumptions cultural theory proceeds to develop an argument. The first step is to argue that out of the infinite number of distinct forms that human society can take, not all attempted combinations will be viable. Many different causes may destroy a human society. War or famine or vast migration may leave a land empty. These dangers are constantly invoked as members of the community put pressure on one another. Such risks may indeed cause the destruction of the community, but cultural analysis is concerned with only one cause of breakdown, the collapse of the normative debate. The speakers in the normative debate hear one another criticize contradiction and rebuke nonsense. Ultimately there is always a touchstone of practicability. A person cannot be in two places at once. One injunction cannot be accepted if it countermands established principle. One person cannot belong to two mutually exclusive groups. Redistribution and saving are at odds. Some kinds of institutions just cannot be added to other kinds because they will be indefensible by any common test. The debate will be in continual danger of falling into uproar or silence because the accepted categories of discourse make no sense.

THE CONSTRAINED DIALOGUE

The idea of the normative debate is very close to Bruce Ackerman's notion that liberalism is based on a constrained dialogue. In a brilliant exercise aimed at analyzing and justifying liberal philosophical principles, Ackerman examines the conditions for a liberal debate. He regards liberalism as "a way of talking about power, a form of political culture" (1980: 6). He finds that it can be defined within three constraints: rationality, consistency, and neutrality. Rationality means the requirement that any claim be supported by reasons. Consistency safeguards the intelligibility of the dialogue demanded by rationality. Neutrality protects the continuance of the dialogue against assertions of intrinsic superiority. "No reason is a good reason if it requires the power holder to assert: a) that his conception of the good is better than that asserted by any of his fellow citizens, or b) that regardless of his conception of the good, he is intrinsically superior to one or more of his fellow citizens" (p. 11).

It is worth distinguishing the use made here of the idea of constrained dialogue. Ackerman's essay is in political philosophy. His initial assumption is that the elementary political contest is a struggle for power, so the dialogue has rules that set constraints on the struggle. Our concern is not with the struggle for power but with the viability of a form of society. However, he maintains that the constraints he argues on behalf of liberal philosophy are sufficiently general to be applied to any of the several forms of political structure identified by cultural analysis.

At this point we need to deal with an objection. Any one who has attended a town meeting or a board meeting knows that the normative debate is a fumbling, half-coherent process. One proposition is made, only to be challenged by a contrary one. Decisions are difficult to reach. They rest on tacit assumptions, not on argued syllogisms. The stability and distinctiveness of a logical pattern is just as improbable as the stability of social forms. It is not plausible to argue that shaky institutions are shored up by equally shaky logical forms: both forms of collective action are so fragile that they are more likely to collapse together. In reply to this, cultural theory will need to save its analysis by recourse to system-sustaining effects that follow from initial decisions in favor of one type of organization rather than another. This is the nub of the argument: institutions stand on different forking paths of decision trees. Once embarked on one path, it is difficult to get back to the choice that would have led another way.

This is the central argument of cultural theory: culture itself is constrained. It cannot make any number of combinations and permutations. Inclusion is logically different from hierarchy; inclusion and hierarchy are different from equivalent exchange. Any human group will be drawn to use one or another of these principles to legitimize its collective action; in doing so it will encounter a specific set of organizational problems. Each initial choice will lead, by the logic of the normative debate, to radically different solutions. Each resultant type of culture will be legitimated upon a different logical base.

By following this argument we can broach the question of stable types from another direction. Assuming that flux and disorder are more probable in social life than order, cultural theory should explain how any type of collectivity can resist pressures to transform. Hierarchy, market, and sect are very different. Given the greater likeliness of disorder, this typological stability is itself curious. Half of the explanation comes from the distinctive legitimizing processes released in the course of the normative debate. The other half follows from the institutional consequences of responding to the logic.

THE TYPOLOGY

The ability of individuals to legitimize coercion is the very question at issue. The list below of initial problems, successful solutions, and institutional reinforcements assumes no illegitimate use of coercion. We assume that the self-sustaining powers of each distinctive system are drawn originally from the legitimating process but will not endure without some system-sustaining reinforcements, in other words, a functional argument. Jon Elster's criticism of the way that functional analysis is often used in explaining social behavior leads him to conclude that in the social sciences good functional arguments may not be quite impossible but they are exceedingly rare (Elster 1983; Douglas 1986). This is partly because they cannot be justified within any overarching theory such as provided for biology by the theory of evolution. However, in a modest way the lack of a major organizing theory can be supplemented by a good little typology of systematic interactions in which system-maintaining loops channel resources back to the collectivity.

The political rhetoric reveals a minimal three types of legitimation, each so distinctive that no speaker in one type can appeal to the justifying principles which uphold another type without landing in contradiction.

The first bases its whole system of relations on bonding insiders together against outsiders. The second upholds the trust necessary for exchange between individuals. The third legitimizes the up-down hierarchical bonding of individuals. Each of these is stabilized in a uniquely specialized normative order. The principles of one cannot be borrowed by either of the others without obvious and grave inconsistency. It makes a good starting place to indicate what problems of collective organization each of the three types is best able to meet and from there to consider the overflow of benefits to the collectivity that follow from each solution.

Inside-Outside

The logical principle of inclusion gives rise to the social type that focuses attention on the relations between insider and outsider. This is a type of organization evolved to solve problems caused by too-easy defection. Anyone who threatens to move out puts the wished-for collective good in jeopardy. Unlike the market, as described by Hirschman (1970), this is a community whose future is at the mercy of defectors. In such a case penalties for defection are not going to work. An attempt to impose penalties will merely make the membership melt away even faster. According to circumstances, and according to their objectives as a community, there are three strategies theoretically open. Two of them would have the effect of moving the community to a different point in this typology.

First, they could theoretically institute a more regulated regime in which each committed member signs an enforceable contract. For example, many communes require that goods be held in common. Then defection is effectively stopped by the heavy loss and disadvantages suffered by a would-be defector who can take no property with him. When the commune adopts this solution, it makes a radical change in the tone of the normative debate. Defection having become difficult, the community generally starts to accumulate centralized authority. It can become a hierarchy. This appears to be what happened with the Mormons. This solution is theoretically feasible. If the normative debate goes in this direction, it escapes what I have called the "sectarian trap" (1986). But this means overcoming individual resistance to collective action. It tends not to be a practical proposition if the objects for coming together in a community are rather restricted and if the members have no wish to give up their scope for seceding; by definition in this argument, no one can force them to accept regulation.

Another theoretically possible solution would be to institute trade. Then the community is turned into the second type, based on exchange. But that is not always possible. Market requires certain conditions, as we will see below. It is not so easy to move out of the first position as defined.

The third solution, in order to avoid the threatened defections, is to find a way of staying together without either exerting authority or giving special enticements to stay. A community without authority tends to be harried by charges of arbitrary behavior. It needs a rule acceptable to all, and only a rule that is demonstrably fair will do. To meet this requirement of fairness the community is drawn to institute equality. If all power and all goods are held equally and in common, no one can complain of arbitrariness. Once the community has founded itself upon the principle of equality, the normative debate has taken a decisive turn. The community has made itself attractive to all: it does not countenance the despoiling of some members by others. But now it has another problem. Equality as a principle of distribution can be monitored in the public debate, but it is not so easy to ensure equal productive effort. Unless it can persuade its members each to "surrender his own will to that of the rest," this kind of community tends to be a prey to free riding and the inertia that Olson sums up as the principle of "Let George do it." The equality rule has not solved the defection problem nor the free-rider problem, though it is adopted as a response to both. Something more has to happen if the commune is to be stabilized, even at a low level of coordination.

In itself the rule of equality has the unintended effect of impeding decision taking and leadership. It has the further unintended effect of exposing the fragile fund of mutual trust to the strains of ambiguity. For the one defense the community has devised against the charge of unfairness is to refuse to define any one individual as distinct from any other, to refuse to institutionalize differences of office or differences of reward. This follows from deciding to take seriously the threat of defection (and rightly, since it would have destroyed the community if it had been ignored).

Now, laboring under ambiguity and lack of leadership and lack of authority, this community is going to be riven by factions. At an early stage in its life the normative debate starts to focus on the theme of betrayal. Members of one faction will seek to clarify by accusing the others of betraying the founding principles. The community would be destabilized early in its career if such accusations did not have unintended positive effects. Axiomatically, this is a society without authority and so one in which delinquents cannot be penalized directly—even if it were possible to agree, in the midst of such ambiguity, on what constitutes delinquency. Accusations of grave treachery against the community have the effect of summoning up enough anger and fear to produce effective collective action. Accusations and threats of expulsion result in greatly clarifying the boundary between virtuous insiders who accept the community norms and all outsiders. A commune (as I shall call it here, in default of a better technical term) generally defines two kinds of individuals, those who truly belong, the insiders, called, saved, elect to salvation, or purer, and the others, the outsiders who, in the light of accusations made against those who have truck with them, are morally inadequate human beings. The measures to institute equality and a normative debate focused on preventing defection finally can combine to make a strong protective constraint.

Defection, which everyone was initially tempted to threaten, now shows in a culpable light: it must be wicked to leave the good and join the bad. So by the moral judgment, which was inherent in the direction the debate was carried, the weakness of the outer boundary is shored up. The normative debate has created a viable institutional form for very difficult conditions, probably the only institutional form which can persist in the face of easy defection.

It is also worth mentioning, in reply to Bruce Ackerman's assumption, that the main concern for many societies is not always the struggle for power and scarce resources. In this common type everyone is worried by fear of losing members.

Exchange

A collectivity based on exchange, such as a market system, rests just as heavily upon the support of its normative debate. When individuals start to exchange and when prices begin to emerge, the embryonic market can be subverted by lack of trust. Without trust transactions are severely limited. One way in which trust can be created is to let the exchanges flow down the lines of pre-existing relationships, reinforcing ties of kinship, friendship, or patronage, thus develop-ing a network of obligatory giving. Then the emergent market system will give way to the gift system, either within a hierarchy or within a commune, and in either case a regime in which free bargaining of private goods is virtually absent.

But let us assume the emergent market overcomes this first hurdle. Essentially the market system depends on open markets, free bargaining, private property, and some protection for contract. These requirements do not combine into a harmonious whole. Markets are built over the tension between the requirement of private property and the requirement of an open market. Private property is basic to a market economy since a market is a method of exchanging property rights. But property rights are by their nature restrictive and the tension within the market is between the restrictions that can be allowed and those that cannot: patents legitimately protect private information; insider trading illegitimately exploits private information. The normative debate has to paper over the cracks in the logic so that a sufficiently strong consensus can emerge to protect the market from subversion. The dialogue has to be something on the lines worked out by Bruce Ackerman for liberalism, a philosophy whose substantive values are essen-tially techniques for keeping the debate itself going.

One threat faced by the market, once established, is monopoly, which will let the most successful trader use the rule of private property to block the rule of free access to the market and so turn his own family into a privileged dynasty or a mafia. How is this avoided? The normative debate pronounces its anathemas against greedy mergers threatening to restrict trade and take over the com-munity. But the normative debate might not be powerful enough by itself, were it not for chains of consequences which it indirectly establishes, consequences which recreate market-sustaining conditions. For example, many informal redistributive mechanisms may prevent the sons of very successful traders from starting with excessive advantage over their rivals. Among the Chimbu in New Guinea, every trader is forced to borrow to the limit of his credit; when he dies his children will be lucky if they can use his estate to pay all his creditors (Brown 1961). Consequently every rich man's son starts from scratch; even if his father did not leave an estate encumbered by debt, what he has to spend by way of a suitably lavish funeral will reduce his circumstances as much as if he had paid an enormous inheritance tax.

A market system needs freedom to expand, to find new outlets, and to justify increased scale of production. Consequently it cannot depend on the exclusive-ness which upholds the insider-outsider type of society. Private property protects it from would-be free riders so it does not need to worry about defectors from the community (unless they try to abscond without settling their private debts, and against such clear delinquency the community will have legitimated sanctions). Nor will the market type be tempted to appeal to the hierarchical principles which uphold the third type, because such principles obviously operate in restraint of trade.

Before we consider the third type, hierarchy, some comparisons of the normative debate in the first two are in order. Commune and market differ in how they work, in where they can flourish, and in the principles on which they can be grounded. As we have seen, the logical problem of the communitarian normative debate is ambiguity; the logical problem in the market is contradiction. The internal arguments of market and commune also generate different conceptions of the individual.

The individual who is most likely to operate successfully in a market society conforms closely to the model of the rational agent to which Herbert Simon brought his famous objection — someone with a mind like a calculating machine, sovereign in control of his own choices, decisive and consistent enough to give clear signals to partners. It is very difficult for such an individual to operate successfully in a commune. The communard needs to be like the saint that the normative debate in the commune upholds as a model, self-effacing and committed, prepared to bow out, quite unlike the ruthless free rider supposed by rational choice theory to exploit the regime when public goods are freely available.

Up-Down, Down-Up

This is the third type, which we have been calling hierarchy, in which authority flows between the top and bottom. A group might start in the midst of a crisis when quick and clear decisions will save the day. This does not necessarily mean that the group will support a strong leader or even stay in existence for long. If the opportunities for defection are plentiful, the group once formed might easily try to stop members from leaving by turning itself into the insider-outsider type of community, but on the other hand, if trade is rewarding it might dissolve its group boundaries and develop into an individualist system of market exchange. In whichever direction the community starts itself off, it is not going to be able to maintain the pattern without effort. For a hierarchy to try to keep centralized leadership with a clear line of authority is probably as difficult a challenge as developing either of the other two forms of organization. If the community were to start a centralized command, privilege would accrue to the power holders, which in itself would help to keep them in power. But unless they divest themselves punctiliously of hereditary advantages, their leadership becomes vulnerable to subversion from below as well as from rival factions in the elite group. The normative debate has to work very hard at monitoring a hierarchy; the whole system depends on the trustful compliance of the people it advantages least. One way of getting this compliance is to create a circular principle of responsibility, by the following stages.

The debate will assert that someone has to be first (thus safeguarding the principle of strong decision), but then it will also declare that the first shall be last, that the chief is the servant of his people, and that the pope is the servant of the servants of God. This is what Dumont describes as the holism which legitimates a hierarchical system (Dumont 1983). Saying is not enough, ritualizing is not enough. It is not enough to keep saying that what is done is for the good of the whole. Putting the principle of mutual dependence into the normative debate allows it to be publicly challenged. The demands of consistency require words to match deeds. Those in command must be seen *not* to be lining their private pockets. The robber baron who abuses the power which has been created for the common good must be seen to be chastised. The powerful lord must be seen to provide the protection to his liegemen that the system implies. Without this self-correcting power from the normative debate, hierarchy will not last. No more than the market can be sustained without support for contract, or the commune without accepting the principle of equality, the hierarchy cannot be sustained without commitment to the circle of responsibility.

Like the other two types, the hierarchy's future can be saved by chains of consequences that follow once it has been set up in the first place. Hierarchical principles easily ensure that material wealth flows toward the center; accumulating there it constitutes a reserve of power that can be used to maintain the system and a store of value that can be redistributed in patronage.

The rhetoric of service which maintains the hierarchy is not going to be acceptable or plausible in either of the others. It may well be easier to live at peace with one's neighbors in a hierarchy than in a commune or market society. First, there are so many good reasons given for the way things are. Contradiction does not so obviously underlie the hierarchy as it does the market, and ambiguity is reduced in a way it can never be in a commune. But it has its special weaknesses. Hierarchy needs information to flow from bottom up as well as top down. The channels of information being organized vertically and authority being centralized, it is a truism of organization theory that sending commands down is easier than receiving news from below, as a truly collegial hierarchy would require. The subversion of the hierarchy into a tyranny is easy. This kind of society works well in situations needing strong, centralized command; to work efficiently it needs good intelligence. But because the system depends on the consent of the subordinate class, the majority who benefit least, reasons must be given for explaining why some (only a few) are in the command positions. The value of the reasons depends on the value of the system as a whole to those it privileges least. They need to perceive an overspill from the powerful individuals' transactions to themselves as a collectivity.

Inevitably the command fears its chain of reasoning is not strong enough to be convincing and it tempted to exclude the voices of the followers. When the normative debate becomes an affair of the elite, there is a tendency to reinforce good reasons with censorship. Censorship spells the end of the flow of information on which hierarchy depends, and digs its trap.

Now we have identified three forms of normative debate, or three forms of culture. Each is comprised of a mixture of sensible strategies and mutual exhortation, both submitted to the best available logic. Each has its own theory of what the individual human is like. The model of the individual is adapted to the model of the social system in which the individual is expected to operate. The individual in the market system is the only one which is held to be driven by self-interest.

As Albert Hirschman has pointed out, the idea that greed is the dominant human motive only came to be generally accepted after the sixteenth century when market itself became dominant and was expected to be a motive force that would curb the passion for power (1977). It is not too fanciful to point out that each of the three cultural types described above has its own specific temptation in the list of deadly sins: if greed is written into the account of the individual operating in the exchange system, envy can be written into the account of the unbuffered individual trying to lead the good life amid the stressful ambiguity of the commune. As for the individual in the hierarchy, pride is the motive underlying his characteristic lust for domination. Only the first, greed, has been incorporated into an axiomatized theory of social forces. But there is no intrinsic reason why the conditions for a society composed of envious or prideful individuals could not be formalized.

My friends will recognize in this typology the familiar outline of grid-group analysis of which there are now several variants used for different kinds of problems. James Hampton originally helped me to develop a two-by-two matrix to capture the features of four distinctive social environments (1982). Michael Thompson turned it into an ecological model driven by the competition between different forms of social organization, each seeking to absorb or eliminate the others (1982). Jonathan Gross and Steve Rayner have provided a formal basis for measuring and comparing these different social environments (1985). Gerald Mars has used the four social environments for identifying kinds of occupational crime (1982). Why then have I only studied three types in this chapter, when colleagues have done so well with four? The answer is the same as it is for Aaron Wildavsky, who has applied this method of analysis to political cultures (1984) and in chapter 3 of this volume. By definition the fourth type is politically mute: it is a social environment which separates individuals, cuts down their communication with one another, and limits their options. Such a social environment with a high degree of regimentation and no clear group affiliation is quite common in complex societies. On the fringe of markets are individuals who have little scope for trading; on the fringe of hierarchies are other individuals who are very weakly enfranchised. They may indeed speculate, but it is hardly realistic for such individuals, whose autonomy is severely limited, to be conducting a normative debate about how their society should be constituted. Their best option is to band together to start a group of their own. Otherwise, they can only try to put in disconnected remonstrances to the debates going on around them.

THE DEBATE ABOUT PUBLIC GOODS

We ought now to be in a stronger position to confront the vexed question of public goods. According to the principles we have explored, the question of public goods arises in different forms in each kind of community, and the different definitions proffered reflect the different social forms which frame the debate. Economists naturally try to focus on relations between persons and things, since that, as Dumont has said, is a distinctive market way of thinking. From the point of view of a community based on market relations, public goods can only be envisaged as a residual class, a set of goods which inherently escape from market conditions, products which cannot be appropriated or costs which cannot be reclaimed. From the standpoint of such a society, the fact that transactions in these goods have to be external to the market will appear as the crucial characteristic, and Samuelson's definition of pure public goods is based on an ideal form of perfect externality. Being without bounds or center, the market type of society is not well placed to think of collective goods except as residual to all the private goods.

On the other hand, this definition hardly would work in a commune of the extreme polar type in which all goods are held in common. Here the private goods are residual. The Hutterite community, for example, allows each member a small box in which to keep personal mementos, but these private goods do not enter into exchanges. The equivalent of public goods in a commune are collective goods. This is where the focus on nonexcludability (characteristic of Olson's definition and of some others wrestling with the problem of collective action) has its full force.

Neither of these definitions works well to describe the nonmarket sphere in a hierarchy. In the extreme polar case of hierarchy most goods would be compulsorily allocated according to status, as part of the definition and requirement for holding a status within the community. This is the so-called gift economy we have mentioned, exemplified by feudal dues. Steiner's definition — any publicly induced or provided collective good — is broad enough to embrace it.

In sum, the effort to find one good definition of public goods is probably doomed. What counts as public does not depend on kinds of goods or kinds of transactions but on kinds of communities.

NOTE

I am particularly grateful for help in the writing of this article to John Ikenberry, Richard Nelson, Steven Jones, and James Douglas.

REFERENCES

Ackerman, Bruce
    1980   *Social Justice in the Liberal State.* New Haven: Yale University Press.
Alchian, A. A.
    1967   *Pricing and Society.* London: Institute of Economic Affairs.
Becker, Gary
    1981   *A Treatise on the Family.* Cambridge: Harvard University Press.
Bourdieu, Pierre
    1979   *La Distinction: Critique Social du Jugement.* Paris: Editions de Minuit.
Brown, Paula
    1961   "Chimbu Death Payments." *Journal of the Royal Anthropological Institute* 91 (1): 77–96.

Buchanan, J. M.
    1965   "An Economic Theory of Clubs." *Economica* 32 (2): 1–14.

Douglas, Mary
    1986   *How Institutions Think.* New York: Syracuse University Press.

Dumont, Louis
    1985   "The Economic Mode of Thought in an Anthropological Perspective." In *Economics and Philosophy,* Peter Koslowski, ed. Tübingen: J. C. B. Mohr.

    1983   *Essais sur l'Individualisme, une Perspective Anthropologique sur l'Ideologie Moderne.* Paris: Seuil.

Elster, Jon
    1983   *Explaining Technical Change: A Case Study in the Philosophy of Science.* Cambridge: Cambridge University Press.

Freilich, Morris
    1980   "Smart-Sex and Proper-Sex: A Paradigm Found." *Central Issues in Anthropology* 2 (2): 37–51.

Gross, Jonathan, and Steve Rayner
    1984   *Measuring Culture.* New York: Columbia University Press.

Hampton, James
    1982   "Giving Grid and Group Dimensions an Operational Definition." In *Essays in the Sociology of Perception*, Mary Douglas, ed. London: Routledge & Kegan Paul.

Hardin, Russell
    1982   *Collective Action.* Resources for the Future. Baltimore: Johns Hopkins University.

Hirschman, A. O.
    1970   *Exit, Voice and Loyalty: Responses to Decline in Firms, Organizations and States.* Cambridge: Harvard University Press.

    1977   *The Passions and the Interests.* Princeton, N. J.: Princeton University Press.

Jones, Steven
    1984   *The Economics of Conformism.* Oxford: Blackwells.

Mars, Gerald
    1982   *Cheats at Work, a Study of Occupational Crime.* London: Allen & Unwin.

Nelson, Richard
    1986   "The Role of Government in a Mixed Economy." Paper for Conference on Privatization of the Public Sector. Wharton School, University of Pennsylvania.

Olson, Mancur
    1965   *The Logic of Collective Action.* Cambridge: Harvard University Press.

Samuelson, Paul A.
    1955   "Diagrammatic Exposition of a Theory of Public Expenditure." *Review of Economics and Statistics* 37 (1): 350–56.

    1954   "The Pure Theory of Public Expenditure," *Review of Economics and Statistics* 37 (1): 387–89.

Sen, Amartya K.
    1977   "Rational Fools: A Critique of the Behavioral Foundations of Economic Theory." *Philosophy and Public Affairs* 6 (4): 317–44.

Simon, Herbert
   1955   "A Behavioral Model of Rational Choice." *Quarterly Journal of Economics* 69: 99–118.

Steiner, Peter O.
   1974   "Public Expenditure Budgeting." In *The Economics of Public Finance,* A. S. Blinder, ed. Washington, D. C.: Brookings.

Tocqueville, Alexis de
   1966   *Democracy in America.* vol. 2. J. P. Mayer and L. Lerner, eds. New York: Harper & Row.

Thompson, Michael
   1982   *Among the Energy Tribes.* Working paper 82–59, Laxemburg, Austria: International Institute for Applied Systems Analysis.

   1980   "Postscript: A Cultural Basis for Comparison." In *Risk Analysis and Decision Processes.* H. Kunreuther and J. Linnerooth, eds. Berlin: Springer Verlag.

Wildavsky, Aaron
   1984   *Moses, the Nursing Father.* Montgomery, Ala.: Alabama University Press.

Wildavsky, Aaron, and Mary Douglas
   1982   *Risk and Culture.* Berkeley: California University Press.

3

FRAMES OF REFERENCE COME FROM CULTURES: A PREDICTIVE THEORY

Aaron Wildavsky

All of us read about the importance of frames of reference. We come to see that by viewing phenomena through different prisms, according to different values and beliefs about facts, people interpret events (and seek out events to interpret) in markedly different ways. Yet it appears that frames of reference are a *deus ex machina* that somehow fall from the sky untouched by human hands. The closest we come to a categorization is economic or class self-interest in which it is alleged that a certain frame of reference is self-protecting. Agreed. But what are diverse frames protective of? Functional theories claim to answer this question: the function (or consequence) of frames of reference is to support the existing social structure. This function mongering led to a premature death, for it could not explain conflict, i.e., the existence in the same society of different frames. Nor could other basic questions be posed or answered: How many frames are there? If they are infinite in number, we are no more the wiser. What kind are they? Why do different people adopt various ones? Unless we can begin to answer such questions, frames of reference becomes an uncaused cause, explaining other phenomena but not itself open to explanation.

I claim that a theory of cultural pluralism can answer these questions, that it can account for the limited number of frames of reference we observe and show how these frames emerge from what matters most to people, namely, how they wish to live with other people. Because this theory generates numerous predictions, moreover, there is ample opportunity for disconformation.

Four cultural types — hierarchy, individualism, egalitarianism, and fatalism — built up out of Mary Douglas's group boundedness and the grid of social prescription, account for most frames of reference. We can therefore explain such critical matters as what kind of frame of reference leads which sort of people to blame certain other people for misfortune. But before we can come to grips with cultural diversity, we have to abandon cultural uniformity.

A POVERTY OF CULTURAL-*CUM*-ORGANIZATIONAL TYPES

In his classic book on *Administrative Behavior*,[1] Herbert Simon spoke of decisions stemming from people's premises about what should count as facts and what they desired, their values. He acknowledged that though these factual and valuational premises could be analyzed separately, in life they are usually found exerting reciprocal influence on one another. Where, then, do these premises from which preferences are derived come from?

Simon thought the premises might exist in the individual, but how they get there remained to be discovered. Cultural theory's answer is that individuals internalize them through their social relations.[2] Preferences for desired social relations serve as the grand theories that provide the values that form the premises on which individual decisions are based. The main stumbling block to understanding how the diverse relationships among people become converted into preferences within them, in my opinion, has been an insufficiently variegated and unsystematic typology of organizations. There are fewer types in our studies than in life, and existing categories are *ad hoc* rather than constructed from the same dimensions.

After a quarter century of studying "organizations," I have become acutely aware of the poverty of organizational types. There has to be something other than bureaucratic hierarchy. And there is — economic markets. But bidding and bargaining is regarded as a purely economic phenomenon rather than an alternative way of life.[3] Consequently one studies either centralized or decentralized bureaucracies, and that is the end of it. There is occasional mention of "clans"[4] or "clubs"[5] but these types do not come from the same matrix, are not built out of the same dimensions, as markets and hierarchies. They are just there. This won't do. There cannot be just one form of organization, one set of shared values and practices, one culture in one society.[6] Corporations, for instance, face externally toward markets, while internally they may be hierarchies, though at certain levels egalitarian relationships may prevail. Similarly, I conceive of countries as conglomerations of cultures — there is more than one culture in one country — though at any one time a single culture may be more powerful than the others in certain spheres of life.

Organizations are more than instruments; they are themselves sources of preferences, for organizations encapsulate ways of life as well as modes of achievement. How, indeed, as Chester Barnard taught,[7] can people be persuaded to commit themselves to organizational life unless the organizations themselves contain the ties that bind — their values legitimating their desired practices?

Richard Cyert and James March's seminal *A Behavioral Theory of the Firm* made us analytically aware that subunits may have different and sometimes opposing objectives.[8] Nevertheless, as the burgeoning development of formal theories of organization reveals, all organizations, at least all bureaucracies, public and private, are treated as if they are alike. An organization is an organization is an.... But if there are different types of organizations whose varying cultures produce different preferences, our efforts to model their behavior can no longer be about any and all organizations, but will have to specify how the shared values and social relations of its members shape their preferences. The cultural context, the relationship among the cultures that make up the organization, be it a bureau, a city government, an interest group, or a voluntary agency, will also have to be specified or else the character of the organization under study will be misspecified. Nor will the assumption of utility maximization prove serviceable because utilities (or preferences) may well vary from one organization to another. Indeed, the organization, with its compound of cultures, may itself be the source of preferences. Assuming the same objective function for organizations, therefore, will be no better than assuming that preferences are externally given. Nor will pasting on the term "organizational culture" or "corporate culture" to cover some ineffable essence, which one is otherwise unable to describe or analyze, rescue the failure to conceive of organizations as culturally pluralistic generators as well as would-be implementers of previously formed preferences.

If there are an infinite and unrelated number of cultures, hence, of cultural premises, no intelligible answer to the question of preference formation can be given except "it depends." History is uniqueness. But if the types of viable cultures are limited in number and interconnected, formed and reformed along the same dimensions, a comprehensible answer can be given: people continuously construct and reconstruct their culture through decision making. The values people prefer and their beliefs about the world are woven together in their institutions. By conceiving of cultures as theories about conceptions of the good life (the desired values) and the way the world works (beliefs about facts) are related to patterns of social relations, we can begin to connect cultures to preferences.

CULTURES AS THEORIES

Here we are helped by intuitive notions of cultures as codes enabling individuals to make much out of little. Thus cultures may be conceived of as grand theories — paradigms if you will, programs if you prefer — from whose few initial premises many consequences applicable to a wide variety of circumstances may be deduced.

Think of cultures as rival theories; they organize experience. If everything is possible, without constraint, there is no need to choose and no way to think, because no act interferes with any other. If nothing is possible, everything being constrained, there is also no way to choose and no point in thinking. In between total constraint and limitless possibility, theories tell us what to take for granted (the assumptions) and what to test (the consequences). Dogma — assuming most things — facilitates skepticism — testing a few things.[9] The impossibility theorems of science, stating what cannot happen, are mirrored by the shared values of cultures, telling members of a society what ought not to occur. Physical impossibilities and moral imperatives serve the same purpose, namely, holding sufficient aspects of life constant to permit a narrower range of hypotheses about what works in physical or social life to be tested.

It is no exaggeration to say that the main task in theorizing or analyzing or explaining is what to leave out. The power of a theory is determined by how much is accounted for by how little. Of all the possible factors that might be involved, only a few can be chosen. Otherwise, the confusion in what is to be understood would merely be mirrored in the theory designed to illuminate its subject. When policy analysts seek to evaluate policies, they are able to manipulate only a few variables. To do more would leave them unable to reach intelligible conclusions. The purpose of the standard sensitivity analyses is to determine whether their conclusions would be altered by a change in the many assumptions they are required to make in order to keep their analysis manageable. History is selectivity. Most of what happened has to be left out or history books would be as large as life. Viewing individuals going through an ordinary day, it is apparent that they cannot base their actions on investigation. Most things have to be taken for granted. The facts to which they pay attention must be severely limited by narrow frames of reference. Otherwise, people, like the man in Dostoyevski's *Notes from the Underground*, who seeks the cause that lies behind the cause that lies behind other causes, are immobilized.

Something has to be added to make the world intelligible to people. What theory or organizing principle helps us cope? On what bases are decisions made about what to leave out as well as what to confront? The single most radical simplifying device is cultural identity. A culture (shared values justifying social relationships) posts lookouts and gives warnings just as assuredly as armies post sentries.

Theories and cultures are resistant to change. Resistance is essential, or meanings would fluctuate so rapidly that no person would know how to behave toward any other. Anyone can undertake a personal experiment by questioning all social forms, asking for evidence of identity, trustworthiness, morality, and the like, discovering for herself how rapidly life becomes intolerable. By the same token, turning the physical universe into random events — one day it is this way and another that way — would make the cumulation of knowledge unfeasible. Correspondingly, if there were as many theories as there are events, there would be no basis for choice.

Resistance to change may be overcome. As evidence builds up against theories or cultures do not pay off for adherents, there may be defections. Rival theories or different cultures come into contention. The ways in which people live are being tested in daily life no less than in laboratories.[10]

On the scientific side, there has been a centuries-long movement to replace man as the passive receiver of physical laws, imposed on him, as it were, from the outside world of nature, with man as the active organizer of his consciousness. This organizing is done by his acceptance of theories that direct attention to different aspects of reality. Even if these theories succeed for a time in organizing perception of a range of phenomena, there is always the possibility that more powerful theories will replace or subsume them (as Einstein's did to

Newton's). A culture is also an hypothesis tested by experience as individuals observe day-by-day whether it makes sense in helping them through life. Evidence plays its part. Information about what works (and what does not) is collected. As in scientific activity, there are always experiences that appear to run contrary to the prevailing paradigm. Life (or science) cannot stand still while each and every bit of evidence that might contradict an accepted theory is tested. Otherwise there would be no stability. As anomalies accumulate, however, the individuals involved consider whether other theories or ways of life might be superior. It is not that one theory is entirely true and another utterly false but rather that one theory (or culture) with its associated facts and research program (or attention-directing mechanisms) is more satisfactory under new conditions and eventually replaces or downgrades another.[11]

As Karl Popper recapitulates his now-classic work on *The Logic of Scientific Discovery*,

> All observations (and even more all experiments) are *theory* [here I would sub-stitute "culture"] *impregnated*: they are interpretations in the light of theories. We observe only what our problems, our biological situation, our interests, our expectations, and our action programs, make relevant. Just as our observational instruments are based upon theories [read cultures], so are our very sense organs, without which we cannot observe.[12]

Similarly, people, may, in effect, try out different political cultures. They may adhere to a given culture until its contradictions become too blatant to be ignored; then, as alternative opportunities arise, they may shift their allegiance. Alternatively, one generation may not change much, but each succeeding generation may contain less of the old, and more of the new, culture, until the balance between one culture and another is overturned.

Culture is the organization of social life. Organization is bias. There is no way to look at all data from all directions, as if our heads were swivels going round at the speed of light. There are only partial ways, selecting some phenomena and rejecting other bits as outside of organized perception. Cultures direct their adherents' attention toward certain phenomena and away from others. Since it is not possible for people to know more than a small fraction of the consequen-ces their actions pose for them in the present (let alone in the future), they must proceed according to an attention-rejecting and directing framework. This most comprehensive of all social theories — culture itself — organizes perception of the immense areas of uncertainty that necessarily surround human action.

PREFERENCES COME FROM CULTURES

If individuals seek to be culturally rational by supporting their way of life, how do they come to know what that entails? First, I will argue that each culture generates characteristic preferences. The reader should view these charac-teristics as part of an "as, if, and when" theory: to the extent that individuals identify with each of the various cultures, they adopt those preferences that they believe, correctly or mistakenly, are likely to help strengthen their culture. Then,

I will suggest, through comparison with alternative approaches, how cultural identifiers come to know what their preferences are supposed to be.

A suggestion by Jon Elster, adjusted to say that it is political cultures into which people are socialized, and where they are kept by continuous affirmation, sets out the structure of the cultural argument. "First a causal explanation of desires, then an intentional explanation of action in terms of the desires, and finally a causal explanation of macro-states in terms of the several individual actions."[13] First, people adhere to cultures. Second, their desires or preferences come from internalizing the social relations these cultures embody and employing them as scanning devices to determine essentially which preferences are culturally supportive. Third, people decide whether to pursue their cultural preference in view of other considerations, the rewards and penalties, that may affect them. The task of the social scientist is to test a theory of cultural causation by treating actors as if they were intentionally acting on the basis of these preferences compared to any other alternative set. The macro- or large-scale institutional behaviors are made up of individuals acting out their cultural biases. By relating to others with a characteristic bias, individuals reinforce their own behavior as well as that of those whose values and preferences for desirable social relations they share.

People use what matters most to them—relations with other people—to make sense out of life. Cultures answer questions about life with people: How is order to be achieved and maintained? Is there to be leadership and, if so, by whom? How are the goods of this world to be secured and divided up? How are envy to be controlled, inequality to be justified or condemned? Which dangers are to be confronted out of the multitude that might face us and which, since we cannot turn every way at once, ignored? What, in sum, is the good (or, at least, better) life?

This is the critical question: What sorts of people, organized into what kind of culture, sharing which values, legitimating which practices, will behave in certain predictable ways in order to do the two things every culture (except the fatalists) tries to do—make its people stronger and the opposing cultures weaker? There follow the predictions cultural theory gives for the four cultures identified in Mary Douglas's grid-group theory. I begin with a summary of the Douglas model. (For the sources of this model, see chapter 2 in this volume.)

Cultural Theory

Cultural theory is based on the axiom that what matter most to people are their relationships with other people and other people's relationships with them. It follows that the major choice made by people (or, if they are subject to coercion, made for them) is the form of culture—shared values legitimating social practices—they adopt. An act is culturally rational, therefore, if it supports one's way of life.

A basic proposition of this cultural theory is an impossibility theorem: there are only a limited number of cultures that categorize most human relations.

Though we can imagine an infinite number of potential cultures, only a relatively small number (here I shall work with four) are filled with human activity; the rest are deserted. What makes order possible is that only a few conjunctions of values are shareable and only a few sets of the corresponding social relations are viable, i.e., socially liveable.

The dimensions of cultural theory are based on answers to two questions: "Who am I?" and "How should I behave?" The question of identity may be answered by saying that individuals belong to a strong group, a collective, that makes decisions binding on all members or that their ties to others are weak in that their choices bind only themselves. The question of action is answered by responding that the individual is subject to many or few prescriptions, a free spirit or one that is tightly constrained. The strength or weakness of group boundaries and the numerous or few, varied or singular, prescriptions binding or freeing individuals are the components of their culture (see Figure 3.1).

Strong groups with numerous prescriptions that vary with social roles combine to form hierarchical collectivism. Strong groups whose members follow few prescriptions form an egalitarian culture, a shared life of voluntary consent, without coercion or inequality. Competitive individualism joins few prescriptions with weak group boundaries, thereby encouraging ever new combinations. When groups are weak and prescriptions strong, so that decisions are made for them by people on the outside, the controlled culture is fatalistic.

The social ideal of individualistic cultures is self-regulation. They favor bidding and bargaining in order to reduce the need for authority. They support equality of opportunity to compete in order to make arrangements between consenting adults with a minimum of external interference. They seek opportunity to be different, not equality of condition to be the same, for diminishing social differences would require a central, redistributive authority.

Hierarchy is institutionalized authority. It justifies inequality on grounds that specialization and division of labor enable people to live together with greater

Figure 3.1   Models of Four Cultures

Number & Variety of Prescriptions	Strength of Group Boundaries	
	Weak	**Strong**
Numerous & Varied	Apathy (Fatalism)	Hierarchy (Collectivism)
Few & Similar	Competition (Individualism)	Equality (Egalitarianism)

SOURCE: Adapted from Mary Douglas, *Natural Symbols* (Harmondsworth: Penguin, 1970), and Mary Douglas, "Cultural Bias," *In the Active Voice* (London: Routledge & Kegan Paul, 1982).

harmony and effectiveness than do alternative arrangements. Hence hierarchies are rationalized by a sacrificial ethic: the parts are supposed to sacrifice for the whole.

Committed to a life of purely voluntary association, egalitarian cultures reject authority. They can live a life without coercion or authority only by greater equality of condition. Thus egalitarians may be expected to prefer reduction of differences—between races, or income levels, or men and women, parents and children, teachers and students, authorities and citizens.

A fatalistic culture arises when people cannot control what happens to them. Since their boundaries are porous but the prescriptions imposed on them are severe, they develop fatalistic feelings. What will be, will be. There is no point in having preferences on public policy because what they prefer would not, in any event, matter.

None of these modes of organizing social life is viable on its own. A competitive culture needs something—the laws of contract—to be above negotiating. Hierarchies need something—anarchic individualists, authorityless egalitarians, apathetic fatalists—to sit on top of. Egalitarians need something—unfair competition, inequitable hierarchy, nonparticipant fatalists—to criticize. Fatalists require an external source of control to tell them what to do. "What a wonderful place the world would be," say the adherents of each culture, "if only everyone were like us," conveniently ignoring that it is only the presence in the world of people who are not like them that enables them to be the way they are. Hence, cultural theory may be distinguished by a necessity theorem: conflict among cultures is a precondition of cultural identity. It is the differences and distances from others that define one's own cultural identity.

Alone, no one has power over anyone. Power is a social phenomenon; power, therefore, is constituted by culture. But the form and extent of manipulation vary. Apathetic cultures are manipulated; fatalists live by rules others make and impose upon them. Manipulation is built into hierarchies; orders come down and obedience presumably flows up. The evocative language of New Guinea anthropology (the "big men" versus the "rubbish men") expresses the growth of manipulation in market cultures as some people no longer possess the resources to regulate their own lives. Egalitarians try to manipulate the other cultures by incessant criticism; they coerce one another by attributing inequalities to corruption and duplicity.

To identify with, to become part of a culture, signifies exactly that—the unviable void of formlessness, where everything and therefore nothing is possible, is replaced by social constraint. Even so, individuals keep testing the constraints, reinforcing them if they prove satisfactory in practice, modifying or rejecting them, when possible, if unsatisfactory. It is individuals as social creatures, not only being molded by but actively molding their social context—running the maze and shaping it—that are the focus of cultural theory. Once in that context, sharing its values, joining its comrades, individuals use their social filter to develop preferences about what sort of behavior they think will support their way of life. I begin with envy because it sets the stage for the crucial drama about who is to blame for misfortune.

Envy

Envy must be an especially difficult problem for egalitarians because they work so hard to control it. Since all members are supposed to be equal, this egalitarianism must show in the outer appurtenances of life — plain food, meals without main courses (as in vegetarianism), simple clothes, redistribution of income, bare furniture, unornamented "worker" housing — the life of the humble style. The spotlight is on all members, but especially leaders, to see that they do not elevate themselves above others. Envy is not correlated with the size of social differences alone but rather with their acceptability. The crucial question for social science is not whether there are large differences in individual or group resources in most places — surely there are — but whether these are rationalized as natural or unnatural, right or wrong, appropriate or illegitimate.

The humble life, to say the least, would hardly be appropriate in individualism, whose rationale depends on the ability of competitors to appropriate the benefits of the risks they take. Conspicuous consumption, or making a fetish out of commodities, may be a rational effort to point to where the power is so as to gain adherents in a network for future ventures. Since some people display many more of the goods of this world than others, however, envy is a possibility to be guarded against. But where egalitarians blame the system, individualists attribute personal success to good luck or good performance and failure to bad. Those who complain are told, "You have had your chance [e.g., opportunity is equal] and will have it again if you work hard." Naturally, fatalists know no envy, because, for them, to use Mrs. Gaskell's evocative term, life is like a lottery. Lacking control over their lives, they take whatever they get.

Control of envy in hierarchy is more interesting because it is more necessary. After all, hierarchy is institutionalized inequality. Ostentation — grand palaces, public works, ornate buildings in which the complexity of design mimics the near-infinite gradations of social structure — is reserved for the collectivity. Hierarchs may wear faded finery at home, but the army and the marching bands and the tombs of founders are bedecked in all splendor. As education inculcates the desirability of differences, envy is deflected by arguing the appropriateness of specialization and the division of labor. Experts do know best. Leaders are to be loved because they reveal the sacrifice of the parts for the whole by going first in battle, or by subsidizing medical care and pensions, or by donating museums and libraries.

Blame

When things go wrong, however, as they do in all cultures, who is to blame? Fatalists blame fate, but hierarchs cannot blame the collective. "System blame," blaming the relationship between the parts and the whole on which they pride themselves, would amount to self-destruction. No, hierarchies are famous for their blame-shedding techniques. Responsibility is hidden or diffused (the same thing) among numerous offices. Investigations are quashed or forbidden by official secrets acts. Blame is shifted to deviants. They do not know their place. They must be subject to reeducation or they belong in asylums. (Apparently, a person would have to be crazy to object to a collective way of life.)

To egalitarians, however, it is precisely the system (some combination of individualism and collectivism) that is insane—coercive and inegalitarian. If they had their way, suicides would be owed redress by the implacable institutions that drove them to their undeserved deaths. Were society differently organized, murderers would not want to kill their prey. Since good people are corrupted by evil institutions, the egalitarian task is to unmask authority by revealing the connection between apparently benign institutions and the evils they actually cause. Cultural solidarity is maintained by portraying external forces as monstrous and by accusing deviants of secretly importing evil ways ("hidden hierarchies") to corrupt the membership. Consequently, egalitarians search for insidious contamination from secret external sources, the turncoats, the "Oreos," the political radishes, the witches, the polluters, who have brought duplicity into their innocent garden.

Now individualists can hardly claim to be innocent; they are supposed to know what they are doing. But not entirely. The whole point is to outguess the future; if it were knowable, there would be no need for entrepreneurs. Hence, individualists can blame bad luck or personal incompetence or any combination thereof, providing only that the system, in their case competitive individualism, is blameless. People may be dumb, as economic individualists say, but markets are always smart.

Inequality

Every regime has to confront inequality of condition. Egalitarians abhor inequality; it can never be justified. Cultures that embody it are guilty of perpetrating institutional oppression—silent death. For fatalists, inequality is the norm; they are ruled by others. Hierarchies give more help because the "unequals" are their own people, for whom they feel responsible. Their justification of inequality is the same as for the system itself: different roles for different parts is healthy for the system as a whole. Essential order, hierarchical collectivists claim, can be achieved only by agreeing to accept inequality. In return, all members of society are supposed to get equality before the law, so that their claims may be adjudicated on a consistent and predictable basis. Adjudicating "who has the right to do what" is essential to maintaining distances and differences in hierarchies.

I have argued that egalitarians advocate equality of results, that collectivists are concerned with legal equality, and that individualists advocate equality of opportunity; that is why, though everyone (except fatalists) speaks approvingly of equality, each means something different. There is a world of difference between equality of opportunity to be different, equality of result to have the same, and equality before the law to legitimate differences. Whether policies are designed to diminish or destroy differences among people is a tell-tale sign, to citizens as well as to social scientists, of what political culture is preferred.

Fairness

For those who have no control over the prescriptions or people who govern their lives (I call them fatalists), fairness is fate. Life is fair for individualists when they have opportunity to enter and to benefit from competition. Failure is fair, too, providing that the markets they enter are unfettered and that they have a chance to acquire resources so as to try again. Cumulative inequalities, to use Robert Dahl's phrase,[14] would eventually prevent competition. In a hierarchical collective, fairness follows function; being fairly treated does not mean being treated like everyone else but being treated according to predictable rules affecting one's own station in life. In egalitarian collectives, fair is equal. No one is to have more of anything, especially power, than anyone else.

Economic Growth

Egalitarians have little interest in (i.e., they do not prefer) economic growth. Abundance increases the temptation to differentiation, which interferes with equality. Far better for egalitarians to concentrate on equal distribution, which keeps their people together, than on unequal development, which pulls them apart.

Wealth creation belongs to the established cultures, but in different ways. The promise of hierarchies is that collective sacrifice will lead to group gain. Thus they plan to reduce consumption to create capital to invest for future benefits. Should its solidarity be threatened, the collective may adopt a limited redistributive ethic, buying off discontent, limiting exchange so as to limit losers. Not so competitive individualists, they seek new combinations in order to create new wealth so that there will be more for all and they can keep more of it.

Scarcity

The idea of resource scarcity is useful to collectivists who can then proceed to allocate physical quantities by direct, bureaucratic means. The idea of resource depletion is also useful for egalitarians who can blame the "system" for exploiting nature, as it does people, and who can then try to get the authorities to change their inegalitarian life-style. The idea that resources are limited, however, is anathema to individualists because it implies that exchange makes people worse off (and therefore has to be curtailed), and because it attacks the central promise of expanding wealth that will eventually make everyone better off. Shortages do not matter to fatalists who must, in any event, make do.

Uncertainty

Just as cultures fundamentally are concerned with moral order (the shared values and social practices that constitute them), so they also must cope with uncertainty about which norms apply in a given circumstance and what the consequences of following prescribed practices are likely to be. Adherents of hierarchical cultures try to negotiate their environments so as to reduce ambiguity in the structure of roles according to which they regulate themselves. They will intervene to dampen economic fluctuations or to punish deviance, giving up efficiency in order to reduce behavior variations that threaten established relationships. Fatalists accept uncertainty, as they do everything else, as beyond their control. Individualists welcome the uncertainty that creates their opportunities. . . . up to a point. Extreme uncertainty, say, large fluctuations in the value of money, may threaten exchange relationships. Individualism copes with extreme uncertainty by doing more of what it does best, i.e., by competing. Large numbers of transactions and large numbers of firms, each bidding back and forth with rapidity, smooth out fluctuations. When one entrepreneur fails, or one resource is depleted, others, if markets work well, rush in to take their place. Overlap, duplication, redundant organization, trial-and-error make up for the absence of central planning.[15] Egalitarians also work with little prescription but they abjure competition. How, then, do they cope with uncertainty? Where the hierarchy stresses clarity in role definition, so that performance can be attached to position, the egalitarian culture embraces ambiguity, so that no one has authority.

Leadership

Hierarchies tie authority to position.[16] Hence hierarchies are proleadership cultures, shoring it up at every opportunity, protecting it when under attack, shedding and diffusing blame, keeping information under close control. Individualistic cultures treat leadership like any other commodity; they pay as little for it as they can. They seek to make it unnecessary by self-organization through bidding and bargaining. When conditions, such as external attack, make a modicum of leadership necessary, it is limited in time and authority, the hope being that the meteoric leader who flames bright and then burns out will retire when the task is completed. Egalitarians actively reject leadership as a form of inequality. When the existence of their organization is imperiled, however, they will accept charismatic leadership as a substitute for authority. Even so, the claim of the leader to inspiration and perfection is precarious; because equality of condition is the guiding cultural norm, leaders are subject to frequent charges of falling away. Observe that this is a cultural theory: charisma cannot occur in hierarchies because they have a detailed structure of their own, nor in individualism, which will not tolerate strong prescriptions, nor in fatalism, because passive people cannot have active leaders. Only in egalitarian collectives, where equality of condition prevails, so that structure and status are weak and ambiguous, can there be not the popular but the charismatic leader who substitutes for the law. (In the words of Jesus, "You have heard that it was said by them of old time. . . . But I say unto you. . . . ")[17]

In a corresponding manner, each culture fears the perversion of its main values. Hierarchs, who elevate leadership, fear the charismatic leader who overturns the law; individualists fear the leader who overstays his welcome; fatalists fear the disappearance of leadership to give guidance; and egalitarians fear the very distinction between leaders and followers, for followership implies inequality.

Apathy

The very same failure to vote (or lack of other political activity) may be appropriate or inappropriate, legitimizing or destabilizing, depending on the social context. Adherents of each culture select out meanings of apathy (as of activity) to support their preferred power relationships.

Egalitarians rationalize rejecting established authority by arguing that there is no real participation. Power is "unmasked" by showing that fatalism is the true location of the mass of citizens. Like the wonderful Steinberg cartoon in *The New Yorker*, where Manhattan grows so large the rest of the country recedes from view, egalitarians see fatalists as most of the people, a nation metaphorically populated by 4,200 oligarchs, 2,000 egalitarians, and 200 million apathetics. All the while egalitarians seek to recruit supporters from fatalists who, they claim, are apathetic because decisions are made for them by the establishment. The hierarchical counterclaim that apathy is functional, because inactivity implies consent, is derided as ideological window dressing. High rates of general participation across a broad scope of issues, by contrast, would undermine hierarchical rule. How could principles of hierarchy be maintained if roles are changed and challenged all the time? Instead, hierarchies try to inculcate civic consciousness, a positive obligation to vote. But not much more than that, for citizens should participate according to their station in life. Within the sphere of competence assigned to them, however, members of hierarchies are expected to do their duty.

Individualists do not have to take the rate and scope of activity as a measure of their manhood. If it is worthwhile for people to participate, they will; if not, they won't. Should an individualist decline to vote, for instance, this might indicate that he calculates the probability of his influencing events is so low that a rational person should not bother. Perhaps people feel the government does too much. ("Don't vote," the old adage goes. "That will only encourage them.") Indeed, the anarchist wing of individualist cultures thinks of government more as the problem than the solution. ("Voting makes no difference; the government always gets in.")

Why, in sum, is there a low rate of voting (if, indeed, there is)? Because, egalitarians answer, the system excludes people or voting is ineffectual; because, supporters of hierarchy reply, voters are so satisfied they are willing to leave things to those who are better qualified; because, individualists respond, voting is not worth the effort it takes.

Turn the tables. Suppose you wish to oppose prevailing policies that you believe confer undue advantage to people who are already well off. You may not get much help from individualists, for they may like large differences or they may well ask whether it is worth their while to participate in view of the low probability of success. Adherents of hierarchy may support existing policy or they may believe that it is not their place to act. Fatalists think there is no point in acting because they will not make a difference. Under such circumstances, you may be grateful for the existence of egalitarians who are prepared to throw body and soul into the fray, who never seem to tire, and who are not easily deflected from what they consider to be a just cause.

THE RULES OF THE CULTURAL METHOD

Shared beliefs and values, though varied, I hold, are not free to float about just anywhere.[18] They are closely tied to the social relations that they help sustain and render meaningful.[19] For instance, beliefs about needs and abilities (human nature) and about resources (physical nature) will be absolutely central to any socially viable pattern of values. Taken together, such socially constructed beliefs about nature — niggardly or bountiful, resilient or precarious, a rebuke or an affirmation of existing authority — determine the line between what is deemed acceptable (in my culture) and unacceptable (in yours). Any strategy or policy, therefore, has to be justified by beliefs concerning what people are about and how the world is — a particular idea of justice and a particular idea of nature. Such pairing of beliefs and their sustained values is visible in all societies — in the New Guinea Highlands, in the China of the Warring States, in the cattle herders of the southern Sudan, in the United States, and in the Soviet Union. It is not the presence or absence of these shared values and social practices that distinguishes these societies, since all societies have them, but the relative strengths of different values and practices and the configurations (the social context) in which they are arranged.

In cultural analysis, context is critical. It is never enough to know whether and to what degree certain people identify with one of a number of possible cultures; always it is essential to know how the culture in question relates to others. What are the relative strengths of the various cultures? What is the scope of the activities within which cultures are meaningful for a given person? It is quite possible for individuals to live in one culture at work, another at home, and still another in leisure pursuits. (Think of the eighteenth-century Scottish entrepreneurs with cut-throat competition on the job but powerful regulation of family life — houses, carriages, food, friends, clothing — at home.) The more the different elements of life come under the same cultural context, of course, the more they reinforce each other.

The term "social structure" is used by social scientists to designate the attributes of social relations they believe are important to explain. Structures are regularities. There is no magic in any particular concept of structure, only its utility in explanation. Social context, the array of cultures, is what I mean here by social structure. Thus, in this theory, cultures are not embedded in something else; they are the thing-in-itself, social structure, if you will, that needs to be explained and that, once known, helps explain such phenomena as political preferences.

Cultures are not countries. There is generally more than one culture in one country at one time. For cultural analysis, what matters are the social contexts, the relative strengths and positions of the differing ways of life *vis-à-vis* one another within any given society.

Cultural theory knows no dualisms. Just as cultural theory refuses to separate shared values from social practices (except for analytic decomposition), so it does not separate mind from body, superstructure from base, physical nature from mental thought. They come together just as do the people who confer meanings on these concepts.

PREDICTIONS

The predictions made in the preceding pages—to the extent people adhere to these four ways of life, they will view the world from the corresponding, culturally induced frames of reference and therefore arrive at the preferences ascribed to them—are meant to be universal. No matter what the material or technological position of people, or where they are located geographically, or in what historical time they live, their objectives can be derived from their cultural frames of reference.

This claim of universality manifestly does *not* mean that history is irrelevant. On the contrary, only history can give us the cultural context. Only history can tell us as well which means or instruments of policy are available and which ones will, based on the experience of these particular people, be seen as relevant to their circumstances. After the American Revolution, for instance, activists with egalitarian tendencies—anti-Federalists, Jeffersonians, Jacksonians—believed that the central government was a source of artificial inequality. Following the disputes between the party of the king and the party of the country in England, they believed that the executive power would be used to undermine republican government. Therefore they sought to keep the central government small and weak.[20] Nowadays, after the advent of the industrial revolution and corporate capitalism, their cultural successors, liberal Democrats, given their quite different circumstances and reading of history, believe that the central government is (or, at least can and should be) an instrument for reducing inequalities. The objectives of egalitarians—to reduce differences—remain constant over time but the means they adopt to that end differ with changing historical circumstances.

Attempts at falsification proceed in a straightforward fashion. Given a problem, say the nature of the struggle between Augustine and Pelagius, or the rise of capitalism, or why there has been no socialism in America, whatever the object of inquiry, the analyst performs three operations. The first is to code the contending parties into their cultural categories.[21] The second is to use their cultural frame of reference to predict or explain how adherents of these cultures would behave under the given historical conditions. If their behavior does not follow upon their cultural premises, the theory is disconfirmed. The third operation, in order to avoid counsels of perfection, compares the predictions and explanations one gets using cultural theory with the existing alternatives. The first two operations are about closeness of fit: how well does cultural theory solve the problem? The third operation is about relative adequacy: how well does cultural theory compare in power to alternative explanations?[22] Frames of reference are demystified by being tied to cultures and by generating numerous predictions in diverse areas of life that are subject to disproof.

NOTES

1. New York: Macmillan, 1947, 1976.

2. The sources of this theory are to be found in Mary Douglas, *Natural Symbols* (Harmondsworth: Penguin, 1970); Mary Douglas, "Cultural Bias," in Mary Douglas, *In the Active Voice* (London: Routledge & Kegan Paul, 1982); Mary Douglas and Aaron Wildavsky, *Risk and Culture* (Berkeley: University of California Press, 1982); and Aaron Wildavsky, "Choosing Preferences by Constructing Institutions: A Cultural Theory of Preference Formation," *American Political Science Review* 81(1): 3–21.

3. E. E. Evans-Pritchard, *The Nuer* (New York/Oxford: Oxford University Press, 1940).

4. William G. Ouchi, "Markets, Bureaucracies, and Clans,"*Administrative Science Quarterly* 25(1) (1980): 129–41.

5. Oliver Williamson, *Markets and Hierarchies, Analysis and Antitrust Implications: A Study in the Economics of Internal Organization* (New York: Free Press, 1975).

6. If information is power (as assuredly it can be), then culturally biased information will give rise to its own distinctive power structure. "If you knew what I know you wouldn't be saying that," says the senior civil servant to his junior, thereby putting him firmly down in his proper place and in the process confirming his own position near the apex of the decision-making pyramid. Were someone foolish enough to try that sort of thing in an egalitarian bounded group, the result would be very different; she would quickly find herself ejected from it. In a market setting, the response would be different again. There the claim to uncommon knowledge leads neither to exaltation nor expulsion but to the simple challenge: "Put your money where your mouth is." For an analysis of the information biases inherent in different forms of organization, see Michael Thompson and Aaron Wildavsky, "A Cultural Theory of Information Bias in Organizations," in Geert Hofstede, ed., "Organizational Culture and Control," a special issue of *Journal of Management Studies* 23(3): 273–86.

7. Chester I. Barnard, *The Function of the Executive* (Cambridge: Harvard University Press, 1948).

8. Englewood Cliffs, N. J.: Prentice Hall, 1963.

9. See the section on "Dogma and Skepticism" in my *Speaking Truth to Power* (Boston: Little, Brown, 1975), pp. 205–79.

10. For speculation on cultural change, see my "Change in Political Culture," *Politics, Journal of the Australasian Political Studies Association* 20(2): 95–102.

11. The same sort of discussion may be traced through the large literature surrounding Thomas Kuhn, *The Structure of Scientific Revolution* (Chicago: University of Chicago Press, 1962). For a view corresponding to my own, see Stephen Toulmin, *Human Understanding* (Oxford: Clarendon Press, 1972).

12. Quoted in Karl R. Popper and John C. Eccles, *The Self and Its Brain* (New York: Springer Verlag, 1977), p. 134.

13. Jon Elster, *Explaining Technical Change: A Case Study in the Philosophy of Science* (Cambridge: Cambridge University Press, 1983), p. 85.

14. Robert A. Dahl, *Who Governs?* (New Haven: Yale University Press, 1961).

15. Martin Landau, "Redundancy, Rationality, and the Problem of Duplication and Overlap," *Public Administration Review* 29(4): 346–58.

16. A more substantial analysis of leadership from this cultural perspective may be found in my "Political Leaders Are Part of Political Systems: A Cultural Theory of Leadership," paper prepared for the Bentley Chair Conference at the Workshop in Political Theory and Policy Analysis, Indiana University, May 17–18, 1985. It will be published under the title, "A Cultural Theory of Leadership," in *Political Leadership: Perspectives from Political Science*, Bryan D. Jones, ed. (Lawrence: University Press of Kansas, 1989).

17. Matthew 5: 21, 22, 27, 28, 33, 34.

18. This section has been written with Michael Thompson. His works on culture include *Rubbish Theory* (Oxford: Oxford University Press, 1979) and *Misplaced Concrete: A Theory of the Built Environment and a Strategic Prescription for the Reform of the Architectural Profession* (London: Ethnographica, 1986). A related book is Gerald Mars, *Cheats at Work: An Anthropology of Workplace Crime* (London: Allen & Unwin, 1982).

19. As Giandomenico Majone explains, "All theories place constraints on the range of observable or imaginable phenomena. Reality, Einstein once observed, restricts the wealth of possibilities; science attempts to discover those restrictions. Scientific laws 'do not assert that something exists or is the case; they deny it. They insist on the nonexistence of certain things or states of affairs, proscribing or prohibiting, as it were, these things or states of affairs; they rule them out.' [Karl Popper, *The Logic of Scientific Discovery*, London: Hutchinson, 1968, p. 69]. Entire branches of physics are based on very general 'prohibitions' or 'postulates of impotence,' as they have been called, and it has been argued that all physical science and perhaps all natural science could some day be derived from a small number of such postulates. 'A postulate of impotence,' Sir Edmund Whittaker writes [*From Euclid to Eddington: A Study of Conceptions of the External World*, New York: Dover, 1958, p. 69] 'is not the direct result of an experiment, or any infinite number of experiments; it does not mention any measurement, or any numerical relation or analytical equation; it is the assertion of a conviction that all attempts to do a certain thing, however made, are bound to fail'." Giandomenico Majone, "The Economist as Policy Adviser," typescript, n.d.

20. See Lance Banning, *The Jeffersonian Persuasion* (Ithaca, N. Y.: Cornell University Press, 1978); and my "Industrial Policies in American Political Cultures," in Claude E. Barfield and William A. Schambra, eds., *The Politics of Industrial Policy* (Washington, D. C.: American Enterprise Institute, 1986), pp. 15–32.

21. Jonathan L. Gross and Steve Rayner, *Measuring Culture* (New York: Columbia University Press, 1986), provide instruction.

22. For examples of comparison, see Mary Douglas and Baron Isherwood, *The World of Goods* (London: Allen Lane, 1978) on theories of consumption and the rise of capitalism; Michael Thompson, "Postscript: A Cultural Basis for Comparison," in Howard C. Kunreuther and Joanne Linnerooth et al., *Risk Analysis and Decision Processes* (Berlin: Springer Verlag, 1983), pp. 232–62; and Aaron Wildavsky, "The Logic of Public Sector Growth," in Jan-Erik Lane, ed., *State and Market* (London: Sage Publications, 1985), pp. 231–70.

4

CULTURE IN ITS PLACES: A HUMANISTIC PRESENTATION

Miles Richardson and Robert Dunton

The humanistic approach in anthropology is similar to the other, so-called mentalistic perspectives in that it strives to interpret culture from the view of the participant. Yet it differs in three ways.

(1) It is not mental structures, however elegantly mapped, that respond to a baby's smile, a lover's kiss, or a friend's death; it is we, we flesh-and-blood, bipedal primates. Consequently, the humanistic approach celebrates the species' physicality: the female's pointed breasts, the male's distended penis, and the naked skin that warms to the hand's gentle caress. Humanistic anthropology is grounded in the reality, experienced even in our most humdrum moments, that we humans *act*. Constrained though we may be, determined though we surely are, we act. Not always in the manner we anticipated and at times, perhaps ultimately, with tragic consequence, we, nonetheless, act.

(2) And when we act, *we* act. We act in consort and in antagonism. We act when we see one another face-to-face, and we act when, alone, in solitude, we hear one another speak. Self and other are complementary objects in a single structure, the we. The we who we are derives from our primate, mammalian heritage and, paradoxically, from the absence in that heritage of tight genetic control. Compelled by genes, you and I, we act to construct in a world in which we then are.

(3) The third way in which the humanistic approach differs is the location of the world in which we are. Both structuralism and cognitive anthropology fix that world inside the individual heads of the participants. Social life is made possible only through participants sharing that knowledge. Even structuralism, which may begin its analysis with a collective product, a myth, for example, ends by reducing the myth to mental formulae situated, if anywhere, in the head of the teller of the myth. In contrast, the humanistic anthropologist places the world in which we are out there, in the intersubjective reality that lies between the me of my I and the you of your you. This reality is not the distant being of

language, which has the bloodless reality of a genetic code, switching our actions on and off, as it passes through its programmed structure; it is the reality of speech, the immediate, red face-to-red face argument in which we engage to convince one another we exist. This world in which we are is not a given code; it is a struggle (Unamuno 1972, 1974).

Thus, although agreeing with its mentalistic kin in its goal to interpret culture from the view of the actor, the humanistic approach differs in its emphases on the act, on the we, and on the placement of the world in which we are. We act and through our social actions construct a reality in which we then exist. Consequently, culture, in humanistic anthropology, is a coming into being.

Since we flesh-and-blood primates are physical creatures, we occupy space. Our coming into being transforms that space into place. In transforming space into place we convert the experiential world of primate gesturing into symbolic discourse. We fix that discourse into material objects, which we use to place ourselves in the world in which we are. Once brought into being, place is not simply a structure that shelters us from nature's elements; it is our coming into being fixed in place, our culture. The question of this chapter is: How does culture come to be in its places?

The presentation of how culture comes to be in its places calls for a perspective that accounts for the emergence of meaning out of social interaction, a perspective that stresses both the flow of experience and the transfiguration of that experience into cultural forms. Such a perspective is offered by the work of George Herbert Mead.

THE MEADIAN DIALOGUE OF BEING

Mead (1863–1931), a social behaviorist and a contemporary of fellow pragmatist, John Dewey, at the University of Chicago, begins his analysis from the position that the act is the unit of existence (Mead 1972: 65). We are as we become. Our becoming, the act, has three phases: the initial, perceptual phase; the inhibiting, manipulatory phase; and the reflective, consummatory, or integrative phase (Mead 1972; Lewis 1981; Richardson 1982).[1]

In the initial, perceptual phase of the act, as we approach one another and the objects around us, we look ahead, into the future, and prepare ourselves to be. Although relative to the perceiving organism, perception is, in Mead's behaviorism, objective (Mead 1972: 114; Reck 1964: 306–19; Lewis 1981). As bipedal primates, moving forward into the world, we perceive the world differently from our brachiating siblings and even more distinctly from our reptilian cousins. The perceptual world that we see ahead is a world that is there, but how it is there comes about through our perception of it. "The object of perception is the existent future of the act" (Reck 1964: 289), and this future is not that which we see but darkly; it is that which *emerges* (Reck 1964: 335). Thus, in the initial perceptual phase, we, through our actions, look ahead and form a preliminary definition of the world, the situation, that is emerging among us.

As we move forward, into the world we are preliminarily defining, we reach — frequently literally, with our hands — to bring the future into the present. "The proximate goal of all perception is what we can get our hands on"(Reck 1964: 294). In the time of the manipulatory (Latin, *manus*, hand, and *pulus*, full) phase, we have the present in our hands. The flow of experience is blocked, and we take the perspective of that which impedes our actions. Here, the stone that we reach for defines the hand even as the hand grasps the stone (Mead 1972: 186); you define me even as you feel the coarseness of my crude grasp within the gentle silk of your own. In the manipulatory phase, the flow of experience — which, in handless creatures, speeds through them untouched, and thus unconsciously — is shaped into objects that tell us we are here (Miller 1973: 105).

In the consummatory phase, the objects that we have sequentially encountered and brought one by one from the future into the present are integrated into an overall pattern. This pattern constitutes an object itself, a generalization of the present, and from its position we get a view of the world in which we now are. The view of the world in which we now are creates, at times more intensely than others, an aesthetic experience. This experience emerges through our grasping of the "complex efforts of men in society to infuse meaning into the details of existence..." (Reck 1964: 296). The consummation of these efforts locates the experience of each of us within the collective work of all; we experience each other's touch.

In his account of the act, Mead depicts how we, you and I, experience — and feel, with our hands — the world as it comes to be in our experiencing. In the genesis of the self, Mead describes how we become conscious of that experiencing and in so doing transfigure the experience into symbolic forms (Strauss 1964: 33–38, 155–65, 191–203). A naturalist and evolutionist, Mead, in the manner of anthropologists searching for the origins of humanity, saw that social interaction must precede the emergence the conscious self. Phylogenetically, and perhaps even ontogenetically, we are first and foremost warm-blooded, big-brained, passionate creatures dependent upon others for our survival. For us to be, we must interact. Consequently, Mead begins his account of the self with the gesture.

The gesture of an animal, a snarl, a touch, a cry, elicits a response from another, whose response in turn elicits a response from the first. This interaction is a "conversation of gestures" (Strauss 1964: 155), and in this conversation, the meaning of the gesture of the first animal lies in the gesture of the second, and the meaning of gesture of the second lies in the gesture of the first.

In the human case, with the emergence of the capacity to designate a response with a vocal gesture which stands for that response, that is to say, to name, the conversation of gestures emerges into a dialogue of words. At the time the first animal gestures to the second, the human animal also gestures to himself. To gesture to himself, he assumes the attitude, the position, of the second animal. From actions of the second animal, he responds to his own responses. If the second animal is also human, that animal also responds to his own actions from the responses of the first. From the position of each other, we gesture back to our own gesturing, and thus we each become the object of our own gesturing. If the gesturing back to our own gesturing is vocal, we become objects of our own vocal gesturing. We name our gesturings. The conversation of gestures transforms into a dialogue of words.

The objects of this dialogue of words are self and other. We name ourselves. I am the me of your naming, you are the you of mine. (More precisely, I am the me of my naming of your naming; I am the me of my gesturing of your gesturing.) Self and other are the objects of speech; we, you and I, are names, symbols, attached to the flesh-and-blood of our primate being. "Men create symbols in dialogue, not to measure space, but to name things, events, and relationships so they can act together" (Duncan 1968: 104). I exist because you have called my name; likewise in my call, you are. In the Meadian conservation of gestures turned into words we are joined, our destinies linked. I cannot be me without you; you cannot be you without me.

We do not relate, however, simply to a series of self and others. We also address ourselves and one another from the position of the group. We turn the experience of social interaction into an object; we name our social experience (often literally) and through our naming, our symbolization, of that experience, we make the experience into an object, a generalized other. Once objectified, we take the position of the reified experience and define our relations to it and to one another. Together we produce a generalized other, and individually, we define ourselves by it.

The outcome of the genesis of the self, the generalized other, parallels — to a degree perhaps unrecognized by Meadian scholars — the consummatory phase of the experiential act. In the consummatory phase, the individual objects we experience are integrated into a pattern, much in the same manner we fit the acts of individual characters into the overall pattern of a story. As an outcome of the genesis of the self, the generalized other is the naming of that pattern and the attributing of the story's pattern with a structure, which becomes the story's world, its self.

Before proceeding, we need to pause and underscore several points.

In his accounts of both the act and the genesis of self, Mead — in accordance with the humanistic insistence on the centrality of human action — stresses behavior. He particularly lauds the role of the hand. A dog, Mead points out, moves directly from the perceptual phase of the act to the consummatory, or in the dog's case, the consuming, phase. There is no intervening manipulatory phase because the dog has no hand. Thus, the dog cannot separate himself from his own actions. In humans, however, the hand isolates us from the flow of experience and allows us to become an object of ourselves, to hold ourselves in our hands, so to speak. Indeed, speech "and the hand go along together in the development of the social human being" (Mead 1972: 237).[2]

Notwithstanding the stress on behavior, Mead does not commit the behavioristic fallacy of seeing consciousness as nothing more than a physiologically produced response. The emergent self is an emergent object. "Social beings are things as definitely as physical things are social" (Reck 1964: 313). Conversely, Mead avoids the phenomenalistic fallacy of seeing the self as antecedent to social behavior (Miller 1973: 89-106). The conversation of gestures precedes the conversation of words; likewise, words are acts; they are gestures with which we indicate to one another the world that is there.

Thinking is talking to oneself, and thinking "is that relationship of the organism to the situation which is mediated by sets of symbols" (Strauss 1964: 187). Thinking, therefore, is not an activity confined to the individual brain. Thinking, to the extent it is the structuring of the world in which we are, is neither a discovery of a structure already fixed in place, nor is it an imposition of pure thought upon a blank nature. Rather, thinking "is the creation of a structure to which the world that is there *answers*..." (Miller 1973: 107).

With these points underscored, we may now unite the trajectory of the act and the genesis of the self into a more compact statement of how culture comes to be in its places.

(1) The perceptual, preliminary definition phase. Even with the material setting of house, church, plaza, or market already built, the space thus indicated is not a fixed determination that condemns us to a ceaseless repetition of what has occurred in the past but a constellation of gestures that beckon us to respond. We respond by contrasting the gestures of the setting before us with those of other settings and note their distinctive patterning. Our noting is not simply visual, but in accordance with our biogram (Count 1958), we look ahead also with sound and smell. We extend our primate sense to establish the nonverbal perimeters of where we are.

(2) The manipulatory, verbal phase. We reach, with both touch and utterance, to bring the future of the preliminary definition into the reality of the present. Encountering one another with hand and word, we assume the role of each and convert primate gesturing into the dialogue of self and other.

(3) The consummatory phase. We generalize our encounters with both the gestures of the material setting and the verbal exchanges with others into a generalized other and bestow upon it a name. From the position of the generalized other we contract an image, a Meadian thought, that distinguishes the place symbolically, as earlier, in the preliminary phase, we distinguished it physically. Space has now been transformed into place, and culture has come to be.

Space is transformed into place and culture comes to be in ball parks, museums, homes, bars, churches, beaches, schools, wilderness parks — wherever humans congregate. Two general modes of being occur (1) where participants are fully engaged in the matter at hand and the matter at hand is being negotiated as to its competitive advantage to self and other and (2) where observers look and marvel at the awful frailty of human life and self and other conclude a pact that from this day they will walk together in honor and in love. An example of the first mode of being is the Spanish-American market; an example of the second is the Vietnam Veterans Memorial.

CULTURE AS SMART: THE SPANISH-AMERICAN MARKET

In the grid-pattern towns of Spanish America, that vast cultural region that begins somewhere north of the Rio Grande and extends southward to the tip of

South America, away from the central plaza, where church and state view one another across flower-lined walkways, to the back region of the community, where the streets are perpetually darkened with oil and fumes, culture comes to be in the market.

The Perceptual, Preliminary Definition Phase

As we approach the market, you and I, each on separate missions but both looking for good buys, we pass the businesses lured here by the concentration of prospective customers: *tiendas*, smaller stores with names like "The Swan" or "The Gypsy Woman" selling everything from toys to liquor; the larger *almacenes* with goods both for wholesale and retail; and *papelerías*, stationery shops that sell single envelopes and typing paper by the sheet. We weave among the carts — some with wooden wheels bound with strips of rubber and others with metal ones that crunch through discarded corn shucks and banana leaves — that men push or pull to unload trucks (battered Chevrolets, whose ancient gears groan in agony, or bright new Datsuns, whose chrome is even now being wiped clean) that have hauled produce from field or warehouse.

In our ear, a lottery vendor cries optimistically, "Tomorrow it plays! What is your number? Your number! Your number! "You consider yourself fortunate that you can buy your number, the one you dreamed last night.

Since today is Sunday, a favorite market day, the streets are full of *campesinos*, small, dark men with their tiny wives and little children, all in clean, freshly ironed apparel. They have already attended mass, and after the market they will spend an unaccustomed free hour in the plaza where they will stroll amid plants not raised with oxen and hoe to eat or to sell but cultivated and pruned to adorn a brief moment given over to the leisure of urbanity.

The church, in whose darkened interior Christ hangs forever in agony, and the plaza, where wild and dangerous nature has been converted to flowery ornaments, contrast with the starkly utilitarian building before us. The older market structures made of plastered brick and roofed with tile, the new ones of cinder block and corrugated tin roof, the building has been reduced to the single, basic function of sheltering merchandise, seller, and buyer. Even the entrance ways, always an occasion for a classical pediment or a baroque curlicue, are naked rectangular cuts in a plain wall. There are no windows, but the larger structures may have skylights that allow the attenuated rays of the sun to enter through dust-coated panes.

Inside, to facilitate the two-party exchange between vendor and customer, the single, uniform space has been checkerboarded into a series of smaller rectangular spaces. In these each vendor displays what he offers to the customer: large stands piled high with fruit (bananas, plantains, mangos), or vegetables (potatoes, tomatoes, string beans), or flowers (gladiolas, roses, carnations), and small cubicles within which the vendor stands surrounded by eggs, cheese, and long twists of sausages, or by harness, belts, and coils of rope, or by the crucified Christ, the Virgin Mary, and lurid scenes of the saints.

The building, as large as it is, cannot contain all there is to sell, and goods spill out along the sides of the building and into the streets: medicinal plants whose cleansing purity flushes out the liver and restores that organ's vital functions; edible clay for women whose pregnancy has brought a compelling urge to devour; and a rich variety of screws, bolts, and nuts, plus a door latch, and, as if by magic, a shiny new socket set.

The profusion of goods is so great that we must squeeze ourselves into narrow aisles already packed with buyers. The vendors, accustomed as they are to this sea of potential profit, call out nonetheless: "What offers itself?" "Tell me what pleases you!" or simply "Speak." At a vegetable stand, you reach with your hand to test a cabbage.

The Manipulatory, Verbal Phase

You with his cabbage in your hand, he with your purse in his eye, buyer and seller, classic antagonists, each prepared to take advantage of the other, yet the value of the cabbage, Mead argues, its price, as it were, is social. The value arises because of your mutual interests, or, more Meadian, because "buying and selling are involved in each other" (Reck 1964: 284). If you are to be the buyer and he the seller, you each have to assume the attitude, the role of the other, and from that position gesture back to yourself so that you each become a symbolic object to one another. You must name each other and in so doing name yourself. The other of the self you are as buyer is he the seller; the two of you linked in each one's determination to take advantage of the other.

In asserting that the value of the cabbage is social, an exchange between self and other, are not we ignoring the impersonal laws of supply and demand? Is not the cabbage a mere commodity the price of which is determined not by you the buyer and he the seller but by the play of the market? While it may be true, as Pfuetze argues in his critique of Mead (1954: 110), that the cabbage in your hand, driven by economic forces, has a value that transcends both you with his cabbage and him with your pesos; yet, for that value, like culture is general, to achieve an empirical existence, to become experientially real, you and he must act.

To get customers to act with them, some vendors speak a string of verbal plosives: PoTaToes, PoTaToes, PoTaToes; others call in more sonorous sounds: mangos, mangos, mangos; still others, less energetic or more seasoned, await the customer in silence. All have to decide between a strategy that maximizes the number of buyers at the expense of the time spent with each and a strategy that seeks a payoff in the care and tending of individual clients. The first may be more appropriate for a vendor who has a small space on the sidewalk in front of the market and a perishable product to move. The second may be more readily adopted by an established vendor with a large compartment inside the market with durable merchandise.

"Two for twenty." The boy thrusts a lettuce at you as we exit the market. Beside him is a small wooden crate that contains several heads of lettuce still wet from the water he has poured over them in the vain hope they will remain fresh. He has yet to make a sale. A man appears to see his investment wilting before his very eyes. "Listen, Carlos," he directs the boy, "Sell them three for thirty," and without a pause, the boy attacks the prospective buyer behind us, "Fresh lettuce. Three heads for thirty pesos."

Earlier, while you were waiting, if impatiently, at the compartment of Don Javier, your husband's godfather, Don Javier was attending a young *señora*, whose name we neither could recall. From the list in her head, she calls out the weekly staples, maize, beans, flour, sugar. "*Si, señora,*" Don Javier replies, polite to each request, and his "Yes, m'am" reminds me of my Southern roots. He wraps each item in newspaper and places it compactly in her shopping bag, a sack spun from the shiny fibers of the sisal plant. Finished, she allows herself a treat and buys a single cigarette. As she lights the cigarette, she motions to the young son at her side. Without a word, he, so short he can barely see above the counter, backs up to the compartment, and Don Javier lowers the packed bag on his back. Bent double by the weight of the week's supply, the boy turns to follow his mother, who, with an even younger son on her hip, has already disappeared into the crowd, the smoke of her cigarette lingering delicately in the air.

Here and there, men are making purchases, one with a Western hat cocked to one side and the ash dangling from his cigarette and another, old and tottery, his few requirements met, disappearing into the crowd of taller, healthier people; the majority of the customers, however, are women: thin, battered figures, with only baggy skirts to testify to their femininity; matrons, middle aged and heavy, each accompanied by a small boy who, staggering under the load of purchases, scurries to keep pace; and young, freshly marrieds, neatly made up in pants and top, their faces composed both in eye shadow and confidence.

Not all the people we pass — you with your native knowledge adroitly, never bumping into anyone, I because of my foreign ignorance clumsily, reeling like a drunk — are buying and selling. In front of us, in the middle of the crowded aisle, stubborn as two rocks in a rushing river, two men, twins in advanced age and hard poverty, crumpled hats, burned skin, and backs bent as if by nature to carry loads, grin in toothless glee at the pleasure of each other's company. A man in a natty gray suit, who has presented himself as an importer of foreign articles for the house and home, grabs me and explains he has a check for 5000, but could I loan him a 100? He recites in some detail the agony of a cousin who has died of cancer of the intestines. He wants me to write my name. He shakes my hand and cautions that if he does not see me tomorrow, it will be the next day before he can repay me.

Behind him and his natty gray, leading her blind father through the crowd, a girl of ten in a ragged dress appears. She approaches two men in sport shirts who are discussing market prices, and each, without breaking the flow of conversation, drops coins in her outthrust hand.

The Consummatory, Image Phase

The transformation of space into place and, consequently, the emergence of culture, are achieved when we, together, integrate the physical features of the market with the behavior occurring within it into an aesthetic whole, an image, which is the results of our generalization of the specific, two-party exchanges between self and other into a generalized other. Movement toward consummation begins even as we first enter the market and as your hand grasps the cabbage, and the consummation continues even as we find ourselves in other places. Yet, since the consummatory phase is the phase during the act when the present is moving toward the past, the phase reaches an intensity at the time we are leaving the market's physical confines.

Your purchases made for this week and my observations concluded for now, we make our way past the *cantinas* where tough, brown men from the fields drink crude cane alcohol with equally tough, brown men from the city's lower ranks. More than one will spend an hour or even a night at the nearby "hotel," and more than one will wake with empty pockets and an aching head, a cost that more than one will pay for the memories to take him through the next hard week of sun and sweat. The lottery vendor reminds us that "Tomorrow, tomorrow, tomorrow, it plays," and his voice calls to us even after we have passed the multipurpose *tiendas*, the larger *almacenes*, and the specialized *papelerías*. Near the plaza now, we admire the fountain whose unnatural task is to send water heavenward. A stranger stops us and asks, "Where is the market?"

At the edge of the plaza, the place of leisured urbanity, we turn together to gesture in the opposite direction. In our gesturing toward the place several blocks away, we also gesture to ourselves. We gesture, and the world that is there gestures back. A generalized image comes to mind, an image of a place where nature has been converted not to an ornament as in the plaza but to a commodity. "The language of the market," Mead himself declared, "is the language of money" (1972: 302). The social relationship between vendor and buyer, no matter how layered over with ties of friendship, kinship, or ritual co-parenthood, rests on the strategy of *listo*. *Estar listo* is to be ready, to be ready to act; *ser listo* is to be cunning, to seek personal gain. These two modes of the Spanish verb of being come together in the marketplace, and there the vendor with his cabbage and you with your purse, classic antagonists, are each ready to be smart.

In the market, where even the ethnographer becomes a participant, self and other are paired in their determination to take advantage of each other, to buy low and sell high, to be smart. The action that takes place in the marketplace is focused on the matter at hand, and the matter at hand is nature converted into object that has monetary value. His cabbage in your hand has a price. You may remark about the weather, he may inquire about your health, but as pleasant as these exchanges may be, eventually, you will ask, "How much?" And he will reply, eventually, "Thirty each." To repeat with Mead, "The language of the market is the language of money."

Humans are complicated creatures and creatures with complexes. Among the complications and complexes is the passion for morality. The passion for morality is so strong that even in the market people seek to do the right thing. Before you left the market, your basket filled and household obligations clamoring in your head, you stopped at the shrine dedicated to Sacred Heart of Jesus in the center of the market to light a candle. Your act and the shrine, however, cannot deny that the market remains the place where participants are fully engaged in the matter at hand and the matter at hand is the competitive advantage the self seeks over the other. It comes to be the place of other places, where we move from being participants engaged in being smart to being observers reflecting upon our duties, that morality emerges as the principal goal.[3]

CULTURE AS PROPER: THE VIETNAM VETERANS MEMORIAL

On a morning in March 1979, after a recurrent nightmare in which he relived the explosion of an ammunition truck that scattered the flesh and bones of his friends about him, Jan Scruggs, former infantryman and veteran of Vietnam, told his wife, "I'm going to build a memorial to all the guys who served in Vietnam.... It'll have the names of everyone killed" (Scruggs and Swerdlow 1985: 7). Three years later, on November 13, 1982, 150,000 veterans, family, friends, strangers — Americans — came to Washington, D.C., and dedicated a low V-shaped wall of black marble on which were inscribed names — Donald S Fujimoto, William A Gilmore, Michael T Majeski, Jesus J Meza, George K Golden, Larry D Knight, Jimmy G Freeman — names that Scruggs promised would be there.

A testament of one man's determination and intended to be free of any comment on the war itself, the Memorial, in the manner of a tool made, a word spoken, a poem written, has escaped the confines of a single vision and has become a public gesture whose meaning is dependent upon our responses. From the beginning, before one name was inscribed, the meaning of the Memorial was at issue.

To finance the construction of the Memorial, Scruggs and others had incorporated their efforts into the Vietnam Veterans Memorial Fund, which then sponsored an open, public competition for the Memorial's design. Judged by a panel of landscape architects, architects, and sculptors, the winning entry was a "minimalist," nonrepresentional, "landscape" design that called for the construction of a V-shaped wall sunk into the ground with the names of the dead listed on black marble. To everyone's surprise, including hers, the winner was an undergraduate at Yale University, Maya Lin.

Initially praised, the design quickly attracted criticism. As nonrepresentational, it was obscure and elitist: "Public monuments should belong to the public." Lacking the usual heroic attributes the design was a "black gash of shame" and "a tribute to Jane Fonda."

Confronted with this criticism, the Vietnam Veterans Memorial Fund, which earlier had worried about attacks from the antiwar movement, found itself having to defend its credentials. James Watt, secretary of interior, refused permission for the construction of the Memorial until suitable additions were made. The Scruggs's group eventually agreed and commissioned Frederick Hart, a representational sculptor, to design an additional memorial. His work resulted in three realistic figures dressed in battle gear, but not engaged in combat and seemingly returning from patrol. While the debate continued on as to whether the three figures, along with an American flag, should be placed at the apex of the V, the two artists became antagonists. The Yale student, Maya Lin, who came to her design independent of any experience with the war or with veterans, called Hart's figures "trite," a "simplification," the "illustration of a book" (Hess 1983: 123). Hart, who claimed to be close friends with many vets and to have drunk with them in bars, said that "Lin's memorial was intentionally not meaningful" and "contemptuous of life," while his, in contrast, was "populist" and "humanist" (Hess 1983: 124). Eventually, the decision was made to locate the figures apart but in view of the V and to raise the flag behind the figures. Following the dedication of the wall in 1982, two years later, the figures were unveiled on Veteran's Day, 1984.

The Perceptual, Preliminary Definition Phase

Coming down 20th Street from George Washington University, as we near Constitution Gardens on the Mall, we discover, each with our own questions, the first attribute of this questioning memorial: Where is it? To our right, in the near distance, is the massive Lincoln Memorial, built to bind a nation's wounds. To the left, in the far distance, is the phallic Washington monument, built to honor the father of our country. Ahead, we see an American flag and through the tree figures indistinguishable from the first tourists of the morning. Across Constitution Avenue, we read a small sign, "Vietnam Memorial," and discover a path leading toward a grassy knoll. Leaving the sounds of the day, traffic picking up from the light on Constitution, a jet plane circling National Airport, and shouts from a soccer game on the Mall, we follow the path's curves, until we come to it, the controversy memorializing a still greater controversy.

In Washington, D.C., memorials, as befit a nation's capital, abound. With few exceptions, they are monuments, truly larger than life. Across the Potomac, in Arlington, we stand at the feet of bronze giants and look upward to see huge hands frozen in the act of planting a flag on Mount Suribachi, a scene whose sheer size evokes the call to heroism in a battle for sacred causes.

Here, in Constitution Gardens, we go down and enter the Memorial. The wall, at first, is below us, at our feet. It rises as we move into the center, until at the apex of the V, the wall extends over our heads. We are in the middle of a black mirror of names: Melvin G Cormier, Walter L Burroughs, Hector S Acevedo, Michael L Poletti, Grady E McElroy, Mary T Klinker.

The Manipulatory, Verbal Phase

The Memorial, like all memorials, like all objects, blocks the unconscious flow of experience. Uniquely, it blocks the flow with another question: What is the order of the names?

"They're not alphabetical," a child, fresh from his triumph over the ABCs, complains to his father. "How do you find your state?" the husband of one couple from Texas puzzles to the husband of one from Ohio. You discover the names are not listed in bureaucratic purity, nor are they grouped according to the bearer's place of birth. What then is their order? you ask. At the apex, the structure that is there answers, its only explicit statement: "The names...are inscribed in the order they were taken from us." At the apex of the V, the left panel begins in 1959; the right panel ends in 1975; at the apex we stand in the middle of the Memorial and at the beginning and ending of deaths. The words are inscribed on the black marble. Your hand, with a will of its own, reaches out to trace the flow of the letters; mine follows. People touch the names, they point them out to one another, they place paper against the names and rub the paper to make an imprint, a name, which they carry home. In the narrow spaces between the panels of black marble, they insert small American flags and flowers. At the base, they place more flags and flowers and a wreath with this card, "20th Reunion, Class of 1965. Paul Fleming and Bob Sowlinsk. We will not forget. South Hadley, Mass."

At the Vietnam Veterans Memorial, the hand meets the word. The hand is the self, the word is the other, and at the wall, the black wall, the two, hand and word, self and other, meet.

The Consummatory, Image Phase

The third phase of the Meadian act is the consummatory, integrative one, the one that brings together the preliminary definition furnished by sight and the inhibitory encounter provided by touch into a generalized image of the reality in which we find ourselves.

As we move from the apex of the V, back from where the names begin and end, we come to the statue of the three men. They walk at an angle to the wall, their heads turn slightly, and they gaze at the wall. What do they see? What is in their look? Not victory, but not despair. Pain? Puzzlement? Pride?

We join them and look forward into our past. From this perspective, the wall becomes the other of the past, a past filled with already half-forgotten names: My Lai, Kent State, Khe Sanh, Gulf of Tonkin. At this distance, the Memorial invites us to replace those strident names with the ones on black marble and reflect, as do the three figures, upon the order "they were taken from us." This is its function as a generalized other, to integrate discourse, the polemics of hawk and dove, into a single document that speaks to us, now.

The Vietnam Veterans Memorial, originally a controversy encapsulating a controversy, achieves its power in the unique meeting of the hand with the word and their reflection in the black marble. It, in its understated manner, recapitulates the experience of the act, the Meadian unit of existence, by which we come to be: self, other, and generalized other; I, you, and place. As a generalized other, the Memorial places the Vietnam War in perspective, the perspective of the three figures, the perspective of the past in the present. In so doing, it ameliorates our nightmares and eases the burden of our guilt.

TWO PLACES, TWO MODES OF BEING, TWO CULTURES

It is difficult to imagine two places that differ more than the Spanish-American market and the Anglo-American Memorial. The market is a commonly occurring, everyday structure that appears in the back regions of every Spanish-American town of any size. Although a few markets may be housed in imposing structures, such as the one in Guanajuato, Mexico, erected during the reign of President Porfirio Díaz, the vast majority of markets are sheltered, if at all, under stark, utilitarian roofs. Markets are truly organic, and in the additions of booths, stands, or frequently the products themselves – medicinal herbs, shiny new socket sets – they spread beyond the building and threaten to engulf the very streets that feed them.

The Memorial is a unique structure, whose very uniqueness is controversial. It is located not only in the front region of a city, but in the front region of a nation, between memorials that honor the nation's savior and its early founder. The Memorial is not even remotely utilitarian; its wall is not a wall that shelters, but a wall that reflects. Unlike other memorials, the Vietnam Memorial is still developing, with the flag, the three men, and soon perhaps a nurse.[4] At the market, located across the plaza from her home, the buyer seeks the vendor to make a purchase in an everyday act that occurs each week. Located far from home, the Memorial is object of a journey made by the tourist-pilgrim, veteran or nonveteran, who comes once a year, or once every several years, or once in a lifetime, not to make a purchase, but to seek an answer to a question.

At the market, in front of a stall, face to face, the buyer and the vendor, classic antagonists, gesture and gesture back with hand and word. "Speak," the vendor directs the buyer, as the buyer's hand lifts the cabbage up for inspection. At the Memorial, in front of the black wall, face to face with himself, the tourist-pilgrim reaches for a word with his hand and touches a name. In front of his reflection, the name speaks, "Mary T Klinker."

The market is the place of *listo*, to be smart, to take advantage of the opportunity as it presents itself, for, as the lottery vendor shouts in his wisdom, "Tomorrow, it plays." The Memorial is the place of the past before us, in the present of our view from the observing position of the three figures. In the market, we are participants, lost in the everyday act of asking, "How much?" At the Memorial, we are observers, exposed in our search of asking, "What does it mean?"

Different as the market and the Memorial are, the Meadian perspective allows us to juxtapose them and describe the realities that emerge from the interaction occurring at each place. Through uniting the trajectory of the act with the genesis of the self into a three-phase process, we achieve an understanding of how people move from perceptual, preliminary definition, through a manipulatory, verbal exchange between self and other, to a consummatory, image phase in which they generalize their specific encounters into an other that allows them to reflect back upon their creative efforts and distinguish where they are in the symbolic world. The Meadian perspective, avoiding both the behaviorist's fallacy of reducing consciousness to physiology and the phenomenalist's error of locating the self antecedent to social action, permits us to describe in specific detail how people, flesh-and-blood primates, bring about a mode of being in which they are smart or proper, Spanish-American buyer-vendor or Anglo-American tourist-pilgrim — in sum, how cultures come to be in their places.

Culture, of course, is a many-placed thing; Spanish America has its proper, memorial side, and Anglo America its smart, market side. The study of cultures, however, does proceeds apace through contrasts, and the placing of two places in juxtaposition highlights their distinctiveness and thereby their meaning.

The humanistic approach differs from its mentalistic kin in the emphases it places on the human act, on the we who act, and on the fragile, yet everyday world we construct. And there is one final characteristic: while not relinquishing its claim to science, humanistic anthropology would become, if its practitioners could but claim the skill, an artistic endeavor. If the application of social science theory to human experience does not convey that experience in its vivid immediacy, then we believe we have failed. We strive for a science that even as it satisfies the intellect rejoices in the market's rich profusion of produce and people and grieves to the Memorial's question asked through a finger tracing the contours of a name carved in black marble. In humanistic anthropology, our goal is an aesthetic social science (Collins 1975), a science that celebrates being human even as it strives to elucidate the species' mystery.

NOTES

Sections of this chapter were presented at the meeting of the Association of American Geographers, 1985, and to the Department of Geography, Syracuse University, where James Duncan, Nancy Duncan, and others, both faculty and graduate students, strengthened the argument with their insightful questions. The section on Spanish-American market draws heavily upon Richardson (1982), augmented with later observations and enriched with a fuller understanding of George Herbert Mead. While the description of the market rests on many hours of observation in several countries, the account of the Memorial depends largely on written portrayals supplemented with two brief trips to the Memorial by Richardson and one longer one by Dunton. We thank Morris Freilich for inviting us to contribute to this volume; his intellectual contribution to our work is clearly evident.

1. In the original formulation, Mead preceded the perceptual phase with an impulse phase (1972: 3–25).

2. In paralleling the development of speech with that of the hand Mead has ignored the grasping ability of our wordless primate siblings. The manipulative skills of the chimpanzee may approximate our own, while even the most enthusiastic assessment of their language skills (Savage-Raumbaugh 1986) severely limits their vocabulary of words.

3. The distinction between being smart and being moral or proper comes from Freilich (1972).

4. As reported in the press, the Vietnam Women's Memorial Project is working toward the placement of a statue to honor the some 10,000 women who served in Vietnam, about 7,000 of whom were nurses.

REFERENCES

Clay, Grady
　　1982　"Vietnam's Aftermath: Sniping at the Memorial." *Landscape Achitecture* 71: 54–56.

Collins, Randall
　　1975　*Conflict Sociology*. New York: Academic Press.

Count, Earl
　　1958　"The Biological Basis of Human Sociality." *American Anthropologist* 60: 1049–85.

Duncan, Hugh
　　1968　*Communication and Social Order*. London: Oxford University Press.

Freilich, Morris
　　1972　"Manufacturing Culture." *The Meaning of Culture*, Morris Freilich, ed. Lexington, MA: Xerox College Publishing.

Haines, Harry W.
　　1986　"What Kind of War?: An Analysis of the Vietnam Veterans Memorial." *Critical Studies in Mass Communication* 3: 1–20.

Hess, Elizabeth
　　1983　"A Tale of Two Memorials." *Art in America* 71: 120–27.

Howett, Catherine M.
　　1985　"The Vietnam Veterans Memorial: Public Art and Politics." *Landscape* 28: 1–9.

Lewis, J. David
　　1981　"G. H. Mead's Contact Theory of Reality." *Symbolic Interaction* 4: 129–42.

Mead, George Herbet
　　1972　*The Philosophy of the Act*. Edited by Charles W. Morris. First published 1938. Chicago: University of Chicago Press.

　　1964　*Selected Writings*. Edited by Andrew J. Reck. Chicago: University of Chicago Press.

Miller, David
　　1973　*George Herbert Mead: Self, Language, and the World*. Chicago: University of Chicago Press.

Pfuetze, Paul E.
　　1954　*The Social Self*. New York: Bookman Associates.

Richardson, Miles
　　1982　"Being-in-the-Market Versus Being-in-the-Plaza." *American Ethnologist* 2: 421–36.

Savage-Raumbaugh, E. Sue
　　1986　*Ape Language: From Conditioned Response to Symbol*. New York: Columbia University Press.

Scruggs, Jan C., and Joel L. Swerdlow
　　1985　*To Heal a Nation*. New York: Harper & Row.

Strauss, Anselm, ed.
　　1964　*George Herbert Mead on Social Psychology*. Chicago: University of Chicago Press.

Unamuno, Miguel de
　　1974　*The Agony of Christianity*. Princeton: Princeton University Press.

　　1972　*The Tragic Sense of Life*. Princeton: Princeton University Press.

PART II

CULTURE AND INFORMATION

Culture, Ward Goodenough has long insisted, is information — not behavior, not the results of behavior, but knowledge. This elegant and valuable conceptualization became a major force inspiring the development of *cognitive anthropology*. In his chapter on Culture: Concept and Phenomenon, Goodenough presents seven possible interpretations of the equation: *Culture* = *information*. Clearly, information is a very complex concept. Those who utilize this conceptualization of culture, therefore, are well advised to study the various meanings of information.

Judith Perrolle provides such understandings in chapter 7, Information, Technology and Culture. Reading Judith Perrolle, we learn that it is useful to distinguish among data, information, and knowledge. We go on to discover an "informational" approach toward "tools" and "technology." Step by step, Perrolle leads us through a conceptual maze with such signposts as computers, artificial intelligence (AI), knowledge engineering, and cybernetic impact. How can we employ informational language for the "better" study of culture? Perrolle's Figure 6.1 provides an instant answer. Slower answers are provided in her sections: Information, Technology, and Culture Change; Information Technology in Agricultural Societies; and Information and the Rise of Capitalism.

Cultural analysis has only recently enjoyed the many insights which come from an informational focus. While the insights achieved have been important, they cannot be described as developing a conceptual breakthrough. Such is not the case with the sister science of biology. Here an informational focus has a long history of important insights and a short history of conceptual breakthroughs. It becomes meaningful to ask: Can modern biological theory provide valuable information for cultural theory? In chapter 8, Peter Richerson and Robert Boyd answer this question with a forceful "Yes." Richerson and Boyd argue that a Darwinian explanation for the evolution of group symbolic traits can be developed. What are required are a focus on the force of indirect bias and a model of indirect bias. These authors provide both. Cultural transmission is indirectly biased when people use some traits displayed by potential models (say, assertiveness) to bias the imitation of other traits (say, short hair). That the indirect bias process actually exists is supported by evidence from (1) social learning theory, (2) studies of the diffusion of innovation, and (3) work in sociolinguistics. Using interesting ethnographic illustrations these authors show that their theory has real explanatory power. Moreover, they use their theory to explain how behaviors which are "merely" symbolic can be defined by people as central to their existence.

Anthropology is moving toward full membership in a relatively new discipline: cognitive science. By using mental models, such as those described by Richerson and Boyd, by Mary Douglas, and by Morris Freilich and Frank Schubert, anthropologists can develop valuable, cross-discipline ties (Dougherty 1985). But, as we learn from Eugene Hunn's contribution, we may have to move with caution. A purely informational approach to culture is, for Eugene Hunn, a useful but incomplete approach. An informational approach leads to rules or a grammar. And grammars, he reminds us, permit us to make grammatical sentences which are nonsense. In chapter 8 Hunn argues that we must go beyond information to effective action. But what, very exactly, is effective action? And how does culture "teach" effective action? These and related questions Hunn very completely answers, and his answers include cases which explicate his reasoning.

Hunn's essay is usefully studied in conjunction with chapter 12 by Freilich and Schubert. Hunn wants to bring effective action "into" culture. In the language of Freilich's model of "Smart/Proper Analysis," Hunn sees culture as smart and proper. His arguments are reasonable and persuasive. Moreover, they are supported by Richardson and Dunton's chapter 4.

In the last analysis neither logic nor persuasive argumentation will win the day. The question will be settled by the answer to the following question: Which model of culture will lead to the most exciting, creative and productive hypotheses?

What is clear and already settled is that culture can still generate fascinating debates. Culture, indeed, is still relevant!

REFERENCE

Dougherty, Janet W. D., ed.
   1985   *Directions in Cognitive Anthropology*. Urbana and Chicago: University of Illinois Press.

5

CULTURE:
CONCEPT AND PHENOMENON

Ward H. Goodenough

Reviewing the state of anthropology in the *New York Times*,[1] Eric Wolf said, "The old culture concept is moribund." He had reference to the various directions taken in recent years by anthropologists of note whose personal agendas as anthropologists have been taken up by their students and admirers and converted into competing schools of thought. The same thing could have been said thirty years ago. The term culture has a long history of meaning different things to different people. One need only compare its treatment in the writings of Alfred Kroeber and Edward Sapir, for example.

The fact is that culture has never stood for a well-defined concept, but since Tylor's famous definition in 1871 as "that complex whole which includes knowledge, belief, art, morals, law, custom, and any other capabilities and habits acquired by man as a member of society," culture has designated a domain for investigation: namely, all those things characterizing humans as members of groups, including the things that remain similar and the things that differ from group to group. A theory that can account for all those things would be a theory of culture at least as Tylor delimited it. It would necessarily be a general theory embracing (1) the interrelationships of physiological and psychological processes with the physical and social environments of individuals within groups, (2) how these processes translate into what characterizes groups as human systems, and (3) how these characteristics are in turn affected by the way these groups as systems interact with their physical environment and with other groups as systems.

As yet, anthropologists have not arrived at any such general theory. But I think we are slowly working toward one. When we get there, it will involve most if not all of the different approaches that seem to divide us today. Each approach deals with a different strand of the problem. Clearly, an ecological approach to the study of human groups as systems is not in conflict with, but necessarily complements, an approach that focuses on human groups as held together by symbols whose various meanings to individual members of the group are so articulated as to enable them to live rewardingly together. There is not only room, then, for the wide variety of things anthropologists are doing, there is also good reason for us to pay serious attention to one another in all our apparent differences as anthropologists in how we approach our subject. For we all have things to contribute to the making of the general theory, although the exact nature of our contribution will undoubtedly end up taking a form somewhat different from the one any of us now envisages it to be.

Within this broad endeavor, the term culture has been used in a variety of ways in reference to a number of things, each of which is itself an appropriate object of investigation. For example, it has been used widely in reference to the patterns of activity that seem to characterize the flow of events within a community, as when we speak of a people's customary way of life. Such patterns of activity characterize colonies of ants and hives of bees as well as human communities, and in this sense culture is not peculiar to humans. Indeed, many of the things that we must consider in developing a general theory of culture are obviously not restricted to humans.

Some anthropologists have focused on those things characterizing human groups that result from learning. In doing so, they use the term culture more narrowly, referring to the end products of the learning process. It is in this narrower sense of the term that I have chosen to discuss culture in my own theoretical writing. What is learned embraces most of the things to which Tylor referred. Moreover, to have a theory that accounts for how the products of human learning both resemble and differ from one another in the many ways that they do we must take account of the same range of physiological, psychological, ecological, and social processes to which I have already referred.

The things that go into making a theory of culture are the things that explain culture as a phenomenon (or as a bundle of interrelated phenomena). What explains the existence of a phenomenon, however, should not be confused with the content of the phenomenon, the things that define or describe the phenomenon in the first place. In my own work, I have concentrated on the problem of the phenomenon of culture as such — the problem of its content and how to describe it and conceptualize it. In the course of this work I have found it convenient to distinguish seven different senses in which the term culture may be used. Every sense is useful for cultural and social theory, and every one of these senses is systematically related to every other. I have already discussed them in *Culture, Language, and Society*,[2] but I shall review them now, since they are clearly relevant to our present topic.

First, we can speak of culture in a general sense as consisting of systems of standards for perceiving, believing, evaluating, and performing, including, of course, standards for systems of meaning. People who live and work together have expectations of one another. These expectations have to do with how objects and events are to be classified as to what they apparently are (e.g., a barn as distinct from a house, a formal dinner party as distinct from a pot-luck supper). They involve understandings about how things thus classified work in relation to one another. They have to do with priorities and with deciding on the desirable and the undesirable. People's expectations also involve what constitute acceptable as against unacceptable performances; and they involve the symbolic and contextual associations of things and events. All these different kinds of expectations constitute what people must learn in order to be able to function acceptably as members of a social group in the activities in which members of the group engage with one another. A person learns not only how to perform acceptably but also how to judge the performance of others in a way that is similar to the judgments of others in the group. When he can do this, he has learned the standards by which he presumes others in the group do this. From his point-of-view and from that of other members of the group, he has learned what he has to know to get along acceptable in the group. He has learned its culture. Since the members of all social groups manage their affairs in terms of such mutual expectations or standards, it is in this sense of the term culture that we speak of it as a universal or general panhuman phenomenon. It is in this general sense of standards that we seek to relate culture to the biological, psychological, and behavioral constitution of humankind.

Second, we can speak of the culture of a group as the specific system or systems of standards a person attributes to the membership of the group as a result of her experience of various of the group's members. I find it convenient to distinguish a culture in this sense from the total content of an individual's knowledge of self and external world (including other people) — what I call one's "propriospect." A person's propriospect may contain several cultures, in this sense of the term, which she attributes to different sets of other persons. This second sense of the term is necessary when we consider specific cultures as products of human learning, for learning has to do with how each person organizes her experience, including experience of other people. This is also the sense of the term that is necessary for understanding what we do as ethnographers when we try to describe specific cultures. Any such description is the product of an ethnographer's learning experience of a set of others, a product he attributes back to them as being their culture and which is in truth his culture for them. A person considers the culture he attributes to a set of other people to be his own culture to the extent that he identifies himself with that group.

The third sense of the term culture relates to what I distinguish as "operating culture," the particular system of standards in a person's propriospect that he selects to interpret the behavior of others or to guide his own behavior on a given occasion. Do I use what I understand to be American or what I understand to be Japanese standards of precedence for going through doors, for example? We deal with this sense of the term when we try to understand the role of culture in social interaction. Since operating cultures are what people exhibit behaviorally to one another, this sense of the term is the one that is relevant when we consider the processes by which people learn cultures and by which they can be said to come to share cultures or to share meanings.

The fourth sense refers to what can be called a group's "public culture." It considers of all the individual versions of the standards that a group's members expect one another to use as their operating cultures in the various activities in which they have mutual dealings. In Washington, D.C., we all expect to use what we individually understand to be the American and not the Japanese order of precedence for going through doors. That expectation delimits our public culture for that activity. Subjectively, each individual's own version of a group's public culture corresponds to the second sense of the term culture: the standards a person attributes to a group of others. Viewed objectively, a public culture is a class or category of such attributions, consisting of all the individual versions of the group's standards in the propriospects of its members. The variance among these versions is contained within limits by psychological processes of corrective selection (as in cognitive learning). A public culture may contain several relatively discrete systems of standards — one for speaking and another for cooking, for example — each forming a distinct tradition within itself. This fourth sense of the term culture becomes relevant when we consider culture as the property of a social group and when we become concerned with how traditions are maintained over time in association with a group.

A fifth sense of the term culture refers to a level in a taxonomic hierarchy of public cultures. It consists of a set of public cultures that are functionally equivalent and mutually apprehensible. Each public culture in the set is a subculture. In this sense, culture is to subculture much as language is to dialect or species to subspecies.

Then we come to the anthropologically common sense of the term in reference to a society's culture, which I like to spell with a capital C. A society's Culture is the overall set of mutually ordered public cultures and subcultures pertaining to all activities within the society. Here we are concerned with culture as it relates to human societies at all levels of social complexity.

But a society's members, taken collectively, have knowledge of more than the public cultures that comprise the overall Culture of their society. In varying degrees, they know something of other cultures that pertain to other societies, as they know something of other languages. All of this additional knowledge in the propriospects of a society's individual members, taken together with their knowledge of the Culture of their own society, constitutes what may be called a society's "culture pool." It serves as a reservoir of resources in knowledge and skills carried by the membership of a society. It is especially relevant to the processes of culture change. Elements are continually being lost from and added to a society's culture pool by one set of processes; and elements in the pool are being brought into the public culture or dropped out of the public culture (although remaining in the pool) by another set of processes.

The foregoing enumeration, I think, makes it evident that, as our study of the phenomenon we call culture progresses, it becomes necessary to conceptualize it in a variety of interrelated ways, each conceptualization being appropriate to a particular kind of question or problem for research. In this respect, there is nothing moribund about culture as a conceptual tool.

There is a sense, however, in which I concur with Eric Wolf that the concept is moribund, or ought to be. It is in its use as a counter to old racist and outmoded forms of biological explanation of human differences in custom and belief. Biology helps explain human behavior but does not determine it. Similarly, culture helps explain behavior but does not determine it, either. Nor does culture explain the differences among peoples; it simply refers to what those differences consist of. Their explanation calls for resort to such things as history and ecology and to an understanding of the conditions in which the social and psychological processes of which culture is an artifact have been at work.

NOTES

Presented at the annual meeting of the American Anthropological Association, Washington, D.C., December 5, 1980.
1. Eric Wolf, "They Divide and Subdivide," *The New York Times*, November 30, 1980, p. E 9.
2. Ward H. Goodenough, *Culture, Language, and Society*, 2nd rev. ed. (Menlo Park, Calif.: Benjamin/Cummings, 1981).

6

INFORMATION, TECHNOLOGY, AND CULTURE

Judith A. Perrolle

> Information is not just one thing. It means different things to those who expound its characteristics, properties, elements, techniques, functions, dimensions, and connections. Evidently, there should be *something* that all the things called information have in common, but it is not easy to find out whether it is much more than the name. If we have failed and are still at sea, it may be our fault: Explorers do not always succeed in learning the language of the natives and their habits of thought. (Machlup and Mansfield 1983: 4–5)

The current revolution in computers and communications technology uses concepts of information that seem far different from the concepts of culture theorists. The selection of symbols as the units of cultural information presupposes a primary concern for meaning. Although it is claimed that computers can "see" through video cameras and can "recognize" letters and numbers, they have not been very successful at handling abstract symbols, especially those referring to the emotional qualities of human experience. Over the theoretical objections of some linguists, computer interfaces are being designed to use natural human languages. Yet it is difficult to imagine in what sense a computer could "understand" words used to express symbols of human emotional experience, as in poetry:

For all the history of grief
An empty doorway and a maple leaf. (MacLeish 1962: 51)

THE SCIENTIFIC STUDY OF INFORMATION

The notion that information can be the measurable object of scientific study appears reductionist to many scholars of culture. The assertion that information is intangible, unmeasurable, and only to be studied through interpretation seems absurd to the scientist who routinely measures it. Yet the possibility that information is indeed one "thing" and that the cultural concept of information is relevant to information science is worth exploring. The emerging field of cognitive science takes this proposition quite seriously (Gardner 1987) and is already informed by Lévi-Strauss's structuralist approach to culture. It is also important to consider the relevance of the mathematical concept of information for the cultural sciences.

Norbert Wiener (1948) and Claude Shannon (1948) define the quantity of information as a statistical measure of a system's organization. In cultural terms, the amount of information would thus be considered a measure of symbolic relationships, an indicator of cultural richness and complexity, rather than a measure of the number of distinct cultural elements symbolized. Shannon defines information as the probability of a message being transmitted. In an electronic transmission system, noise is the highly probable, randomly generated part of the transmission, such as the static during a telephone conversation. The signal is the nonrandom, information-bearing part of the transmission, for example, the voice you are listening to in a noisy room. In Shannon's formulation, low probability signals contain more information than high probability ones. If you are told something you have been told many times before (and that you expect to keep on hearing over and over), there is not much information in the message. From this perspective, a new artistic expression has more information than a repetition of a traditional cultural form.

Shannon's approach to measuring information is now most commonly used in the fields of telecommunications and electronics. There, the focus is on the speed and accuracy with which data can be transmitted through a variety of media. The meaning of information to humans is not really considered. Thus linguists have criticized Shannon's definition by pointing out that the sentence "Fred is a dog" contains more information than the less probable sentence "Fred is a mammal," where Shannon's theory predicts it should contain less information. However, his theory was intended to deal with message transmission, not with symbolic meaning. Nor is it suggested in Shannon's theory that more information transmission through computer networks will automatically add to our cultural knowledge.

Cybernetics

From Wiener's perspective, information is the key to the way both machines and living organisms modify their behavior to take into account the outcome of their previous actions. He defines cybernetics as the study of communication and control mechanisms. *Feedback* is the information process that allows an organism or a machine to be self-regulating, in the way a thermostat works to maintain room temperature. Information about how hot the room is causes the thermostat to turn the furnace on or off, changing the temperature of the room in the desired direction. Put another way, when you reach for a moving object, you see where your hand is in relation to the object, then use that information to correct the motion of your hand. This sort of feedback is an essential part of the way humans survive in their environments.

One of the first observations of feedback in culture was Adam Smith's concept of the "invisible hand" that regulates economic exchange. Feedback has been applied to political organization by Karl Deutsch (1966) and to social structure more generally by Talcott Parsons (1951) and Herbert Simon (1969). The association of cybernetic concepts with American structural functionalism has led many scholars to dismiss them as conservative attempts to characterize and defend the cultural status quo. However, cybernetic concepts can be applied to dynamic, and even revolutionary, models of cultural change.

Entropy

Entropy is a measure of the natural tendency of physical systems to become disordered. For example, most of us comb our hair every morning; by afternoon it has become tangled "all by itself." Throughout our lives we put energy into activities like combing hair or straightening up our rooms. By random processes of the wind blowing and our putting things down anywhere, our hair and our rooms get messy. Of all the possible ways our heads and houses could be arranged in space, only a few are "neat"; the vast majority are not. Thus the untidy state is much more probable than the neat state.

Wiener related information to negative entropy by showing that it had the same mathematical properties. Information is analogous to negative entropy because we use it to create improbable, organized systems. When we pick up a room, we scan the situation, locating objects in space and comparing their distribution to our mental pattern for "clean room." We select each object that is out of place and put it where it belongs. As we identify, select, and relocate objects, we are using information to identify objects and feedback to observe and control our cleaning activity. As we work, the arrangement of objects in the room gets closer to our mental goal. To appreciate the way we use information to create order, try cleaning a room in the dark. Unless you are blind and used to identifying objects by touch and sound, you may find it quite difficult in the absence of visual information.

We cannot create order unless we have in our minds a set of criteria for selecting and arranging the objects we are trying to organize. These nonrandom mental criteria for identification, selection, and action are themselves a form of cultural information. The entropy concept underlies one important relationship between the material and symbolic components of culture: the production, maintenance, and transmission of cultural information is naturally prone to disorganization, distortion, and loss. Culture is not immune to the laws of physical science: it requires energy and systematic effort on the part of its members for its preservation. The implications of Wiener's concept of information for the relevance of culture to scientific systems of knowledge is that the creation of order is accomplished with reference to preexisting information. In other words, as Kuhn (1970) and Polanyi and Prosch (1975) point out, we cannot develop scientific knowledge independently from our cultural beliefs.

Data, Information, and Knowledge

The cybernetic view of information as an ordering of symbolic relationships makes it useful to distinguish among the concepts data, information, and knowledge. *Data* refer to representations of what we believe to be "facts" about the world (for example, the word "trees," a photograph of trees, or the phrase "four trees"). *Information* refers to relationships among facts (for example, the sentences "There are more trees in Idaho than in Rhode Island" or "The maple is a common urban tree"). Finally, in evaluating and understanding the world, we develop *knowledge* like "Oak makes better furniture than pine" and "Trees help maintain humidity and prevent erosion on hillsides." Like the distinctions made between signs and symbols in the cultural sciences, distinctions among data, information, and knowledge allow us to discuss structural relationships among representations and the connection between representation and meaning.

Higher orders of symbolism, as in the mythic symbol, "the tree of life," can also be distinguished to describe additional levels in the conceptual structure of human thought. *Myths*, which explain the relationship of human beings to time, life, death, and the sacred, are the form in which our earliest scientific knowledge was passed from generation to generation (de Santillana and von Dechend 1969). Although a myth has the form of a story, it is a high-level symbolic expression of the workings of the universe. Myths today still have the power to explain the human condition in symbolic terms. The Greek myth of Prometheus, who was punished for bringing technology to humanity, has been used by contemporary scholars to symbolize the unforeseen consequences of technological change. In applying it to computers, Patricia Warrick (1980) argues that the Promethean theme is a warning that nature has placed limits on humanity's ability to create and control.

As an example, a telephone book contains data representing the names, addresses, and telephone numbers of people in a city. The information in the phone book is the relationship between name and phone number and the alphabetical order of the names. A phone book for the whole world would contain more data than a city directory, but it would not necessarily have more information unless it were organized by region or in other useful ways. Knowledge about phone books includes an understanding that the names refer to people and the numbers are codes enabling one person to operate a machine in order to speak with another. It also includes normative rules for the circumstances under which telephones are to be used and the behaviors to be employed during phone conversations. The meaning of telephones is also part of more general cultural concepts of technology and communication, including contemporary myths of technological progress.

Technology

Information technology represents the introduction of new tools for communication and remote control. Technology, however, is more than tools. It comprises the social processes which produce tools, the social behaviors involved in using tools, and the culturally defined meanings of tools. Information about tools, whether their design or the techniques for using them, is an essential

CARL A. RUDISILL LIBRARY
LENOIR-RHYNE COLLEGE

component of technology. In its most general sense, a tool can be defined as an object or agent through which human activity is directed toward some goal. Tools are often used as extensions of the human body, to gather information about and to manipulate the physical world. Microscopes and telescopes extend our vision; hammers and spaceprobes extend the reach of our hands. Tools like cameras or tape recorders store sensory information; tools for writing and painting allow us to make a durable record of our inner ideas and visions that can be shared with others. Information storage media, from stone carvings to data bases, facilitate the communication of information from person to person and from generation to generation.

Computers can be very specific tools (to play a video game or to regulate a single machine tool's performance) or very general purpose (such as the programmable digital computer). Although many people consider the computer to be useful only for computation, computers are tools for communication and control of all types of information. Analog computers handle nondigital processes (like monitoring an electric current or the temperature of a room); graphics capabilities enable us to process visual images and create pictures or charts; peripheral devices such as remote sensors can process sound, pressure, and a host of other data.

As an information-processing tool, the computer's major characteristic is the speed with which it processes extremely large quantities of data organized in complex ways. Although computers are popularly noted for their perfect accuracy, all large and interesting computer systems are prone to error. Hardware and software "bugs," human errors in data entry, and built-in possibilities for less than perfect performance (such as the ability to "guess" or "forget" that is a feature of the heuristic programs used in artificial intelligence) mean that computer technology is not the way to perfection.

The control over geographically dispersed information is an extremely important feature in business and military applications, as well as in the communications industry. Remote sensors used in satellites and space probes extend our ability to gather information on subjects as diverse as the vegetation of Africa or the rocks of Mars. With telecommunications equipment we can hear from any part of the earth and far into space. Via robotics, we can work from a safe distance on the ocean floor or with hazardous chemicals. Also, and more dangerously, computerized weapons have vastly extended our ability to throw deadly objects at one another.

Computer-based decision making is at the heart of the integrated software systems now being designed for industrial and military uses. These systems coordinate decisions, from the purchase of raw materials through automated plant operation to customer billing. Although the expression, "Computers only do what you tell them to do," has become almost a folk saying, decision making by computer is becoming increasingly sophisticated.

Perhaps the most striking characteristic of the computer is its *extension of the human mind*; both our memories and our abilities to calculate and reorganize information have been enhanced by computers. Edward Feigenbaum and Pamela McCorduck (1983) believe that we will enter into a partnership in which computers perform calculation and memory functions, while humans exercise their analytic capacities. The danger in this, expressed by Joseph Weizenbaum (1976), is that we will neglect those areas of human judgment and reason which cannot easily be computed. He fears that the new doors opened by computer extensions of the mind will close other, more important doors of human thinking.

Technique

In order for any tool to be used successfully, the technique for using it must be understood. A *technique* can be thought of as a method for performing a task, without necessarily including a full scientific or social explanation of what is being done. The technique for driving a car can be learned without any under-standing of how an internal combustion or diesel engine works. No knowledge of traffic rules or the consequences of driving head-on into a truck is necessary to insert the key, start the engine, engage the gears, and go. The techniques of safe driving include a broader understanding of the social consequences of making a car run. The techniques of automotive design include a much fuller scientific knowledge of the principles behind the car's motion. The techniques of social impact assessment would include an understanding of the consequen-ces of the automobile for such phenomena as patterns of urban residence, air pollution, energy resource use, and the industrial structure of the economy.

Technique can be taught explicitly through demonstration or written instruc-tion, but it can also be embodied in ritual. Though analysts may consider rituals to be declining in cultural significance, many contemporary individuals learn to use technology in magical, ritual ways. What distinguishes their approaches to technology from the group rituals of traditional culture is that these are private, personal rituals of human/machine interaction rather than symbolic affirma-tions of collective life.

Technology and Reification

By building tools and developing techniques we make our imagined designs real. But sometimes, as we embody our ideas in machines, we reify social relation-ships as well. In other words, we imagine that our relationships to one another are "in" the technology. An example of this is lie detection technology—polygraphs or the newer, computerized, voice stress analyzers. Lying is a very human phenomenon. We often present ourselves to others as nicer, smarter, more attractive, or more competent than we secretly feel. People deliberately distort information for their own advantage or to avoid hurting others. Although we have strong norms against lying to gain power over others, we expect "white lies" in polite conversation. We often say "I'm fine, thanks. How are you?" when we feel terrible.

Lie detectors, according to a review by the United States Congressional Office of Technology Assessment (Saxe 1985), do not detect lies. They detect the physiological changes that occur with emotional stress. There are many sources of such stress besides guilt or fear of being caught at lying. If someone lies without guilt or fear, the technology detects nothing. An honest answer to an embarrassing or disturbing question will show evidence of stress. Yet some people treat lie detectors as if they were a technology to reveal the "truth" in others' minds without having to go through the social interaction processes that establish trust in one another. Trust based on social interaction has been replaced by trust in information technology.

INFORMATION PRODUCTION

In order to "make" information, new connections must be made among data. This can be done by physically rearranging the data, as when a person or a computer sorts records into some kind of meaningful order. If we put data on people's smoking habits together with data on lung cancer, we can produce information about the risks of smoking. One of the goals of information science has been to create "intelligent" information technology. Computer languages that make sense in human conceptual terms and computer programs that apply human selection criteria to information are believed to be both possible and desirable by practitioners of the new field of artificial intelligence.

Artificial Intelligence

Artificial intelligence (AI) involves the design of computer programs and automated equipment, such as industrial robots, with a limited capacity to behave in ways that at least resemble human thought processes. (For a technical survey, see Barr and Feigenbaum 1982; Hayes-Roth 1983; or Coombs 1984; for a sympathetic popular history, see McCorduck 1979; for a critical review, see Athanasiou 1987.) Information from the outside world can be sought, interpreted, and used as the basis for heuristic decisions which in humans would be called "best guesses." The programs can, within the narrow range of the world to which they are applied, draw inferences, suggest solutions to previously unsolved problems, select relevant information according to their own internal criteria, and modify their own behavior as a result of the outcomes of their previous actions.

Knowledge Engineering

The knowledge engineering area of artificial intelligence promises that its software will "capture" the knowledge of experts in programs that enable a less skilled person to achieve expert results:

> Knowledge is a scarce resource whose refinement and reproduction creates wealth. Traditionally the transmission of knowledge from human expert to trainee has required education and internship years long. Extracting knowledge from humans and putting it in compatible forms can greatly reduce the costs of knowledge reproduction and exploitation...skill means having the right knowledge

and using it effectively. Knowledge engineering addresses the problem of building skilled computer systems, aimed first extracting the expert's knowledge and then organizing it in an effective implementation. (Hayes-Roth, Waterman, and Lenat 1983: 5,13)

The theoretical possibility of representing human knowledge and decision-making processes in computer programs has been fiercely debated on both scientific and moral grounds, with the strongest objections coming from the philosopher Hubert Dreyfus in *Mind over Machine* (1986) and the artificial intelligence expert Joseph Weizenbaum in *Computer Power and Human Reason* (1976). One important issue is the degree to which human decision making is believed to be rational and logical. Intelligent software has been most successful for those applications in which the knowledge of human experts is very well understood and rather routine. Critics of knowledge engineering doubt that computers actually can be designed to handle any but the simplest symbolic meanings.

While the debate between those who argue that machines can think and those who argue that they can't continues (Boden 1977; Goldkind 1987; Haugeland 1981), the practical success of intelligent programs that play chess, infer chemical structures from molecular data, and diagnose illnesses indicates quite clearly that artificial intelligence is being put to work at industrial and professional tasks, despite the reservations of many theorists (Perrolle 1988). Weizenbaum questions Feigenbaum's assertion that computers will produce the future knowledge of the world; he asks how we are to understand just what information the computer produces and how it does so (Weizenbaum 1983). But if information itself is seen as a product made for profit by efficiently organized employees, then information can be produced by the computer in the same way that products were made by the factory machinery of the first Industrial Revolution (Perrolle 1986). Wiener's mathematical quantification of information represents an important step in "the establishment of socially recognized standards of measure" that Marx identified as an important characteristic of commodities (1967: 199). Current social and legal trends toward greater recognition of information as a form of property are providing the cultural context for much broader property rights in information (Perrolle 1987: 183–204).

INFORMATION TECHNOLOGY AND CULTURAL CHANGE

Information technology plays a role in cultural change because it modifies the way a society interprets and interacts with its environment. Information is the way we organize our understanding of the world; tools are means to our acting in it. Figure 6.1 illustrates these interrelationships.

The Social Interpretation of Reality

In addition to our own perceptions, socially shared experiences and preconceived cultural conceptions contribute to our understanding of the world. In a

Figure 6.1   Information and Tools Modify the Relationships Between the Social System and the Physical Environment

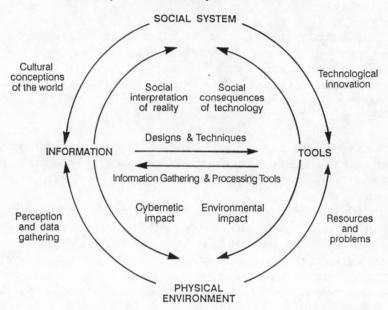

review of empirical research on environmental perception, Holahan (1982) points out the importance of cultural contexts for an individual's ability to perceive shapes. In a classic experiment involving optical illusions Allport and Pettigrew (1957) found that rural Zulu children were less likely than their urban counterparts to be fooled by a rotating trapezoid's visual resemblance to a swaying rectangular window, since rectangular windows were not a part of their cultural experience. In experiments with the apparent motion of a fixed spot of light in a darkened room (the autokinetic effect), observers who were told to expect that the light would write out words observed that to occur (Rechtschaffen and Mednick 1955). Research on the interaction between visual images of traffic accidents and verbal accounts containing different information shows that people's memories of perception can be influenced by what others say to them about it (Loftus, Miller, and Burns 1978). This tendency for members of human groups to influence one another's perceptions and to share a systematic pattern of information selection is essential to such recreations as watching cloud pictures with a friend or enjoying a magician's performance. It is also an essential part of the way humans develop and share a common culture.

Our sensory system is a biologically based data-gathering and processing system. However, the meaning of this direct experience is provided by our culture. Although many animal species have genetically preprogrammed responses to environmental stimuli, human cultures, through their languages, beliefs, and habits, encourage individuals to select information from the world in socially appropriate ways and provide interpretations of the meaning of the information selected. Consider the different ways skiers, Eskimos, and others experience snow. Eskimos and skiers have large vocabularies to describe snow according to its properties. Their activities depend upon their ability to distinguish different kinds of snow and to understand the meaning of those differences. For most of the rest of us, snow is not important enough to be perceived in such detail. Even the sensory data we do pay attention to is modified by our perceptual mechanisms for sight, hearing, touch, taste, and smell. We receive input from the world only after it has been filtered through both our nervous system and our culture.

New information technology alters our ability to predict and control physical and social events as we presently understand them. As we change our ability to predict and to act in the world, our cultural concepts of the world will change as well. In computer modeling, for example, we create abstract mathematical representations of our environments and even our internal biology. With these models we are able to make predictions or gain new insight into how the world behaves. Sometimes these models become metaphors for features of society, the physical world, or the human nervous system, which are spoken of as if they were computers or computer programs. In fields such as neurophysiology the computer has become so popular a metaphor that critics have to remind us that brains are not actually computers any more than they were the clockwork mechanisms of earlier models (Gregory 1981: 226–40; Calvin 1983).

Besides providing new paradigms for the nature of the physical and biological world, changes in information technology affect cultural values. Computer system metaphors for the world make it easier to conceive of complex wholes and to see ourselves as part of a single environmental and social system. This sense of being part of something much larger and more important than oneself is often considered part of traditional culture's concept of the sacred quality of human life. In this case, a new kind of experience with information technology strengthens a traditional value. By adding a new dimension to the question, What does it mean to think? artificial intelligence research addresses existing cultural concepts of self and consciousness. While cognitive science's goal of achieving a scientific understanding of mind may appear as an expression of positivistic hubris to theorists of culture, this emerging effort to develop a new science of consciousness is likely to have a profound impact on contemporary culture.

Sherry Turkle (1984) found young computer users placing higher value on emotion and feelings to define what it means to be human. They associated the ability to calculate and reason logically with the machines they played with. As a consequence of her findings, we can predict that the experience of using computers will cause us to devalue calculation and logical reasoning. Daniel Bell (1980) believes that information will become more highly valued, with the ability to use it becoming our most important skill. Joseph Weizenbaum (1976) has suggested that computer-based data will become so important that we will neglect our cultural traditions and fail to explore new, nontechnological areas of human experience. Echoing the theme of the Promethean myth, he fears our fascination with the power of the computer to let us design and control imaginary worlds will lead us to tragedy in the real world of social cooperation and conflict.

Since the meaning communicated through information exchange is the basis of social interaction, one important impact of information technology is the way it changes the process of interpersonal communication. From the individual's perspective, power is both the ability to affect the physical environment and the ability to make other people do what you want them to do, even against their will. From a social perspective, power is the ability of groups to interact successfully with one another and the physical world. The capacity to motivate individuals for cooperative purposes is an essential part of a society's ability to survive. Although we may think of our power in terms of military strength or superior technology, our abilities to investigate problems and negotiate solutions are just as important. Power is more than the ability to control others; it is also the capacity to organize effective action.

The exercise of power requires information. We cannot influence people unless we can communicate with them. We cannot offer them material rewards to do our bidding unless we can come to an understanding about the exchange. We cannot even forcibly move people or objects without knowledge of where they are vulnerable to our efforts. Planning long-term actions requires procedures to gather new information, evaluate it in terms of shared goals, and use it in choosing a course of action. Information technology is a source of power for those who use it to gain an advantage over others. In other cases, the use of information technology has made it easier for people to negotiate and to reach decisions (Koh 1984).

Interactions with the Environment through Tools

The environment can be thought of as presenting us with a set of problems of subsistence and survival and also providing us with materials for the solution of those problems. Another way to put it is that the physical world contains resources which we use to satisfy biologically and culturally defined needs. Through the process of technological innovation societies have developed new tools to deal with the physical world as they perceive and interpret it. Some of these problems, like food and shelter, are basic to our species' biology. Other problems, like war and peace or economic production and distribution, are central to human interaction within a society, as well as to the way societies interrelate. Historically, agricultural technology has provided food; weapons have been the means for aggression and defense; craft and manufacturing tools have supplied products defined as socially desirable or necessary. Theories of technological innovation do not assume that an environmental problem, such as food shortages, will automatically produce a technical solution, like improved agriculture. Instead, these problems provide societies with a strong incentive to innovate.

Once developed, tools have an environmental impact on the world. The environmental effects of new technology have often been unexpected and undesirable. The use of tools to solve one set of survival problems, such as generating energy, can create another set of problems, like environmental pollution and the greenhouse effect. For this reason, gathering information about the consequences of technology and trying to anticipate potential new problems are important for human survival. It was conventional wisdom a few years ago that the ecology movement and the computer revolution were in "fundamental harmony" (Hyman 1980: 126). Unlike our older smokestack industries, information technology was viewed as "environmentally sound, non-polluting, and non-destructive of the ecology of an overcrowded planet" (Martin 1978: 4). Recent experience with environmental pollution in the computer industry has drastically altered our understanding (LaDou 1984; Burton 1985). Information technology has a great potential as a tool for solving environmental problems, but its own environmental impact must be carefully assessed.

The Social Consequences of Technology

Tools affect the social system out of which they were developed. Although we are used to computers doing what we tell them to, it is also the case that using computers and other tools changes what people do. Once we have told a computer what to do, we have created an environment that may define our pattern of activity. Thus, we often find ourselves limited to defining tasks and problems according to the computer system's capabilities and requirements. If it is easy to do on the computer, we do it. If it is difficult or impossible, we do not.

The effects of a new tool can change individual social interactions. The use of a two-person saw requires a particular working relationship between two people. If they are then put to work using new single-person power saws, the social relationship of the sawing team will be broken. Many problems associated with the introduction of new computer systems are caused by this sort of alteration in people's social interactions. While computer professionals have grown used to considering how "user-friendly" a program is to a single user, it is also important to consider how computer systems change people's interactions with one another. Even people who respond enthusiastically to computer networks report a reduction in social contact with co-workers (Diebold 1984).

Information technology also has consequences for larger patterns of human activity. The widespread use of data processing systems can radically change the number and kinds of jobs available to members of a society. It is this sort of feedback from tool use to the social pattern that produced the tool which makes technological innovation a major source of social change. To understand the consequences of a tool, one must understand the context in which it is used and something of how it came to be developed. This entails an examination of the tool's unintended social and psychological effects as well as its intended purpose.

Once we understand the consequences of our technology, we can choose to use it or not. Our choices, however, are severely limited by what is available, what is considered culturally appropriate, what we can afford, and whether we are influenced or threatened. If computers are expensive and we have little money, we cannot easily choose to own one. If the company we work for installs a computer system, our choice to use it or not is usually the choice of keeping our job or not. Technology is a social product. Those who develop and finance it often have a particular interest in replacing older ways of doing things because to do so would be to their economic advantage. Other proponents of new technology feel that it will increase their prestige or give them more influence over other people. Since new technology is rarely of equal interest to everyone in a society, a considerable amount of conflict can occur during the innovation process. For this reason, an understanding of society's economic and political processes is also necessary in order to understand technological change.

The Cybernetic Impact

The concept of cybernetics provides a useful model of one way information contributes to cultural change. It assumes that human groups develop new meanings and behaviors based on feedback about the results of their past experiences. Cybernetic impact refers to the way the informational content of culture affects the physical world. Although Figure 6.1 shows information to have a direct impact on the world, this is a simplification of a more indirect relationship. The assertion that ideas by themselves can alter the physical world is generally confined to religious and mystical belief systems. Although the media in which information is expressed and stored appear in the material world as cultural artifacts, it is the way in which ideas guide human behavior that has the greatest effect.

Our mental models, the way we organize information and apply it to activity, are part of our cybernetic impact. Research into how we create and use mental models has been spurred by the fields of artificial intelligence and cognitive science. But it through the study of culture from a diversity of perspectives that we understand the highest levels of symbolic expression. Without the concept of culture, our attempts to understand cognition can succeed at only the lowest levels of meaning.

INFORMATION TECHNOLOGY AND HUMAN COMMUNICATION

One source of continuity between the contemporary revolution in information technology and much earlier forms of cultural change is the human use of information. Nonverbal communication developed before the evolution of modern human speech and is still an essential ingredient of social interaction. (Indeed, one of the technical difficulties of natural language software is human reliance on body posture, eye contact, and gesture to communicate meaning.) The first two innovations in information processing were art and spoken language. Paleontological evidence indicates that visual representation of objects had begun by the time humans were hunters of large animals. By then, people had learned to store information in carvings and pictures. They had also begun to bury their dead with flowers, suggesting that they had begun to ponder the symbolic meaning of their existence.

Lieberman (1984) dates the evolution of rapid symbolic communication from the flourishing of Cro-Magnon culture 35,000 to 40,000 years ago, basing his argument on fossil evidence for changes in vocal physiology. Some of our oldest myths and religious traditions refer to the long, food-gathering part of our past, when we lived in a "garden" and began to give names to animals and things. One explanation for the cultural theme that symbolic representation through art and words is sacrilegious (as in the Judeo-Christian prohibition against graven images) is that face-to-face, emotional communication is an important source of group solidarity. In many religious traditions, such as the Greek mysteries or some modern forms of group prayer, a sacred silence helps produce feelings of connection among humans and between humans and the sacred (Basso 1972). Contemporary studies of computer-mediated communication identify the loss of face-to-face contact as a problem for groups of people working together.

Rapid symbolic communication contributed to more complex forms of social and economic life. Songs, stories, art, and myth communicated to each new generation the wisdom of the past. This process of cultural information accumulation has contributed much more to our evolution than the slower processes of genetic selection (cf. Boyd and Richerson 1985).

Information Technology in Agricultural Societies

From observations of contemporary gathering and hunting societies we can theorize that the process of transmitting information was structurally differentiated as the division of labor developed in human societies (for an anthropological review of the origin of the division of labor, see Leibowitz 1983). Transmission might occur through ritual initiation into sacred knowledge. Technical skills like tool making might become specialties passed down from craftsman to apprentice. As food surpluses appeared in hunting societies, laws regulating distribution added to the informational complexity of culture. In the minds of influential men and women who could interpret and magically influence events, cultural information was accumulated, reorganized, and transmitted. For most of our history on earth, memory has been the storage medium for information; the sudden death of a shaman or elder might erase a good portion of a group's knowledge.

Sometime during the last 20 to 30,000 years, communities of people scattered across the globe learned to raise plants and animals for food (cf. Braidwood 1960; Harlan 1976). This early agriculture was seminomadic, similar in many ways to gathering wild plants. More rapid population growth and the low productivity of early agriculture pressured human groups to improve their food-producing technology (Boserup 1965). Archaelogical evidence suggests that, by at least 10,000 B. C., people had begun to settle in villages organized around permanent farming plots. Compared to previous cultural developments, information and social organization evolved rapidly. During the next few thousand years humans developed a variety of extraordinarily complex cultural forms (cf. Renfew 1983; Lewin 1986). The reproductive habits of plants and animals were learned and formalized as a set of myths and customs, as part of the new techniques of food production. Fertility, weather, and the seasons took on a central role in religion. As early as 30,000 B. C. (which is as far back as carbon-14 dating can be done reliably) the inventory of tools included calendars which could predict the annual agricultural cycles. These were analog rather than digital devices, dependent on the relative positions of sun, moon, and stars to compute the changing seasons. Because we have no similar evidence (like counting sticks or the sand table abacus) for any development of mathematics that early, it appears that our first information technologies were developed before computation (cf. Menninger 1969.) Our earliest calculators expressed relationships in terms of visual sacred symbols, such as the signs of the zodiac or the image of the sun god being pulled across the sky by horses.

With the establishment of early forms of private property and inheritance, information about both kinship and ownership became an important part of culture. New social arrangements were based on food surpluses that freed some individuals from agricultural tasks. Leaders assumed more important informational roles in society, interpreting both social rules and religious traditions. Over time, those with the power to define cultural meanings and to remember official history rose in status and privilege. As early forms of agriculture established the division of labor by age and sex, so settled agriculture divided labor by social class, while the ideal of personal property in the form of food, tools, or ornaments that could be used was transformed into the idea of private wealth that could be amassed by a privileged group.

As the state, with its monopoly on the legitimate use of force, appeared in human society, information gathering and processing became increasingly important. Agricultural surplus, in the form of taxes, was extracted from villagers. Specialized staffs of warriors, priests, craftsmen, artisans, and slaves were employed in keeping track of imperial resources. China, the oldest of the agrarian empires, was the originator of major innovations in information technology (cf. Needham 1956). As the 5000-year-old oracle bones of China indicate, early writing developed from pictures and was part of a religious information system. The important advantages of writing as a method of information transmission, as opposed to oral or nonverbal communication, are that information is stored outside the human mind and is less subject to memory loss or idiosyncratic changes as it is passed from person to person. It also made it easier to centralize control over information, since written records can be accumulated. Along with the invention of the abacus, writing provided the Chinese state with the means to build and administer an empire, based on irrigated rice cultivation, which lasted several thousand years. A strict class division between the educated elite and the common people appeared. For the elite, the arts flourished. Progress in mathematics was made as part of administrative and ritual calculations; paper, invented for wrapping delicate bronze mirrors, turned out to be a solution to problems of producing and storing written records.

Agricultural civilizations also developed in other parts of the world. Although they shared with China some of the patterns of extreme class inequality, there were some important differences in their cultures' use of information. Languages like Egyptian evolved away from pictographs, toward the representation of sounds by individual symbols. The invention of phonetic alphabets greatly simplified written language, resulting in a wider diffusion of literacy (Goody and Watt 1962). Few members of the lower classes in agrarian societies had the free time to become literate. Alphabetic languages lowered the barriers between social classes because much less time was required for mastery of them. Alphabetic languages facilitated information processing for encyclopedias, libraries, and other early data bases. The burning of the Great Library at Alexandria, Egypt, destroyed a major part of the Mediterranian world's knowledge, and demonstrates the vulnerability of early information storage. Although several methods of storage were used, all were expensive and time-consuming. Literacy was rare. Manuscripts had to be copied by hand (with the inevitable addition of errors) or printed the way artists make woodblock prints. Not until the widespread use of paper and Gutenberg's invention of the modern movable-type printing press did written materials become widely available in Europe. By then, in the middle of the fifteenth century, Europe was on the threshold of the "long 16th century" (Wallerstein 1974) that brought about the Industrial Revolution.

INFORMATION AND THE RISE OF CAPITALISM

Karl Polanyi (1944) called the Industrial Revolution a "great transformation" during which land, labor, and capital were freed from the restraints of traditional culture and reorganized as commodities in a new form of economy.[1] While the Industrial Revolution is often considered a revolution based on tools— Jacquard's 1801 loom with its punch card controls being particularly important for later data-processing technology—it was also a revolution in cultural conceptions of the world. The rationalization of economic activity was only part of a new conception of a rational universe. The Reformation's challenges to religious authorities and the rise of rational scientific inquiry were precursors to the Industrial Revolution. The age of scientific reason created a view of the world as a rationally organized mechanism that could be understood, predicted, and controlled. The appearance of public clocks marked a new temporal rationalization of society. Beginning in the monasteries and moving into the early factories, clocks organized people to pray and work in unison (cf. Landes 1983; Mumford 1963).

Information technology also developed rapidly during the Industrial Revolution in the form of timepieces, mechanical calculators, Charles Babbage's 1833 design for the first digital computer, and Lady Ada Lovelace's conceptualization of computer programs. Information technology was envisioned as a means to rationalize the intellectual labor of calculation by Leibnitz and by Babbage in the seventeenth century (D. E. Smith 1959: 156–64; Babbage 1832). Marx, following Babbage's analysis of machines as divisions of labor in which a single engine links particular operations performed by single instruments, saw factory

workers as becoming components of the commodity production process (1973:
110–26). But Marx and theorists working in the Marxian tradition (especially
Braverman 1974) did not consider the production of information to be commodity production. Although modern information technology has its origins in
the Industrial Revolution, the culture concept of information changed very little.

Secrets are not new. Throughout history, both individuals and groups have
guarded particular forms of information. The best location for fishing or finding
flint for arrowheads, the techniques for working metals, magical hunting or
healing techniques — all of these have been made secret. The Egyptian priesthood kept knowledge of land surveying to themselves. Each year following the
Nile floods, they ritually recalculated property boundaries, with the result that
their own lands tended to get larger. Some of the first makers of iron weapons
tried to prevent the diffusion of metallurgical technology, hoping to gain military
superiority. Medieval European urban guilds used the secrets of their crafts to
gain some independence for their cities against the political rule of feudal
landowners. At the beginning of the Industrial Revolution, England prohibited
the export of weaving technology; the first textile machinery in the United States
was smuggled to Rhode Island piece-by-piece. Once assembled and copied, this
illegal technology became the basis of New England's cotton industry, a major
competitor for England. Yet most of this secret information was not property
in the modern sense.

In nonindustrial societies, information was rarely for sale. Cultural tradition
defined who was allowed to know what. In India, occupational techniques could
be used only by persons of the same caste. Similarly, in many societies (including
the American South) it was forbidden to teach slaves to read. Since information
about supply and demand is essential to the operation of a free market, early
capitalist manufacturing and trading organizations pressured their governments to provide more information about resource availability and prices. With
equal fervor, however, they tried to protect information about their own activities from their competitors and their governments. Information was not
transformed into commodity property in the way that land and labor had been.
However, we can find the origins of information products in the printed maps
and travel records of the fifteenth and sixteenth centuries. Although guarded
by nations and individual navigators, the widespread copying of such documents
helped broaden Europe's knowledge of geography and trade routes (Mukerji
1983: 79–130). Innovations in accounting and bookkeeping also contributed to
the rise of capitalism, but the market for the business information services we
take for granted today developed very slowly. We can find their origins in railway
schedules and shipping announcements of the 1800s and in the growth of
banking and mail service.

The most important changes in social views of information during the rise of
capitalism occurred in the political and religious spheres and challenged traditional beliefs about who should know what. The ideas of political democracy
put into practice by the American and French Revolutions included the belief
(expressed in the First Amendment of the United States Constitution) that

citizens should be able to exchange information freely. With the spread of literacy, newspapers, and other publishing, freedom of information became one of the cornerstones of democracy in industrial societies. This linkage between the origins of political democracy and the Industrial Revolution does not imply that capitalism and democracy will necessarily continue to coexist or that industrialization is automatically the route to democracy in the developing countries of the world (de Schweinitz 1964). The historical link between democracy and the Industrial Revolution was a common cultural value for free inquiry and innovative ideas.

Archibald Cox (chief Watergate prosecutor) described the way in which the freedom to communicate information is linked in the Constitution to religious and political freedom:

> The authors of the First Amendment moved from religious liberty through the freedoms of speech and the press to political rights to assemble peaceably and to petition the government for the redress of grievances. Thus, as the freedoms of speech and of the press are linked to spiritual liberty on the one side, so they are tied to and find justification in political liberty and democracy on the other. (1981: 2)

Although information, like land and labor, was gradually freed from traditional social constraints during the rise of capitalism, it did not generally become private property. Instead, through the spread of literacy and scientific knowledge, modern information became a new collective property. And education became a major way for individuals to acquire personal knowledge from the expanding cultural storehouse. Our public schools, libraries, and support for scientific research are indicators of the extent to which information is still defined as collective cultural property. A large-scale redefinition of information as a commodity would have a sweeping effect upon our institutions.

NOTE

1. See Perrolle (1987: 58–69, 1985). For a more general discussion of the origins of the Industrial Revolution, see Hobsbawm (1968: 34–55); Weber (1958); Wallerstein (1974); Giddens (1971).

REFERENCES

Allport, Gordon, and T. Pettigrew
    1957   "Cultural Influence on the Perception of Movement: The Trapezoidal Illusion among the Zulus." *Journal of Abnormal and Social Psychology* 55: 104–13.
Athanasiou, Tom
    1987   "High-Tech Politics: Artificial Intelligence." *Socialist Review* 17(2): 7–73.
Babbage, Charles
    1832   *On the Economy of Machinery and Manufactures.* London: Charles Knight.
Barr, Aaron, and Edward A. Feigenbaum
    1982.   *The Handbook of Artificial Intelligence.* Stanford: Heuris Tech Press.

Basso, K. H
    1972   "To Give Up on Words: Silence in Apache Culture." In Pier Paolo Giglioli, ed. *Language and Social Context*. New York: Penguin.

Bell, Daniel
    1980   "The Social Framework of the Information Society." In Michael Dertouzos and Joel Moses, eds. *The Computer Age: A Twenty-Year View*. Cambridge: MIT Press.

Boden, Margaret
    1977   *Artificial Intelligence and Natural Man*. New York: Basic Books.

Boserup, Ester
    1965   *The Conditions of Agricultural Growth*. Chicago: Aldine.

Boyd, Robert, and Peter J. Richerson
    1985   *Culture and the Evolutionary Process*. Chicago: University of Chicago Press.

Braidwood Robert J.
    1960   "The Agricultural Revolution." *Scientific American* 203(3): 130–48.

Braverman, Harry
    1974   *Labor and Monopoly Capital: The Degradation of Work in the Twentieth Century*. New York: Monthly Review Press.

Burton, K.
    1985   "Studies Relate Birth Defects to High-Tech Toxins in Water." *Computerworld* (January 28): 84.

Calvin, William H.
    1983   *The Throwing Madonna: Essays on the Brain*. New York: McGraw-Hill.

Coombs, M. J., ed.
    1984   *Developments in Expert Systems*. New York: Academic.

Cox, Archibald
    1981   *Freedom of Expression*. Cambridge: Harvard University Press.

de Santillana, Giorgio, and Hertha von Dechend
    1969   *Hamlet's Mill: An Essay Investigating the Origins of Human Knowledge and Its Transmission through Myth*. Boston: Godine.

de Schweinitz, Karl, Jr.
    1964   *Industrialization and Democracy*. Glencoe, Ill.: Free Press.

Deutsch, Karl
    1966   *The Nerves of Government: Models of Political Communication and Control*. New York: Free Press.

Diebold, John
    1984   Findings reported at the First World Conference on Ergonomics in Computer Systems, New York (September 27).

Dreyfus, Hubert, and Stuart Dreyfus
    1986   *Mind Over Machine: The Power of Human Intuition and Expertise in the Era of the Computer*. New York: Free Press.

Feigenbaum, Edward, and Pamela McCorduck
    1983   *The Fifth Generation: Artificial Intelligence and Japan's Computer Challenge to the World*. Reading, Mass.: Addison-Wesley.

Gardner, Howard
    1987   *The Mind's New Science: A History of the Cognitive Revolution*. New York: Basic Books.

Giddens, Anthony
  1971   *Capitalism and Modern Social Theory*. Cambridge: Cambridge University Press.

Goody J., and I. Watt
  1962   "The Consequence of Literacy." *Comparative Studies in Society and History* 5: 304–45.

Gregory, R. L.
  1981   *Eye and Brain*, 3rd ed. New York: McGraw-Hill.

Harlan, Jack R.
  1976   "The Plants and Animals that Nourish Man." *Scientific American* 235(3): 88–97.

Haugeland, John, ed.
  1981   *Mind Design*. Cambridge: MIT Press.

Hayes-Roth, Frederick
  1983   Roundtable Discussion at Carnegie-Mellon University (June 3).

Hayes-Roth, Frederick, Donald A. Waterman, and Douglas B. Lenat, eds.
  1983   *Building Expert Systems*. Reading, Mass.: Addison-Wesley.

Hobsbawm, E. J.
  1968   *Industry and Empire*. London: Pelican.

Holahan, Charles J.
  1982.   *Environmental Psychology*. New York: Random House.

Hyman, A.
  1980   *The Coming of the Chip*. New York: New English Library.

Koh, T. T. B.
  1984   "Computer-Assisted Negotiations." In H. Pagels, ed. *Computer Culture: The Scientific, Intellectual, and Social Impact of the Computer.* New York: New York Academy of Sciences.

Kuhn, Thomas S.J
  1970   *The Structure of Scientific Revolutions*, 2nd ed. Chicago: University of Chicago Press.

LaDou, J.
  1984   "The Not So Clean Business of Making Chips." *Technology Review* (87): 23–36.

Landes, David S.
  1983   *Revolution in Time: Clocks and the Making of the Modern World.* Cambridge, Mass.: Harvard University Press.

Leibowitz, Lila
  1983   "Origins of the Sexual Division of Labor." In Marion Lowe and Ruth Hubbard, eds. *Woman's Nature*. New York: Pergamon.

Lewin, Roger
  1986   "Myths and Methods in Ice Age Art." *Science* 234(21 November): 936–38.

Lieberman, Philip
  1984   *The Biology and Evolution of Language*. Cambridge: Harvard University Press.

Loftus, E. F., D. G. Miller, and H. J. Burns
  1978   "Semantic Integration of Verbal Information into a Visual Memory." *Journal of Experimental Psychology, Human Perception, and Performance* 4: 565–72.

McCorduck, Pamela
    1979   *Machines Who Think*. San Francisco: W. H. Freeman.
Machlup, Fritz, and Una Mansfield, eds.
    1983   *The Study of Information*. New York: John Wiley & Sons.
MacLeish, Archibald
    1962   "Ars Poetica," in *Collected Poems of Archibald MacLeish*. Cambridge, Mass.:
            Riverside Press.
Martin, James
    1978   *The Wired Society*. Englewood Cliffs, N.J.: Prentice Hall.
Marx, Karl
    1973   [orig. pub. 1847] *The Poverty of Philosophy*. Moscow: Progress Publishers.
    1967   [orig. pub. 1867] *Capital*. Vol. 1. New York: International Publishers.
Menninger, Karl W.
    1969   *Number Words and Number Symbols: A Cultural History of Numbers*.
            Cambridge: MIT Press.
Mukerji, Chandra
    1983   *From Graven Images: Patterns of Modern Materialism*. New York: Columbia
            University Press.
Mumford, Lewis
    1963   *Technics and Civilization*. New York: Harcourt Brace.
Needham, Joseph
    1956   *Science and Civilization in China*. Cambridge: Cambridge University Press.
Parsons, Talcott
    1951   *The Social System*. Glencoe, Ill.: Free Press.
Perrolle, Judith A.
    1987   *Computers and Social Change: Information, Property, and Power*. Belmont,
            Calif.: Wadsworth.
    1986   "Intellectual Assembly Lines," *Computers and the Social Sciences* 2(2): 111–21.
    1985   "Computers and Capitalism." In John Williamson, Linda Evans, and Michael
            Rustad, eds. *Social Problems: The Contemporary Debates*. Boston: Little, Brown.
Polanyi, Karl
    1944   *The Great Transformation*. Boston: Beacon Press.
Polanyi, Michael, and Harry Prosch
    1975   *Meaning*. Chicago: University of Chicago Press.
Rechtschaffen, A., and S. Mednick
    1955   "The Autokinetic Word Technique." *Journal of Abnormal and Social
            Psychology* 51: 436.
Renfew, Colin
    1983   "The Social Archaeology of Megalithic Monuments." *Scientific American*
            249(5): 152–63.
Saxe, Leonard
    1985   "Umpiring the Controversy: Liars and Lie Detection." *Society* 22(September/October): 39–43.
Shannon, Claude
    1948   "A Mathematical Theory of Communication." *Bell System Technical Journal*
            27: 379– 423 623–56.

Simon, Herbert
   1969   *The Sciences of the Artificial.* Cambridge: MIT Press.
Smith, Adam
   1937   [orig. pub. 1776] *The Wealth of Nations.* Edwin Cannon, ed. New York: Modern Library.
Smith, D. E.
   1959   *A Sourcebook of Mathematics.* Vol. 1. New York: Dover.
Turkle, Sherry
   1984   *The Second Self: Computers and the Human Spirit.* New York: Simon & Schuster.
Wallerstein, Immanuel
   1974   *The Modern World-System.* New York: Academic.
Warrick, Patricia
   1980   *The Cybernetic Imagination in Science Fiction.* Cambridge: MIT Press.
Weber, Max
   1958   *The Protestant Ethic and the Spirit of Capitalism.* New York: Scribner's.
Weizenbaum, Joseph
   1983   "The Computer in Your Future." *New York Review* 30(October 27): 58–62.
   1976   *Computer Power and Human Reason: From Judgment to Calculation.* San Francisco: W. H. Freeman.
Wiener, Norbert
   1948   *Cybernetics: On Control and Communication in the Animal and the Machine.* Cambridge: MIT Press.
Wittfogel, Karl A.
   1957   *Oriental Despotism.* New Haven: Yale University Press.

7

A DARWINIAN THEORY FOR THE EVOLUTION OF SYMBOLIC CULTURAL TRAITS

Peter J. Richerson and Robert Boyd

The last decade has seen numerous attempts to use neo-Darwinian evolutionary theory to explain human behavior. For the most part, these studies have been functional in nature, aimed at understanding how contemporary human behavior enhances Darwinian fitness. This approach seems wrong-headed to many anthropologists for two reasons. First, a great deal of human behavior seems either afunctional or even maladaptive. Perhaps even more important, the functional approach misses the fact that much of human behavior is symbolic (Shweder and LeVine 1984). Sahlins (1976a, b), in particular, argues that the application of sociobiological theory to human behavior is of limited interest because human behavior is strongly affected by meaningful cultural symbols whose evolution is governed by an autonomous process, "cultural reason." For Sahlins, the key feature of cultural reason is that it frees human evolution from any functional imperatives, whether derived from the action of natural selection or from other processes.

There is more to Darwinism, however, than adaptive functionalism. The great evolutionary biologist Ernst Mayr (1982: 487–88) argues that the idea that natural selection can lead to adaptations was not Darwin's most fundamental intellectual contribution. Rather, it was his methodological insight that the analysis of the dynamics of heritable variation in populations was the key to understanding organic evolution. To understand long-run evolutionary change, Darwin showed, we must understand how events in the lives of individuals affect the frequency of behavioral and morphological variants in a population and how these variants are transmitted from one generation to the next. He believed that several processes besides natural selection influence heritable variation, including chance, acquired variation, and sexual selection, and that at least one of these processes, sexual selection, often acts in systematic opposition to ordinary natural selection.

It is especially important to keep in mind the distinction between the methodological and substantive aspects of Darwinism when it is applied to humans. In our species there is a second system of heritable variation, culture, which can be approached in two ways from the Darwinian perspective. Using the main substantive result of Darwinism, we might assume that the cultural system is an adaptation shaped by natural selection and seek to explain culturally acquired behaviors in terms of their adaptive functions. Applying its methods, we might be interested in analyzing how cultural transmission works and how the frequency of alternative cultural variants changes through time.

Here we argue that theory which combines the substantive and methodological aspects of Darwinism is most likely to be of use to anthropologists. It is difficult to doubt that natural selection acting on genes played an important role in human origins, as even Sahlins (1976b: 208–9) seems to accept. Thus the human capacity for culture, and cultural traits themselves, must, at least in part, be understood as adaptations (Keesing 1974). On the other hand, to have a satisfactory understanding of the causes of human behavior, we need a theory that specifies how cultural and genetic processes affect the frequency of alternative culturally transmitted behaviors in human populations.

We will illustrate the application of Darwinian methods to culture by considering how a particular pattern of cultural transmission, which we call "indirectly biased" transmission, can lead to the evolution of apparently nonadaptive (or even maladaptive) symbolic cultural traits. During enculturation people acquire beliefs and values from others by teaching, imitation, and other forms of social learning. We call this process "cultural transmission." Many kinds of biased cultural transmission are possible. We say that indirect bias occurs when individuals choose whom to imitate, based on some cultural trait like prestige, and then imitate that person's other traits without further decision making. We are all familiar with the role that especially attractive, popular, and successful people play in the spread of fads and fashion. This is a simple example of indirectly biased transmission. Indirect bias makes adaptive sense because it is a mechanism for acquiring useful beliefs and values. By imitating prestigious or successful people, a naive individual can increase the chance of acquiring beliefs and values that lead to prestige or success. This will be particularly important when it is difficult or costly to learn what behaviors are best in the local environment. The interesting thing is that this mechanism of cultural transmission can also cause maladaptive beliefs and values to become common.

ELEMENTS OF A DARWINIAN THEORY OF CULTURE

Darwinian methods are applicable to culture because culture, like genes, is information that is transmitted from one individual to another. Although there has long been substantial debate on just how to define culture (Keesing 1974; Kroeber and Kluckhohn 1952), virtually all definitions involve the idea that information about how to behave is communicated among individuals by nongenetic means. Although the mechanical details of cultural transmission are very different from genetic transmission, the general similarity between the two processes is strong. Important determinants of individual behavior are passed from generation to generation by both systems. Recently, theorists from several disciplines have taken advantage of the analogy between genetic and cultural transmission to attempt to understand cultural evolution.[1]

The idea that unifies this literature is that culture is a form of heritable variation. That is, humans differ from one another in large part because they have learned different things from other humans. Cultural transmission sets up patterns of traditional variation within and between human societies. Casting the basic insight of anthropology in this bit of biological jargon suggests that we might use similar methods to understand both cultural and genetic variation. Evolutionary biologists have developed a substantial body of concepts, experimental and observational methods, and mathematical tools to understand one specific kind of heritable variation. With suitable modifications to take account of the differences between genes and culture, the same basic analytical methods should apply to any system of of heritable variation.

Application of the Method

The real work in applying the Darwinian method to culture comes in the specification of the evolutionary processes that cause cultures to change. Some care must be taken because the analogy between cultural and genetic transmission holds only at a very general level. In detail they are quite different. People other than the biological parents are often important in socialization, such as peers and grandparents. The cultural analogs of generation length and the mating system are often rather different from, and more variable than, the genetic system. Further, the individual acquiring an item of culture is an active participant in the transmission process. To some extent, we choose what traits we learn from others, but a zygote does not choose its genes.

These structural differences lead to differences in the processes of change, what biologists call the "forces" of evolution, that act on cultural variation, compared to the genetic case. Forces which are closely analogous in the two transmission systems, such as random errors and natural selection, will not necessarily produce the same sorts of results when the structural differences between genes and culture are taken into account. For example, if a significant amount of cultural transmission is nonparental, natural selection can favor cultural variants that are maladaptive from the genetic perspective (Pulliam 1982; Richerson and Boyd 1984: Werren and Pulliam 1981). If priests play an important role in socialization, then beliefs that make it more likely that an individual enters the priesthood may spread, even if they are genetically maladaptive (say because priests are celibate).

In addition, entirely novel forces result from human decision making. Decision making, when coupled to the possibility of imitating someone else's decisions, gives rise to two types of evolutionary forces. First, behaviors resulting from individual learning, strategizing, and invention can be imitated by others. We know that the inheritance of acquired variation is incompatible with the genetic system of inheritance; however, this "Lamarckian" process does affect cultural evolution. Second, the transmission process itself can be biased. For example, modern young adults usually observe a variety of drug use among older individuals and peers. Many people drink coffee and alcohol, smoke, use marijuana or cocaine, while others abstain. How does one decide whether or not to adopt such behaviors? In the simplest case, an individual might try out each of the variants of a cultural practice he or she observes and adopt the one that seems best by some decision-making criterion. Is the use of the particular substance pleasant or unpleasant? More complex possibilities include the use of information about the frequency of the practice as a guide to adoption (say a conformist rule like: adopt the trait of the majority of one's friends), or the use of information about the status of individuals as a guide for which ones to imitate. Do people whom one admires and respects use the substance or not? It is this last type of bias, which we term "indirect bias," that will be used as an example of the application of Darwinian methods in this chapter.[2]

Substantive versus Methodological Hypotheses

The substantive approach to applying Darwinism to human behavior is well developed in the work of human sociobiologists.[3] The idea that human sociobiologists have in common is that the processes of cultural evolution are governed by evolved predispositions. Natural selection, the argument runs, should have structured cultural transmission by favoring decision-making rules that increase the frequency of cultural traits that enhance ordinary genetic fitness. Despite the complexities introduced by culture, we can depend upon the same adaptive reasoning used in biology applying to the human case.

This argument cannot be lightly dismissed. Unless the whole thrust of modern evolutionary biology is quite wrong, natural selection (acting on genetic variation) must be responsible for the main features of evolutionary change, including human capacities for culture. Hypotheses derived from the fitness-maximizing assumption often show quite reasonable predictive power, as in the case human foraging activities (Smith 1983), even when the proximal causes of the behavior are cultural.

Nevertheless, the methodological approach strongly suggests that using the substantive approach alone will result in an incomplete theory of culture. The key problem is that the application of strong decision-making rules to guide cultural evolution is probably prohibitively costly. People simply cannot decide for themselves on a case-by-case basis what is the best way to behave. (Think of any even moderately complex skill that you have learned. Could you have invented it for yourself? Did you exhaustively research all the alternate ways of achieving the same results and choose the best one on the basis of careful comparison?) It seems likely that the main advantage of learning from others is that social learning is much less difficult than individual learning (Bandura 1977). One of the by-products of substituting social learning for individual learning is that cultural traits are thereby sufficiently heritable to respond to selection and other evolutionary forces. If the costs of using individual decision-making processes are high, selection on genes over the long run of human history may not have favored decision-making forces which would completely compensate for the genetically maladaptive effects of cultural evolutionary processes. We mentioned those due to nonparental transmission above. Even if the forces that act on nonparentally transmitted cultural variation do not favor the ends of genetic fitness on a trait-by-trait basis, the structural features of culture that allow the divergent evolution may still confer a genetic fitness advantage. So long as nonparental patterns of cultural transmission provide economy in information acquisition, selection on the genes that underlie a capacity for such transmission may be favored. Given that the genetic evolution of the decision-making forces that constrain cultural evolution is relatively slow and that the cost of acquiring information limits the specificity of decision-making rules, the genetic fitness advantages of a particular form of cultural transmission will be averaged over many individuals in many cultures.

If this argument is correct, there is no reason to expect that any particular human trait in any particular society should conform to the predictions of ordinary Darwinian theory. To understand why humans behave the way that they do we must first understand how the existing cultural transmission system interacts with social and environmental contingencies to create a pattern of behavior. To understand the evolution of human behavior we must further understand why the system of cultural transmission has the form that it does, including an understanding of why selection on the genes that affect cultural transmission favored or permitted that form.

THE FORCE OF INDIRECT BIAS

The purpose of the rest of this chapter is to make this abstract discussion more concrete by considering in detail one process that can change the frequency of cultural variants. This process, indirect bias, will be of interest to anthropologists because it provides a Darwinian explanation for the evolution of group functional and afunctional or dysfunctional symbolic traits in the human species. Indirect bias provides a particularly clear example of how the use of Darwinian methods to understand cultural evolution can lead to quite different results from direct substantive applications of Darwinian biology to humans.

Indirectly Biased Cultural Transmission

Cultural transmission is indirectly biased when people allow some traits displayed by potential models, such as indicators of prestige, to influence their adoption of other traits, such as dialect or subsistence technique. In other words, some attributes of one person are used by another as a basis for choosing to imitate a more general class of traits possessed by the same model. It is useful to distinguish three classes of characters when thinking about this mechanism of cultural evolution. (1) Indicator traits are displayed by models and used as a basis for weighting their importance by potential imitators. For example, suppose that imitators are inclined to admire and then to imitate successful individuals, and that success is estimated using particular indicator traits – number of cows, quality of car, or taste in music. (2) Indirectly biased traits are acquired as a by-product of choices based on indicator traits. Once a particular model is chosen on the basis of an indicator trait, naive individuals might tend to acquire animal husbandry lore, beliefs about what sort of person to marry, or a set of work habits from this model. Friends, once chosen on one basis, tend to exchange a variety of habits, opinions, and tastes. (3) Preference traits are the criteria by which naive individuals judge indicator traits. In some cases, a simple more-is-better rule might be used. Other times, intermediate values of an indicator trait may result in the strongest weight. For example, contemporary middle-class Americans seem to admire people with intermediate-sized families, rather than the childless or those with very large families.

An example will illustrate how indirect bias works as an evolutionary force. Suppose that graduate students commonly use the apparent self-confidence and assertiveness of professors as an indicator trait. Students might prefer as mentors those professors among those available who appear to have the strongest confidence in their own ideas. Once the mentor is chosen, students are likely to acquire research methods, ideas about which problems are important, career advancement strategies, and perhaps even mannerisms and irrational prejudices from the mentor without exercising much additional choice. If certain traits are regularly associated with self-confidence and assertiveness among professors, these traits will increase. If, for example, quantitative skills and methodological rigor generate self-confidence among their users, then indirect bias will cause a disproportionate number of graduate students to acquire these as a research strategy. However, it might also be that a dogmatic and irrational faith in one's own simple explanations is more effective at generating self-confidence. In this case, indirect bias will lead to a dogmatically contentious rather than to a methodologically rigorous discipline.

Three bodies of empirical literature suggest that the process of indirect bias is an important process in cultural evolution:

(1) Evidence from social learning theory. Laboratory studies of human imitation have shown that naive individuals use some attributes of models (indicator traits) to bias their attention to models and their acquisition of other behaviors (Yando et al. 1978: 62–65; Rosenthal and Zimmerman 1978: 251–54). Yussen and Levy (1975) exposed groups of preschool children and third graders to warm and friendly and to emotionally neutral teachers. Warm teachers increased student's attention, reduced their susceptibility to distraction, and enhanced their recall of modeled behaviors compared to neutral teachers. Children apparently learned most things better from friendly teachers even though teacher personality has nothing directly to do with the quality of what is exhibited for the children to imitate.

(2) Evidence from the diffusion of innovations. Rogers (1983: 271–311) reviews how patterns of information flow during the adoption of innovations are affected

by sociological attributes of adopters and models. They report that a class of individuals whom they label "opinion leaders" plays a disproportionate role in the spread of innovations within a local community. These individuals are usually somewhat higher than average in status in the local community, but the differences between opinion leaders and followers is relatively slight compared to the total variation in the status hierarchy. If opinion leaders adopt an innovation, it spreads to the rest of the community; if not, few adopt the innovation.

(3) Evidence from linguistics. Linguists have shown that patterns of the spread of new linguistic variants are related to social class in a way that is very similar to the patterns observed in the diffusion of innovations. For example, Labov (1980) shows that the leaders of dialect evolution in Philadephia are upper-working-class women with high status within their neighborhoods and with wide-ranging contacts in and outside of their local communities.

It is easy to imagine that indirect bias is a functional mechanism for acquiring cultural traits (Flinn and Alexander 1982). Successful, happy, outgoing people who manage to acquire the trappings of prestige in a society on average probably have useful skills and attitudes. By copying the successful, naive individuals can increase the chance that they will acquire the beliefs and values that lead to success without bearing the costs of hard thinking and costly, time-consuming experiments. In the case of diffusion of innovations, for example, Rogers suggests that copying opinion leaders is a sensible way for potential adopters to decide whether to adopt an innovation. Potential adopters of new techniques have a wide range of abilities and resources to devote to judging the utility of new techniques, and it makes sense for adopters with moderate resources to use opinion leaders with more resources as models of what to adopt. On the other hand, the choice of a model of very different status is unlikely to be an effective strategy because the circumstances of life of such a model are likely to be too different to provide a good guide for optimal techniques. A poor peasant does not have the same access to capital or the same ability to bear risks as a rich farmer, so his approach to farming is necessarily different. The evidence is that people make fairly sophisticated use of the indirect bias decision rule.

A Model of Indirect Bias

Indirect bias in human societies is undoubtedly a very complex process. It seems likely that real prestige systems involve many indicator, indirectly biased, and preference traits which interact with each other and the rest of the cultural repertoire in complicated ways. In this section, we briefly describe the structure of a very simple model that we think captures the bare bones of the problem. Despite its simplicity, the model produces interesting and surprising results. A more technical and detailed account of the model is given in Boyd and Richerson (1985: 241–79).

We begin by assuming that each individual can be characterized by the values of two cultural traits. The first trait is an indicator trait that affects the individual's attractiveness as a model, and the second is a preference trait that determines which variant of the indicator trait the individual finds most attractive. To keep the model simple we do not include any indirectly biased traits other than the preference trait. Instead we assume that different variants of the indicator trait are characterized by different genetic fitness. The model also lacks any explicit details about the genetic system. We merely assume that selection on the (cultural) indicator trait favors a variant that is optimal in terms of genetic fitness. The two traits themselves are modeled as quantitative characters; it is assumed that they can be measured as real numbers rather than taking on discrete values. (Height is a quantitative character and eye color discrete.) A quantitative character model is quite apt for traits like wealth that do vary continuously, but might not be a very good representation of a trait like religion or class that may have only a few discrete variants.

Next we assume that cultural transmission begins with an episode of simple unbiased transmission in which young children acquire both traits by faithfully imitating their parents. This is followed by an episode of indirectly biased transmission in which adolescents may modify one or both traits after observing the behavior of a number of nonparental adults. The extent to which a particular adult influences a particular adolescent is affected by both the preference trait that the adolescent acquired parentally and the adult's indicator trait. That is, adolescents use the preferences learned from their parents to select a set of nonparental models based on these models' easily observable characteristics, their indicator traits. For example, children brought up in religious households may be more prone to learn from adults who are religious than from people who obviously are not. The adolescents then modify their original indicator and preference traits on the basis of the models chosen. This is not an either/or choice; rather, the adolescent imitators weight the influence of the models in accord with their preferences and the models' indicator trait values. Then there is the episode of natural selection favoring the value of the indicator trait that maximizes genetic fitness. Finally, there is an episode of parental transmission to the next generation, completing the life cycle.

Even given the simplicity of these assumptions relative to real episodes of culture transmission, it is far from immediately obvious what will happen as many individuals follow these rules for many generations in a particular culture. Unfortunately, all but the very simplest evolutionary processes, such as the most basic models of natural selection, are impossible to understand by direct inspection or intuition. Fortunately, almost a century of theoretical work in population genetics has been devoted to developing the mathematical tools to keep track of the intricate logic of evolutionary processes. By the standards of this admittedly somewhat arcane discipline, the evolutionary model implied by our assumptions is only moderately difficult to analyze.

Results of the Model

Rather than present the analysis of the model in detail here (see Boyd and Richerson 1985: 247–69), we simply summarize its results and apply it to the problem of the evolution of symbolic traits. The model suggests that cultural evolution under the influence of indirect bias has two distinct modes:

(1) Stable fitness maximization. If the strength of indirect bias acting on the preference trait is weak compared to the combined forces of selection and preference-based choice on the imitation of the indicator trait, then the preference trait will eventually reach a stable equilibrium at the value that maximizes genetic fitness. In other words, indirect bias will evolve so that naive individuals tend to imitate models with the optimum value of the indicator trait. This occurs when selection is strong enough to ensure that the indicator trait remains a good index of fitness, and individuals are usually able to imitate the indicator trait they prefer. (Imagine a case where hunting success confers prestige and where good hunters have an appreciably better chance of survival than poor ones.)

(2) A runaway case. If indirect bias acting on the preference character is strong compared to the combined forces of selection and preference-based choice acting on the indicator character, then according to the model the values of both the indicator trait and the preference trait will run away, becoming indefinitely larger or smaller depending on the initial condition. Clearly, this cannot be literally true; nothing can really grow or shrink without bound. Some process not accounted for in the model will eventually restrain the evolution of the population. The correct qualitative lesson to be drawn is that when the evolution of a preference trait is affected by indirect bias, the resulting process may be inherently unstable. Where it exists, such instability is likely to result in preference and indicator traits that are some distance from their genetic-fitness-optimizing values.

How the runaway process works is difficult to see intuitively because of the interaction of the indicator and preference traits in the evolutionary process when the preference trait itself is subject to indirect bias. In the case of the rather analogous runaway process in sexual selection in biology, reasonable models of the process have only been analyzed in the last few years (Lande 1981; Kirkpatrick 1982).

To see how the runaway process might work, consider a hypothetical example in which individuals choose models based on the value of a character marking prestige, for example, their style of dress. Further suppose that for still un-specified reasons the majority of the population admire an elegant but otherwise maladaptive mode of dress. Elegant clothing requires emphasis on visually interesting designs and costly fabrics. Individuals who dress practically are better protected from the weather and spend less on clothes, but are less admired and therefore less likely to be imitated. In other words, we assume that natural selection acting on cultural variation favors practical dress and indirect bias favors elegant dress. Nevertheless, an adolescent who admires elegant dress will choose models who tend to dress elegantly. From such models, adolescents can learn how to dress elegantly, knowledge which they in turn transmit to their children, albeit with some selective penalty in terms of number of children they produce. It is easy to see that if most people admire elegant dressers, indirect bias could act to increase the frequency of elegant dressers in spite of the selective penalty of fewer offspring, at least until the degree of elegance becomes a substantial selective disadvantage.

What is less obvious but more interesting is that indirect bias can actually increase the frequency of individuals who admire and tend to imitate elegant dressers. Suppose that individuals tend to acquire their beliefs about what style of dress make a person admirable and their own style of dress from the same individuals. This assumption has two important effects:

(1) The cultural transmission process will cause people who dress elegantly to admire elegant dress. Because people tend to acquire their mode of dress from people they admire, elegant dressers will tend to admire elegant dress.

(2) The process that increases the frequency of elegant dress will also act to increase the frequency of the people who admire elegant dress. As we have seen, elegant dressers will tend to admire elegant dress. Because elegant dressers are more likely to be imitated, people who admire elegant dress will be more likely to pass on their preferences than those who admire practical dress. This will cause the proportion of the population that admires elegant dress to increase.

Thus, after one generation both the frequency of elegant dress and the admiration for elegant dress will have increased. It turns out that under some conditions the frequency of admiration of elegant dress will increase more than the frequency of elegant dressers. This means that during the next generation both frequencies will increase even more. Thus both traits will run away, increasing both the frequency of the maladaptive mode of dress and the preference for that mode of dress.

Evidence for the Runaway Process

Is there any evidence that the runaway process actually occurs in human societies? The ideal data to answer this question would allow us both to trace the trajectory of an indicator trait from an initially adaptive state to an exaggerated state and to demonstrate that indirect bias was the agent responsible for the exaggeration of the trait. As far as we know no such data exist. For the present, we must be satisfied with circumstantial evidence in the form of the existence of traits that seem consistent with an origin and maintenance by the runaway process. Such traits should have the following properties: (1) more exaggerated variants should be associated with greater prestige; (2) The values of the trait observed should not make sense from an adaptive point of view; and (3) the observed variant should be plausibly interpreted as an exaggerated version of an indicator trait that once did make adaptive sense. Here we will discuss one such empirical example.

Markers of Prestige on Ponapae

According to William Bascom (1948), on the Micronesian island of Ponapae a man's prestige is partially determined by his ability to contribute very large yams to periodic feasts. Each year several feasts are given by the chief of each district. In addition to staple foods like fresh breadfruit, coconut, and seafood, the head of each farmstead contributes a "prize" yam, or yams. Everyone at the feast examines the yams and praises the contributor of the single largest yam for his generosity and his skill and ability as a farmer. Moreover, as Bascom reports, "Success in prestige competition is regarded as evidence of not only a man's ability, industry, and generosity, but also of his love and respect for superiors" (p. 215). The chiefs raise men who are consistent contributors of large yams to titled positions.

Several lines of evidence suggest that this practice is not simply a good way to provide food for a party, but instead represents an exaggerated marker of prestige. First, prestige is not correlated with a man's real material contribution to the feast. The contributions of other important foodstuffs like fresh breadfruit or seafood are irrelevant to the prestige competition. So too is the total amount of yams that a man contributes; all that counts is the size and, to a lesser extent, the shape of the largest individual yam. Moreover, these yams are huge; they sometimes exceed nine feet in length and three feet in diameter and require up to twelve men to carry them! The yams used by families in their everyday diet are much smaller and much easier to grow per unit weight. Individual farmers go to very great and special effort to raise large yams. Appropriate varieties must be found and maintained, special laborious cultivation techniques are used, and great care must be taken to prevent neighbors from spying out the size of a man's yams. Bascom concludes that "the labor expended in growing prize yams is far greater than would be necessary to produce the same quantity of foodstuff from a larger number of smaller yams of the same variety" (p. 217). Nor should it be thought this extravagance is possible because there are never shortages of food on Ponapae, as "Not infrequently families go hungry at home when they have large yams in their farms ready for harvest" (p. 212).

It is easy to construct a plausible scenario to explain the evolution of the practice of growing very large yams, based on a runaway process. Suppose that at some earlier time Ponapeans did not devote any special effort to growing large yams. It seems reasonable that under such conditions more skillful or industrious farmers might have tended to bring larger yams to feasts and thus that the size of a man's yams would provide a useful indicator trait for skills and beliefs associated with farming. By imitating the people who grew large yams, naive individuals could increase the chance that they would acquire cultural variants that would cause them to be successful farmers. Once the size of yams became an indicator trait, beliefs or practices that led to larger yams would increase. Individuals who acquire from their parents a stronger tendency to admire large yams will be more likely to acquire these beliefs in later episodes of cultural transmission than those whose parents were less admiring. This will cause the two traits to be correlated. Therefore, when the practices that lead to larger yams increase, so too will the admiration for the ability to grow large yams.

Giant yam growing is a striking practice, but it does not seem to us especially unusual. All cultures have similarly bizarre practices that can be plausibly attributed to the runaway process. Plausible attribution is far from convincing demonstration, but we find it hard not to think of runaway evolution when we contemplate contemporary fashions or are invited to admire the latest possessions of our friends.

INDIRECT BIAS AND CULTURAL SYMBOLS

Indirect bias can be used to understand the relationship between several common interpretations of the role of symbols in human evolution. The relationship between the three major hypotheses about the nature of symbols in human evolution can best be seen as different cases of the indirect bias mechanism. If this argument is correct, we can begin to see what processes will have to be measured to distinguish among alternative hypotheses. It also illustrates, we believe, how Darwinian methods applied to culture can be used to clarify long outstanding problems in the social sciences.

Three Hypotheses for the Evolution of Symbols

The key defining feature of symbols is that they are arbitrary. A sign is something that stands for something else. According to semiotic theory three basic varieties of signs can be recognized (Jakobson 1971: 345ff, 697ff): icon, index, and symbol. More properly each of these concepts can be thought of as a quantitative dimension by which a sign can be classified. An icon is a sign that has a factual similarity to the thing or process signified. For example, a technical drawing picturing a farming technique is an icon. An index has a factual connection with the thing signified. For example, a bulging storage bin or fat cattle is an index of a farmer's skill and energy since each is correlated with farming talent. A symbol is a sign that stands for a thing by conventional agreement. In language, usually it does not matter what sound pattern or series of letters are used to signify a particular thing or concept, it only matters that the members of a speech community agree on its meaning.

The giant yams of Ponapae are at least partly symbols. Since special skills are needed to grow them, which may be different from the skills required to grow other crops, giant yams are not necessarily an iconic sign of farming skill, or even a good index of horticultural talent. Convention could specify quite other means of signifying prestige in such a horticultural society, say by the growing of small, perfectly shaped, "bonsai" yams.

Nevertheless, giant yams are taken quite seriously as symbols, or at least indexes, of prestige by Ponapeans. Perhaps the ability to grow giant yams even *is* prestige on Ponapae, not just a sign of it. However arbitrarily symbolic giant yams appear to us, they are important to their growers, while bonsai yams would be irreverent or perhaps humorous. Thus Sahlins (1976a) would say that giant yams are meaningful to Ponapeans, much as giant autos are to Americans.

The problems that symbolic anthropologists pose for us are how behaviors that are objectively "mere" symbols can come to be taken by people as central to their existence and whether (and in what sense) such behaviors can be functional. On the one hand, the arbitrariness of symbols with respect to function suggests, as Sahlins argues, that the forces of what he calls "practical reason" cannot affect their evolution, while on the other the evident efforts their users devote to them suggest that they cannot be neutral with respect to natural selection. This is the paradox we would like to use the theory to understand. We will consider three hypotheses:

(1) Under some circumstances, the evolution of symbols may be autonomous because the use of alternative symbolic variants has no effect on genetic fitness (or other criteria of function). In this case symbols may be arbitrary without conflicting with a genetic-fitness-maximizing hypothesis or other varieties of functionalism. We call this the "weak interaction" hypothesis.

(2) In other cases, the runaway dynamic may result in group selection of symbolic traits, so a "group functional" hypothesis of symbolic evolution must also be entertained.

(3) Finally, we believe that the runaway case of indirect bias provides an evolutionary basis for Sahlins's postulated cultural reason, or something like it, without violating the criterion of a plausible natural origin for nonadaptive or maladaptive cultural traits. Here this hypothesis is labeled "afunctionalist."

The Weak Interaction Hypothesis

The evolutionary dynamics of a symbolic system are quite different from that of ordinary adaptations. The variant words for "cat" in different languages are all functionally equivalent. For each symbolic trait we observe, there is a very large number of alternatives that are equivalent in terms of fitness. The simplest hypothesis we might have is that symbol systems can evolve by the random jiggling of mean usage, combined with selection or bias against variants that are so distant from the mean as to cause problems in communication. To the extent that symbol systems function simply for communication within a culture, these forces might be sufficient.

We call this the weak interaction hypothesis because the relationship between the content of the symbolic system and adaptation or function is quite tenuous (Cohen 1974; Durham 1976). We can easily explain by a sociobiological hypothesis, for example, why humans have symbolic capacities for culture. The main adaptive functions include interpersonal communication and memory organization. Both of these functions may contribute to more efficient social learning and hence to more effective use of the various advantages of cultural transmission. However, since these functions are served equally well by any well-organized symbolic system, we cannot explain much of the difference between the structures of different cultural systems by adaptive arguments. The Chinese language is not an adaptation to life on the Yellow River Plain, nor is English an adaptation to living in the British Isles, except in the very limited sense that it is useful to speak the language that happens to be common in a given place.

The weak interaction hypothesis thus requires a nonfunctional theory to explain which specific symbols come to have a particular function, but it does not allow symbolic evolutionary processes to affect functional ones strongly. Assuming that the sociobiologists are correct that function derives ultimately from selection on genes, this hypothesis allows little scope for substantive debate between sociobiological and symbolic explanations. The same conclusion would hold for other theories of function in human societies.

Symbolic Functionalism

If symbolic traits are especially prone to runaway evolution as a consequence of indirect bias, the between-group variation generated by this process may be subject to the group selection of cultural variation. This in turn could favor cultural variants which enhance the cultural success of the group, even at the expense of harming that of the individual. The symbolic functionalism hypothesis is sharply different from sociobiological hypotheses because the latter usually identify function with individual or kin group advantage.

The runaway dynamics that result from indirect bias can increase the relative strength of selection among groups for the following reason. In the runaway process, small differences in initial conditions result in very different unstable trajectories. If an ancestral society is divided, any new symbolic trends evolving under the control of indirect bias are likely to differ at least slightly. Such small initial differences will ultimately generate large amounts of variation between groups as each group runs away on an independent trajectory. This variation could lead to strong group selection, which depends on group variation being large relative to individual variation within groups.

Imagine, for example, a one-dimensional continuum of prestige systems: At one end, reckless displays of individual valor are admired, at the other end people esteem conspicuous peaceful public service, with cautious selfishness valued in the middle. Suppose that individual selection favors cautious selfishness, but also suppose that indirect bias can create counterbalancing preferences for the more extreme prestige behaviors. Next, assume that a series of daughter societies are produced by the subdivision of a parent society in which cautious selfishness is valued. If the conditions for the runaway process hold, the prestige systems of daughter societies may be carried toward one or the other extreme. The prestige system which characterized any particular daughter society would depend on chance events surrounding the origin process. Depending on circumstances, selection among groups might favor one or another direction along the line. Groups with a highly martial prestige system might be favored under conditions of pastoral subsistence and a low level of political organization, while a stable rule of law in settled towns and cities might favor groups that value public service. In essence, the runaway process can act as the group-level analog of mutation, creating random variation among groups. The runaway process itself might generate equal numbers of societies with public service prestige norms and martial ones both among evolving pastoral and urban societies, but martial systems may be the only ones that can survive the chronic warfare of pastoral life, and only public service systems the rule of law in towns.[4] This example is based on Lattimore's (1951) reconstruction of the evolution of pastoral and urban societies in North China and Mongolia.

This result is attractive because it may explain why the altruistic, group-functional behavior of humans seems to be so commonly embedded in symbolic systems of supernatural sanctions and costly rituals. Why should group-functional behavior require the support of sacred postulates, rather than a mere mundane conformance to group-functional rules? As Rappaport (1979: 232) remarks, the idea that the rules that support the social order are sanctified is almost a truism. Campbell (1975) alludes to this problem by noting that religion may provide a stronger source of adaptive wisdom for people living in modern societies than sciences like psychology have yet done. Part of this adaptive wisdom is the means by which urban societies solve the problem of cooperation in large groups. Rappaport writes of his proposed functions of Tsembaga ritualized warfare among a people who can hardly be called urban:

> It is by no means certain that the representations of nature provided us by science are more adaptive than those images of the world, inhabited by spirits whom men respect, that guide the action of the Maring and other "primitives." To drape nature in supernatural veils may be to provide her with some protection against human folly and extravagance.(1979: 100)

Rappaport elsewhere makes it clear that that the sharing of cognized models by whole groups often results in group level adaptations:

> We may conclude, I think, that whatever may be the case among other species the use of language, which makes possible such conceptions as honor, morality, altruism, honesty, valor, righteousness, prestige, gods, heaven, and hell, makes group selection important among humans. By *group selection* I mean selection for and perpetuation of conventions enhancing the persistence of groups, even though these conventions can be disadvantageous to those individuals whose actions accord most closely with them. (1984: 401)

Similarly, Freilich (1980) argues that the most symbolic culturally transmitted traits lead to "proper," group-functional behavior and are opposed by less symbolic, "smart" traits that are related to individual advantage. Goode (1978) has interpreted prestige itself as a means of social control. In his functional view of prestige, status and recognition are normally accorded to those who are most altruistic and effective at promoting the welfare of the group as a whole. Military heroism is an oft-cited example of traits of this kind. Warriors seem to be motivated to face the very substantial individual risks of battle by ideas of the prestige of heroism, the risks to one's honor of cowardly conduct, and rewards in a supernatural world for death in battle. A willingness to undergo these risks is usually marked by public rituals invoking sacred postulates, ranging from war dances to swearing of oaths of loyalty.

The observation that selfless and honest behavior is often associated with sacred rituals does not explain how they work to cause such behavior. Symbolic displays and other forms of communication ought to be easy vehicles for deception because using symbols to communicate intentions is ordinarily cheap relative to carrying them out (Maynard Smith 1982: 148). A selfish warrior might well display every ritual indication of his heroism, but cynically plan to take minimum risks in any actual fight. Yet, on the group-functional hypothesis, invocations of the sacred in ritual contexts frequently act to motivate or guarantee honorable performance, rather than provide a gratuitous opportunity to lie (Rappaport 1979: 223–43). Since the runaway process can create a deep belief in the rightness of a symbol system, once the symbol system has been subject to group selection the willingness to perform the sacred rituals will be correlated with actual intentions to perform group-beneficial acts. Once enough individuals become committed to a given correlated set of norms and rituals, they can cooperate to punish violators of sacred symbols *and* mundane failures of cooperation. Individuals who fail to demonstrate proper respect for the sacred are indeed also likely to have failed to acquire the group-functional traits embedded in the symbol system. That it is not unusual for societies to treat impiety and heresy as seriously as "real" crimes is perhaps testimony to this correlation.

In its most extreme version, this hypothesis inverts the usual sociobiological interpretation of prestige. Irons (1979), Dickemann (1979), and others have argued that the fact that in many societies males who are prestigious are also polygynous is strong confirmation of the hypothesis that cultural traits enhance genetic fitness. Group selection acting on cultural variation may greatly complicate this reasoning. Suppose, for example, that prestige is accorded mainly for group-functional behavior, say military heroism or devotion to public affairs, and that prestigious males tend to have greater mating success. Then group selection acting on cultural variation could increase the frequency of genes which increase the success of the group but which would reduce individual fitness in the absence of the culturally acquired mate preference. In effect, the human genome could be "domesticated" by culturally transmitted traits. Much as a prize bull has high genetic fitness because he contributes to a farmer's profit, a prestigious figure may be allowed extra opportunities to reproduce because his genotype produces individuals who tend to be active on behalf of their culture. For a mathematical model of the domestication effect, see Richerson and Boyd (1989).

Afunctionalism

Marshall Sahlins's cultural reason hypothesis represents a more radical departure from sociobiological hypotheses than the weak interaction or even symbolic functionalism proposals. The latter hypotheses ultimately leave function itself to be explained by some form of natural selection, even if it is selection on culture rather than on genes. Sahlins objects:

> All these types of practical reason have also in common an impoverished conception of human symboling. For all of them, the cultural scheme is the sign of other "realities," hence in the end obeisant in its own arrangement to other laws and logics. (1976a: 102)

While we hesitate to claim that any version of Darwinian theory directly translates into Sahlins's cultural reason, we think that the runaway process does resemble it in several respects.

How does the runaway process create meaningful symbols? The runaway process creates symbolic indicator traits, beginning with icons and indexes, in the following sense: We assumed that initially the admired variant was a good indicator of adaptive superiority. All other things being equal, it is plausible that the best farmers tend to grow the largest yams. Thus at the outset the indicator trait is an index of farming skill, not yet a symbol of prestige. If the runaway process ensues, the most admired variant of the indicator trait will not be the most useful index of an individual's adaptive traits. It will confer prestige only because the rest of the population believes that it is prestigious. It is likely that farmers could devote the time and energy necessary to grow gigantic yams to more adaptive purposes. It is true that we can explain the connection between the indicator trait and prestige by understanding the dynamics of the runaway process, so the connection between the symbol (giant yams) and the meaning (prestige) is not completely arbitrary. However, as we noted above, it is in the nature of the runaway process that very small differences in initial conditions can give rise to very different results. The growing of giant yams has not been incorporated into the prestige system of every Pacific Island. The striking diversity of symbolic behavior among human societies is quite consistent with the operation of indirect bias.

The runaway process can also be thought of as deriving its dynamics from cultural factors. Once the runaway process has been initiated, the main force acting on the indicator trait results from the choices made by naive individuals, choices which are based on their values of the preference trait. Thus we imagine that the mean amount of time and effort devoted to raising giant yams increases because people admire and imitate those who grow large yams. The main force acting on the preference character is due to indirect bias acting on the same cultural preference. The size of yams that people find most admirable increases because they have a tendency to acquire their attitudes about yams from people who grow large yams. Once it has been initiated, the runaway process proceeds according to its own internal logic. If this hypothesis is correct, a large amount of cultural variation might be comprehensible only in terms of the internal logic that drove the runaway process in each culture. This logic will, however, have more in common with aesthetic than functional design.

Notice that, in the case of the cultural runaway process, colorful displays are not as likely to be limited to the male sex as is the case with the genetic analog. Apparent examples of runaway sexual selection usually occur in species where gaudy males who meet female choice standards can mate many times. Thus, sexual selection can overcome even quite strong natural selection against the costly display trait because if even a few colorful males survive they can take advantage of multiple matings to perpetuate the sexually selected trait complex. Similarly, a prestigious male or female can have an unlimited number of cultural "offspring" by nonparental transmission; there is a close analogy to the polygynous mating system of sexually selected animals. The fact that women as well as men participate in elaborate symbolic behaviors, such as religious observance or stylish dress, is more consistent with a cultural than a genetic runaway explanation based upon ordinary sexual selection.

Even the afunctional hypothesis can be consistent with the notion that the human cultural inheritance system is adaptive. Indirect bias provides a good general inheritance rule because it allows an efficient shortcut to directly evaluating adaptive consequences of alternative cultural variants. Thus it is possible that, averaged over many different traits and many different human groups, indirect bias is adaptive, even if for some traits in all groups it leads to the elaboration of maladaptive markers of prestige. This is just a special case of the costly information hypothesis discussed above. The cost of individual evaluation of traits may favor indirect bias even if cultural traits are frequently entrained in the maladaptive runaway process.

CONCLUSION

Anthropologists (Harris 1971: 150) and biologists (Dobzhansky 1962: 20) commonly note that culture and genes have a complex set of similarities and differences. We argue that the similarities are sufficiently great that the theoretical concepts and methods used by population biologists can be used to investigate the problems of cultural evolution, including the problem of the relationship between genetic and cultural evolution. These concepts and methods themselves are mostly silent substantive issues. The synthetic power of Darwinian models is a result of their being an accounting system for transmissible determinants of behavior that can be used to represent a quite wide variety of hypotheses.

Among contemporary biologists there is a certain amount of dispute about exactly how organic evolution works. There is disagreement, for example, about the relative importance of selection, drift, and mutation in determining the surprisingly large amount of genetic variation detected using biochemical techniques, such as gel electrophoresis; there is also disagreement about the nature of the processes that cause the larger-scale patterns of evolution as observed in the fossil record. Yet, virtually all of the protagonists in these disputes agree on the basic Darwinian approach to evolutionary theory. Organisms inherit information that, together with their environment, determines their phenotypes. To understand why a population of organisms is characterized by some phenotypes and not others, one determines what processes in the lives of individuals act to increase the frequency of some variants relative to others. Since formal theory was married to a broad range of empirical techniques around the turn of the century, population biology has made steady progress by following the conceptual path laid down by Darwin (Provine 1971).

In this chapter we have argued that, by applying a similar approach to understanding cultural evolution in humans, one can provide a satisfactory explanation of otherwise puzzling features of human evolution. Humans inherit information culturally that, together with their genetic endowment and their environment, determines their behavior. In the particular case of the indirect bias force, we have tried to illustrate its utility by showing three things:

(1) The interactions of genes and culture in the human evolutionary process is intrinsically complex. Using indirect bias as an inheritance rule may contribute substantially to genetic fitness on average, but it may also lead to frequent departures from the fitness optimum for specific traits. If so, the substantive application of Darwinian ideas alone will be insufficient to understand human behavior.

(2) Darwinian models of cultural evolution are capable of explaining the interesting differences between humans and other animals. Among these differences, people make lavish use of symbols and cooperate in large groups. The indirect bias mechanism is a plausible explanation for how symbolic behaviors arise in human societies, why different societies are very different in the symbols they use, how symbolic behaviors play a role in the evolution of large-scale cooperation, and how the apparently maladaptive nature of some symbolic traits might be explained.

(3) The theory sets up clearer tests of hypotheses and is thus a vehicle for resolving the "repetitive and cyclical opposition" (Sahlins 1976a: 102) that seems to characterize the social sciences. The strengths of preference-based choices, indirect bias, and selection determine whether the runaway or fitness-maximizing case of cultural evolution with indirect bias will occur. These forces are susceptible to empirical investigation; indeed, social scientists frequently measure closely related processes for other purposes. One of the most important tasks of theory is to cast seemingly irreconcilable oppositions in common terms so as to show what empirical measurements would actually decide the issue.

THE FUNDAMENTAL RELEVANCE OF CULTURE

From the point of view of the methodologically Darwinian approach, culture is interesting if it is a system for transmitting heritable variation. One justification for a purely substantive application of Darwinian ideas to human behavior rests on an argument that culture is not such a system, that it resembles ordinary mechanisms of phenotypic flexibility like individual learning (Alexander 1979: 75–82). In essence, Alexander argues that individual decision making about what cultural traits to imitate is so powerful, and so firmly based on genetically transmitted rules, that people do not depend to any significant degree on simple imitation of pre-existing cultural variation. Elsewhere we have reviewed some of the empirical evidence that can be brought to bear on this issue (Boyd and Richerson, 1985: 32–80, 157–71). We are convinced that people do depend to a substantial extent on simple unbiased imitation and on low-cost decision rules such as indirect bias. If so, the complexities we have illustrated are likely to be important, and the concept of culture is fundamentally relevant to understanding human behavior.

This conclusion accords closely with the strong emphasis on the culture concept in anthropology. What the Darwinian approach offers is a set of formal tools for building a more sophisticated theory of properties of culture. We emphasize that the application of Darwinian methods to culture does not prejudge most of the substantive issues that have divided social scientists. As in biology, Darwinism should play a synthetic and unifying role because of its ability to cast many hypotheses in a common framework rooted in the realities of information transfer between individuals living in populations. Such a framework will not end debate, but will make it more productive of scientific progress.

NOTES

The authors wish to thank Peggy Barlett, Peter Brown, Donald Campbell, Morris Freilich, Daniel Rancour-Laferriere, Bobby Paul, Joan Silk, E. O. Smith, and Eric A. Smith for providing useful critiques of various versions of this manuscript.

1. Social scientists (Campbell 1965, 1975; Cloak 1975; R. Cohen 1981; Durham 1978; Ruyle 1973) have used Darwinian ideas as the basis for a general theory of culture. Several biologists have considered how culturally transmitted behavior fits into the framework of neo-Darwinism (Boyd and Richerson 1985; Lumsden and Wilson 1981; Pulliam and Dunford 1980). Other biologists and psychologists have used the formal similarities between cultural and genetic transmission to develop theories describing the dynamics of cultural transmission (Cavalli-Sforza and Feldman 1981; Cloninger et al. 1979).

2. The other biased transmission forces have been the subject of considerable theoretical investigation (Boyd and Richerson 1985; Cavalli-Sforza and Feldman 1981; Lumsden and Wilson 1981; Pulliam 1983).

3. The most important contributions to this literature are Alexander (1979), Durham (1976), Lumsden and Wilson (1981), and the authors represented in the volume edited by Chagnon and Irons (1979), among many other sources. There are many important differences among these writers (Boyd and Richerson 1985: 157–66) and not everyone agrees that all this work should be collected under a single heading.

4. A subtler version of the runaway process might allow the development of the prestige system to be guided by group selection in the first place (Boyd and Richerson 1985: 275–76).

REFERENCES

Alexander, Richard D.
    1979   *Darwinism and Human Affairs.* Seattle: University of Washington Press.
Bandura, Albert
    1977   *Social Learning Theory.* Englewood Cliffs, N. J.: Prentice Hall.
Bascom, William R.
    1948   "Ponapean Prestige Economy." *Southwestern Journal of Anthropology* 4: 211–21.
Boyd, Robert, and Peter J. Richerson
    1985   *Culture and the Evolutionary Process.* Chicago: University of Chicago Press.
Campbell, Donald T.
    1975   "On the Conflicts between Biological and Social Evolution and between Psychology and Moral Tradition." *American Psychologist* 30: 1103–26.

1965   "Variation and Selective Retention in Sociocultural Evolution." In *Social Change in Developing Areas: A Reinterpretation of Evolutionary Theory.* H. R. Barringer, G. I. Blanksten, and R. W. Mack, eds. Cambridge: Schenkman.

Cavalli-Sforza, Luigi L. and Marcus W. Feldman
1981   *Cultural Transmission and Evolution: A Quantitative Approach.* Princeton: Princeton University Press.

Chagnon, Napoleon A., and William Irons, eds.
1979   *Evolutionary Biology and Human Social Behavior: An Anthropological Perspective.* North Scituate, Mass.: Duxbury.

Cloak, F. Ted, Jr.
1975   "Is a Cultural Ethology Possible?" *Human Ecology* 3: 161–82.

Cloninger, C. R., J. Rice, and T. Reich
1979   "Multifactorial Inheritance with Cultural Transmission and Assortative Mating. II. A General Model of Combined Polygenic and Cultural Inheritance." *American Journal of Human Genetics* 31: 176–98.

Cohen, Abner
1974   *Two-Dimensional Man. An Essay on the Anthropology of Power and Symbolism in Complex Society.* Berkeley: University of California Press.

Cohen, Ronald
1981   "Evolutionary Epistemology and Human Values." *Current Anthropology* 23: 201–18

Dickemann, Mildred
1979   "Female Infanticide, Reproductive Strategies, and Social Stratification: A Preliminary Model." In *Evolutionary Biology and Human Social Behavior: An Anthropological Perspective.* N. Chagnon and W. Irons, eds. North Scituate, Mass.: Duxbury.

Dobzhansky, Theodosius
1962   *Mankind Evolving.* New York: Columbia University Press.

Durham, William H.
1978   "Toward a Coevolutionary View of Human Biology and Culture." In *The Sociobiology Debate,* A. Caplan, ed. New York: Harper & Row.
1976   "The Adaptive Significance of Cultural Behavior." Human Ecology 4: 89–121.

Flinn, Mark V., and Richard D. Alexander
1982   "Culture Theory: The Developing Synthesis from Biology." *Human Ecology* 10: 383–400.

Freilich, Morris
1980   "Smart-Sex and Proper-Sex: A Paradigm Found." *General Issues in Anthropology* 2: 37–51.

Goode, William J.
1978   *The Celebration of Heroes: Prestige as a Control System.* Berkeley: University of California Press.

Harris, Marvin
1971   *Culture, Man, and Nature.* New York: Crowell.

Irons, William
1979   "Cultural and Biological Success." In *Evolutionary Biology and Human Social Behavior.* N. Chagnon and W. Irons, eds. North Scituate, Mass.: Duxbury.

Jakobson, R.
   1971   "Quest for the Essence of Language:. In *Selected Writings II. Word and Language*. R. Jakobson, ed. Hague: Mouton

Keesing, Roger M.
   1974   "Theories of Culture." *Annual Review of Anthropology* 3: 73–97.

Kirkpatrick, Mark
   1982   "Sexual Selection and the Evolution of Female Choice." *Evolution* 36: 1–12.

Kroeber, Alfred L., and Clyde Kluckhohn
   1952   "Culture, A Critical Review of the Concepts and Definitions." *Papers of The Peabody Museum of American Archeology and Ethnology* 47(1): 1–223.

Labov, William
   1980   "The Social Origins of Sound Change." In *Locating Language in Time and Space*. W. Labov, ed. New York: Academic.

Lande, Russell
   1981   "Models of Speciation by Sexual Selection on Polygenic Traits." *Proceedings of the National Academy of Science, USA* 78: 3721–25.

Lattimore, Owen
   1951   *Inner Asian Frontiers of China.* 2nd ed. Washington, D.C.: American Geographical Society.

Lumsden, Charles J., and Edward O. Wilson
   1981   *Genes, Mind, and Culture.* Cambridge: Harvard University Press.

Maynard Smith, John
   1982   *Evolution and the Theory of Games.* Cambridge: Cambridge University Press.

Mayr, Ernst
   1982   *The Growth of Biological Thought: Diversity, Evolution, and Inheritance.* Cambridge: Belknap Press of Harvard University Press.

Provine, William B.
   1971   *The Origins of Theoretical Population Genetics.* Chicago: University of Chicago Press.

Pulliam, H. Ronald
   1983   "On the Theory of Gene-Culture Evolution in a Variable Environment." In *Animal Cognition and Behavior*, R.L. Mellgren, ed. Amsterdam: North-Holland.

   1982   "A Social Learning Model of Conflict and Cooperation in Human Societies." *Human Ecology* 10: 353–63.

Pulliam, H. Ronald, and C. Dunford
   1980   *Programmed to Learn: An Essay on the Evolution of Culture*. New York: Columbia University Press.

Rappaport, Roy A.
   1984   *Pigs for the Ancestors.* 2nd ed. New Haven: Yale University Press.

   1979   *Ecology, Meaning, and Religion.* Richmond, Calif.: North Atlantic Books.

Richerson, Peter J., and Robert Boyd.
   1989   "The Role of Evolved Predispositions in Cultural Evolution: Or Human Sociobiology Meets Pascal's Wager." *Ethology and Sociobiology* 10: 195–219

   1984   "Natural Selection and Culture." *BioScience* 34: 430–34.

Rogers, Everett M.
   1983   *The Diffusion of Innovations.* 3rd ed. New York: Free Press.

Rosenthal, Ted, and Barry Zimmerman
  1978   *Social Learning and Cognition.* New York: Academic.
Ruyle, Eugene E.
  1973   "Genetic and Cultural Pools: Some Suggestions for a Unified Theory of Biocultural Evolution." *Human Ecology* 1: 201–15.
Sahlins, Marshall
  1976a   *Culture and Practical Reason.* Chicago: University of Chicago Press.

  1976b   *The Use and Abuse of Biology: An Anthropological Critique of Sociobiology.* Ann Arbor: University of Michigan Press.
Shweder, Richard A., and Robert A. LeVine
  1984   *Culture Theory: Essays on Mind, Self, and Emotion.* Cambridge: Cambridge University Press.
Smith, Eric A.
  1983   "Anthropological Applications of Optimal Foraging Theory: A Critical Review." *Current Anthropology* 24: 625–51.
Werren, John H., and H. Ronald Pulliam
  1981   "An Intergenerational Model of the Cultural Evolution of Helping Behavior." *Human Ecology* 9: 465–83.
Yando, R.M, V. Seitz, and E. Zigler
  1978   *Imitation: A Developmental Perspective.* Hillsdale, N. J.: Lawrence Erlbaum.
Yussen, S.R., and V.M. Levy
  1975   Effects of Warm and Neutral Models on the Attention of Observational Learners. *Journal of Experimental Child Psychology* 20: 66–72.

8

ETHNOECOLOGY: THE RELEVANCE OF COGNITIVE ANTHROPOLOGY FOR HUMAN ECOLOGY

Eugene Hunn

Anthropologists have defined culture variously in their pursuit of diverse theoretical goals. Keesing (1974) distinguishes two fundamentally distinct perspectives on the study of culture, the adaptational (or materialist) and the ideational. Examples of the first approach include cultural ecology and cultural materialism. They are characterized by a focus on the adaptive value of culturally patterned behaviors. In cultural materialism "culture" reduces to learned behaviors (Harris 1979). Ideational theories define cultures as semiotic systems. The relations between such systems of signs and the realities of behavioral adaptation is of only peripheral interest. Keesing contrasts ideational theories associated with Lévi-Strauss, Geertz, Schneider, and Goodenough, the last of which is cognitive anthropology, the guiding perspective of this chapter.

Keesing, as an ideational theorist, like Harris on the materialist side, reflects the widely held view that adaptational and ideational perspectives are fundamentally incompatible. I would like to argue to the contrary—that our best hope of developing an effective theory of culture is to bridge the chasm separating adaptationist and ideational positions. The synthesis I propose here may be called "ethnoecology" (but not as described by Fowler 1977). This synthesis should combine the strengths of modern ecological anthropology with those of cognitive-semiotic anthropology while avoiding the weaknesses of both.

The strength of the adaptational approach is its recognition that human behavior both affects and is affected by a complex environment, the social and ecosystems of which humans are but one part. This strength becomes a weakness if it is not clearly recognized that social and ecosystems are composed of individual organisms, each of which is pursuing its own "selfish" plans (Dawkins 1976). The functionalist fallacy results from attributing goal direction to systems rather than to individual actors (Richerson 1977). This problem is avoided by more recent models based on evolutionary ecology, in which adaptation is interpreted in terms of the effect traits have on the individuals who express them, rather than the effect such traits might have on the encompassing system *qua* organism (Smith 1984).

The strength of ideational approaches lies in their focus on symbolic thought and communication. Learning may take place in the absence of symbolic means of expression. Thus culture, defined as learned behaviors, may also exist without such communication. However, such learning is limited in quantity and adaptive flexibility, and thus nonsymbolic culture remains rudimentary. The fact that humans possess a highly elaborated, species-specific, and universal capacity for language should be sufficient motivation to give symbolic expression a central role in our theories of human adaptation.

Some adaptational theories, such as Harris's cultural materialism, treat the symbolically coded information by which human behavior is planned, evaluated, replicated, and manipulated as if it served primarily as an ideological smoke screen that it is the analyst's task to dispel. Other adaptationists perceive only a quantitative difference between nonsymbolic social learning (by imitation) and symbolically mediated cultural transmission (see Richerson and Boyd in this volume). On the other hand, ideational theorists of culture have often devoted inordinate attention to expressive, in preference to instrumental, aspects of culture (Hunn 1982). This emphasis on the noninstrumental may then be combined with a radical relativism and/or a virulent antipositivism (positivism being used loosely as an epithet for modern science) that borders on a rejection of the possibility of a science of human culture. Such ideational theorists define the proper goal of cultural analysis as interpretation rather than explanation. Ideational theorists are also prey to the same functionalist fallacy that waylaid early cultural ecology, subordinating the individual actor to the controlling influence of the encompassing system, whether social, cultural, or ecological.

COGNITIVE DEFINITIONS OF CULTURE

Cognitive anthropology among the ideational theories seems best suited to propose a theoretical marriage of ideational and adaptationist approaches. Cognitive anthropology seeks to develop a scientific approach to ethnography, one that can produce systematic and replicable descriptions of particular cultures (or segments thereof) as a first step toward valid cross-cultural generalizations (Kay 1970). Cognitive anthropology focuses on the individual as the bearer and creative user of culture. The cognitivist culture concept was first clearly articulated by Goodenough, who defined culture as that which one needs to know to act appropriately in all the normal social contexts of the society in question (1957: 167). Culture is thus information, not behavior, a point of agreement with leading cultural evolutionary theorists such as Cloak (1975) and Boyd and Richerson (1985). This definition was inspired by a reaction to the positivistic excesses of behaviorist psychology and descriptive linguistics. This same reaction gave impetus to the Chomskyan revolution in linguistics (Chomsky 1959) and led to the development of cognitive psychology (Neisser

1975). Mental phenomena were not to be ignored as impenetrable and insubstantial, but were to be explained by reference to testable cognitive models. Observed behavior was seen as a superficial phenomenon generated by underlying cognitive processes interacting with — not simply reacting to — external reality. For anthropologists this meant that the seemingly infinite variety of human behavior could be understood in terms of cultural rules learned by individuals in society. Systems of such cultural rules, or cultural grammars on the linguistic model, were necessarily finite and otherwise constrained by the limits of human mental capacity.

This notion of culture as a grammar for behavior — derived from the equation CULTURE : BEHAVIOR :: LANGUAGE : SPEECH — is flawed, for grammars define what is the appropriate form of a sentence, saying nothing of what is its appropriate content. Chomsky's famed nonsensical sentence, "Colorless green ideas sleep furiously," is grammatically correct but "ecologically" absurd. An ecologically appropriate culture concept must address not only what is formally appropriate, but also what is ecologically effective. We should therefore amend Goodenough's definition of culture as follows: Culture is what one must know to act effectively in one's environment. (The environment is understood to include both natural and social components from the individual actor's point-of-view.)

This definition retains an essential ambiguity. What do we mean by "effective"? In Goodenough's original definition there was no question: appropriateness of behavior was to be judged by the native, just as the grammaticality of a sentence must be judged by a native speaker, through introspection. The standard of cultural appropriateness may be equated with Freilich's "proper culture" (1980). But cultural effectiveness includes as well Freilich's "smart culture." Both are emic standards, relevant to culturally defined goals, the one social, the other individual. Alternatively we might adopt an etic standard of effectiveness, that is, by reference to culturally external standards. To a human ecologist effectiveness may refer to the efficiency of energy conversion or ultimately, in evolutionary ecology, to maximizing inclusive fitness. I suggest that ethnoecology adopt as a working hypothesis the assumption that, other things being equal, the effective pursuit of culturally defined goals is the proximate mechanism for realizing the ultimate goals imposed by the biological and cultural evolutionary systems of which the human individual is a part (cf. Durham 1979, 1982).

Thus ethnoecology provides a framework for understanding the mechanisms of human cultural evolution, mechanisms that have only recently been seriously considered by cultural adaptationists (Ruyle 1973; Cavalli-Sforza and Feldman 1981; Cloak 1975; Dawkins 1976; Durham 1979; Pulliam and Dunford 1980; Boyd and Richerson 1985). I believe the analogy CULTURE : BEHAVIOR :: GENOTYPE : PHENOTYPE is more productive than the original Goodenough formulation, promoting a view of a culture as a system of information that serves as a blueprint for a way of life and that is ultimately judged by how well it sustains and promotes that way of life.[1]

In this view, behavior is the result of culture, the product of cultural plans. It is my view that such cultural plans are frequently conscious, that is, symbolically coded in and thus accessible through the native language of the culture bearer. Though learned behaviors and thus culture are not necessarily governed symbolically or consciously, conscious, linguistically encoded plans constitute a very large and highly invested segment of human cultural life, the analysis of which should yield substantial progress toward an understanding of the more general phenomenon of the evolution of learning.

It needs to be stressed that such cultural plans are context sensitive, in that the behaviors they call for will vary depending on the conditions of the environment at the time and place the plans are expressed, as biological phenotypes vary depending on the environment of gene expression. Furthermore, such plans serve as blueprints, and a blueprint of a house is not the same thing as the house it describes, though it contains the information required to organize the material means necessary for the house's construction and thus embodies the material need for shelter the house is designed to satisfy. This shift of emphasis from models of cultures as autonomous formal structures to processual models of cultures as adaptive systems parallels the shift toward pragmatics in linguistic analysis (Silverstein 1976) and toward praxis in Marxian theory (Ortner 1984).

IMAGE AND PLAN

If culture consists of the information necessary for effective action, what is the nature of that information and how is it organized, stored, acquired, and passed on? Such questions with regard to genetic information have received a great deal of attention from scientists analyzing biogenetic evolutionary mechanisms. Similar efforts will be needed in the study of cultural evolution.

At one level cultural information is coded neurophysiologically, but among humans it is most often transmitted and manipulated symbolically via language. Thus a substantial core of human cultural information will be manifested in the language of the culture bearer. Cognitive anthropology is concerned primarily with the form and content of cultural information as it is expressed linguistically. This strategic focus on natural language as the medium of culture is shared by Schank and Abelson, leading artificial intelligence (AI) theorists, who note that "a great deal of the human scene can be represented verbally" (1977: 5).

A primary distinction relevant to understanding how cultural information is encoded is that between systems of information organized by similarity and those organized by contiguity (cf. iconicity versus indexicality). The former focus on features intrinsic to the "things"[2] classified and relevant to their identification regardless of context. The latter refer to extrinsic features of things, i.e., relationships between things and their contexts, which are primarily relevant to understanding how things function, their roles in events.

Models of human knowledge and memory based on abstract similarity have dominated cognitive theorizing in cognitive psychology and cognitive anthropology into the mid-1970s. Concept formation by reference to similarity has traditionally been judged a more "mature" mode of thought than that based on functional association (Bruner, Goodnow, and Austin 1956: 6–8), being characterized as "abstract" (because context free), as opposed to the "concrete" associations of contiguity. Semantic theories of memory conceive of memory as "organized in a hierarchical fashion using class membership as the basic link" (Schank and Abelson 1977: 18), with class membership typically defined in terms of shared similarity. Cognitive anthropology has viewed cultural knowledge similarly, defining as the primary units of analysis "semantic domains" by reference to shared similarity (cf. Sturtevant 1964). Culture in this view is an Image of the world (cf. Boulding 1956) that includes cultural "maps," "taxonomies," and "paradigms" as particular organizational forms. The Image is analogous to the lexicon in models of natural language. It consists of "models of," not "models for," a way of life (Geertz 1973: 93).

Relations of contiguity have recently been emphasized in models of the conceptual organization of human behavior, that aspect of cultural knowledge more directly involved in interpreting events and selecting courses of action than in describing what the world looks like (Randall 1977, 1987). I will contrast such models of the cultural Plan (cf. Miller, Galanter, and Pribram 1960) with those of the Image. A cultural Plan includes "information processing rules" (Geoghegan 1973); "scripts, plans, goals" (Abelson 1976, 1981; Schank and Abelson 1977); and "routine action plans" (Randall 1977, 1987) as particular organizational forms. It involves episodic rather than semantic memory (Schank and Abelson 1977: 18). "Hierarchical decision trees" (Gladwin 1980) may be incorporated as required.

Cognitive anthropologists have made substantial progress in the analysis of the cultural Image, of Image domains such as color, kinship relations, folk biological taxonomies, and folk anatomy. Considerable progress is also evident in the study of decision trees, cultural rules, and routine planning. What is lacking is an effective integration of our models of Image and of Plan (see Figure 8.1). I will discuss below several cases of cognitive anthropological research that suggest the direction such an integration of Image and Plan might take. Each illustrates how cognitive anthropologists have addressed the ecological relevance of cultural knowledge.

Preliminary Illustrations

Case 1. "Cultural Ecology and Ethnography," Charles Frake (1962).

In this brief note Frake illustrates how a local settlement pattern of scattered homesites in the southern Philippines could be "generated" from just three cultural "rules." The rules were the bases on which individuals selected sites preferred for constructing their houses. They sought simultaneously to minimize the distance between home and fields and to maximize the distance to their nearest neighbor's house, while also minimizing the labor of fence construction around the periphery of their fields. The rules were readily elicited in the native language and clearly define appropriate choices of action in terms of social and ecological variables. Thus the observed settlement pattern is the collective

Figure 8.1.   A Model of Image and Plan

Natural Environment

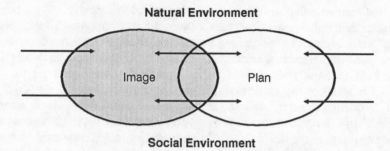

Social Environment

behavioral expression of many individual culturally and environmentally governed choices. The behavioral pattern may change, that is, we may observe cultural evolution, without change in the cultural rule, if environmental parameters, such as population density, should change.

Case 2. "Residential Decision Making among the Eastern Samal," William Geoghegan (1970).

In this classic study Geoghegan constructs an "information-processing model" of residence mode selection in a Philippine Island community. The rule is graphically represented as a flow-chart — a popular convention in cognitive anthropological studies of choice — each node of which represents an environmental assessment relevant to the choice of "appropriate" residence mode. The validity of the model is tested against census data from the original community as well as from a population of war refugees. Predictions were 98 percent and 94 percent confirmed for the two populations. Marvin Harris (1974), in a critique of this and similar cultural accounts of behavior, argues that this demonstrates that etic outputs require etic inputs. However, Harris redefines etic here as "real" versus "imagined." This is a distortion of Pike's (1956) original formulation of the emic-etic contrast. Furthermore, the inputs required by Geoghegan's model are emic in the proper sense of that term, being distinctions relevant to the actor's cultural frame of reference. That cultural rules incorporate information — linguistically encoded — about the "real" world does not make them etic. Clearly, if cultural Images of reality were not more or less faithful to that reality, cultural Plans based on such information would be ecologically ineffective. So Harris is right to demand that cultural systems effectively link objective environmental states (his "etic inputs") to behavioral practice (his "etic outputs"). He is wrong only in suggesting that cognitive anthropologists believe otherwise.

Case 3. "Ice and Travel among the Ft. Norman Slave," Keith Basso (1972).

Basso shows how an elaborate Slave Indian ice taxonomy, incorporating thirteen named varieties of ice of three major types, is relevant to subsistence and survival in the boreal forest environment. The well-worn example of the elaboration of Inuit snow terminology is presumed to illustrate how cultural knowledge reflects adaptive requirements, though no one has actually demonstrated such a relationship. Basso does so for his Ft. Norman Slave case. The thirteen named ice varieties are associated with seven contrasting combinations of mode of travel (on foot, on snowshoes, by sled) and strategies of approach to water barriers (cross at full speed, test before crossing, circumnavigate) encountered by hunters during winter travel. These relationships between named environmental conditions and behavioral options are explicitly taught to the younger generation by means of a word game in which the child is given two of the three conditions and must select the appropriate third element. In this case the Image is an efficient repository of information about the environment essential to ecologically effective choices of action. The importance of language in cultural transmission is also clear in this example.

Case 4. "Talking About Doing: Lexicon and Event," Michael Agar (1974).

Agar argues that the specialized terminology of the heroin addict subculture in the United States is better represented in terms of events characteristic of the addict's life-style rather than in terms of semantic domains defining an Image of the addict's world. In other words, relations of contiguity regarding actors, actions, means, and locations provide a more meaningful characterization of this subculture than do relations of similarity defining, for example, taxonomies of such actors, means, and locations, as had been traditional in ethnoscience. The terms characteristic of the addict subculture, when arranged as in an English sentence, with terms filling slots in the sentence representing actions (verbs), agents (subjects), objects of actions, and means and locations of the labeled actions succinctly summarized "what one needed to know to act appropriately" within the addict subculture.

The possibility that all human languages are built upon an underlying universal "case grammar" (Fillmore 1968, 1977) suggests that the human understanding of events may be as regularly structured as human semantic memory. Schank's Conceptual Dependency Theory (1975) and the various computer simulations of how people understand natural language accounts of human events represent parallel efforts by psychologists and AI researchers to develop a theory of human knowledge of "the world of psychological and physical events occupying the mental life of ordinary individuals…[of] the common sense…assumptions which people make about the motives and behavior of themselves and others — and also a kind of 'naive physics,' or primitive intuition about physical reality" (Schank and Abelson 1977: 4). From this theoretical perspective the cultural Image (as well as the Plan) is primarily structured by functional relations of contiguity; thus the Image, the Plan, and the grammatical structure of human language share a common analytical framework.

Case 5. "Making Plans to 'Make a Living' in the Southern Philippines," Robert Randall (1977).

Randall's analysis of Linungan fishing plans is an ambitious attempt to describe what one must know to "make a living" in this particular ecological setting. His analysis adds a dimension of ethnographic reality to the efforts of AI theorists to account for human understanding of everyday life. Randall stresses the significance of having or acquiring the means necessary for successful action, an environmental constraint on the selection of culturally appropriate behaviors. Randall carefully distinguishes how routine choices of action are implemented, in contrast to the selection of exceptional or marked alternative actions when unusual obstacles or opportunities are encountered (Randall 1987). His analysis describes some microevolutionary changes in Linungan subsistence plans.

These studies are but a sample of cognitive anthropological research relevant to cultural ecology. Basso demonstrates that cultural knowledge has adaptive significance. Frake, Geoghegan, and Randall show the ecological relevance of cultural plans. Geoghegan, Agar, and Randall propose general models of such cultural plans. I will now describe in greater detail an ethnobiological case from my own research to suggest the form an ethnoecological ethnography might take.

Sahaptin Root Digging

This example begins with a traditional ethnoscientific analysis that organizes terminologically labeled elements of the Image as a taxonomic domain structured by relations of perceptual similarity (Kay 1971; Berlin, Breedlove, and Raven 1973; Hunn 1976). The elements of the Image are analyzed in terms of their role in the cultural Plan. The two perspectives are then contrasted.

I have recorded over 200 basic plant taxa for the Columbia River dialects of the Sahaptin language of the Plateau of northwestern North America.[3] A basic category is distinguished from more or less inclusive categories in the same domain by a characteristic combination of features, including high information content, an unmarked name, and a cognitive representation as a prototypical image (Hunn 1976; Berlin 1978; Rosch 1978). The fact that most of these 200-odd categories correspond to scientific species or closely approximate them demonstrates that perceptual similarity is the primary basis for the classification of individual plants into basic level categories. In this respect Sahaptin resembles other folk biological classification systems. However, Sahaptin is unusual in comparison with other well-known folk biological systems in its minimal hierarchical structure. Morphologically based "life form" taxa and folk specific taxa are virtually nonexistent. (Life forms are defined by Berlin, Breedlove, and Raven [1973] as taxa inclusive of a range of "folk generic" or basic-level taxa, while specifics are defined as subdivisions of folk generics characteristically labeled by names of binomial form.) The Sahaptin taxonomic hierarchy thus reduces to a nearly unstructured list of basic level categories.

I would like to be able to say more than this about Sahaptin ethnobotany. To do so I must consider more than the perceptual basis of Sahaptin folk classification. I must consider not only relations of similarity among plant taxa but also relations of contiguity between plant taxa and other conceptual elements of the Sahaptin Image. One way to approach this task is to describe what I call the "activity signature" of each plant (Hunn 1982), which is the set of Sahaptin sentences incorporating each plant name. Activity signatures are lists of admissible predications for which the plant serves as an argument. Those sentences delimit a set of contexts that collectively define the plant's cultural relevance.

Context-defining sentences may be compared among a set of plants to appreciate the contrasting relevance of each plant. As an initial step in this ethnographic program I have drawn from open-ended, native language texts on gathering activities that I recorded from several Sahaptin elders. From these texts I have abstracted an outline of a root gathering plan, a cultural context central to the meaning of the Sahaptin ethnobotanical category *xni-t*, "plants that are dug, roots." I then asked my Sahaptin teacher, James Selam, to review and correct my interpretations.

The basic plant categories grouped under the heading *xni-t* correspond closely to scientific species. Nineteen of the twenty-six roots, or 73 percent, correspond perfectly to scientific species, while the remaining seven are near misses. The perceptual basis for these basic-level taxa is thus clear. However, the collectivity of roots represents a diverse assortment of plants from several plant families. This category includes the edible species of some scientific genera and families while excluding other very similar but inedible species of the same genus or family. Clearly, the category *xni-t* is not based on perceptual similarity. Rather it reflects the common role each such species plays in the cultural Plan. All roots, for example, are appropriate as objects of the transitive verb *xni-* "to dig [something]." The similarity here is a functional equivalence; the members of the category may substitute for one another in a particular role within a characteristic activity, in this case an ecologically fundamental one.

If all twenty-six kinds of roots are functionally equivalent, why bother to name each separately? This seems wasteful of mental effort and of memory capacity. Why not call them all simply *xni-t*? Such a strategy is, in fact, adopted with regard to two categories of useless plants in Sahaptin, *latít* (flower) and *c'ic'k* (grass) (Randall and Hunn 1984). However, all roots on closer inspection are not precise functional equivalents. Though all roots may be harvested with the same digging movement, in the larger context of using these roots, highly salient contrasts appear. To appreciate the cultural need for naming so many roots we must describe root digging in more detail.

The actual act of digging the root from the ground is but one step — albeit the conceptually central one — in a sequence of connected activities. Applying ethnoscientific elicitation techniques in this case is useful. If we ask *táynam-chi á-xni-sha k^w'áaman?* (why one digs this root or that), the answer will be, *tk^{w}átat-yaw* (to eat it). One doesn't just dig roots and then discard them! Root digging is a goal-directed activity. If we ask *míshniki-nam á-xni-xa k^w'áaman?*

Table 8.1   A Sahaptin Root Digging Plan XNI-T*

I. Primary goal: to eat *tk^{w}áta-sha*
  A. Have means to eat , e.g., is there food? *i-wá tk^{w}áta-t*
    1. If yes, go to B. If not, select means, e.g., option 1d.
      a. Fish *np'íwi-sha*: select means, for example,
        1) Fish by hook-and-line *wac'ílak-sha*
        2) Fish by bone choker *shapá?axch-sha*
        3) Spear fish *tayxáy-sha*
        4) Dip-net fish *twalúu-sha*
        5) Set-net fish *tapatúk-sha*
        6) Fish by weir *shapá-xaluu-sha*
      b. Hunt *tk^{w}áynp-sha*
      c. Pick fruit *á-tmaani-sha*
      d. Dig roots *á-xni-sha*
      e. Use stored foods *yáxaynakt-pamá*
    2. Enact root digging plan *wishushuwa-sha xnít-atash*
      a. Have means to dig roots *wás-nas xnit-pamá,e.g.,* digging stick *kápin*, twined bag *wápas*?
      b. If not, acquire means. If yes, initiate plan.
        1) Plan trip *wishushuwa-sha wína-tash*
        2) Pack up gear *i-wiwalak^w'ik-sha kutkut'áwas-na*
        3) Go for roots *máana-sha*
        4) Travel to camp *wishána-sha wáwtukash-kan*
        5) Go around [looking for a camp site] *waqit-sha wáwtuk-awas*
        6) Camp overnight *wishwáwtuk-sha*
        7) Find digging site *á-yax-sha xnit-pamá-na*
        8) Look around for roots *q'inuq'inú-sha xnit-pamá-na*
        9) Select root species, e.g., bitterroot *pyaxí,* camas *wáq'amu,* Indian potato *anipásh*
       10) Dig roots *á-xni-sha*
       11) If bitterroot, strip skin *á-chapyax-sha*
       12) Put in twined bag *á-nich-sha wápas-pa*
       13) Repeat 10) & 12) until bag is full *káakim,* then go on
       14) Collect in large bag *á-yakta-sha ánpsh-pa*
       15) Repeat 14) until full, then continue
       16) Pack roots back to camp *k^{w}náyti-sha*
    3. Prepare roots, select means, e. g., option 3b.
      a. Store underground *á-tamki-sha,* go to I, A, 1, e.
      b. Eat them now *áw tk^{w}áta-sha,* go to A4.
      c. Keep them for winter *á-nich-sha ánwich-tash,* initiate sequence
        1) Wash roots *áw-iix-sha*
        2) Peel roots *á-miik-sha*
        3) If bitterroot, go to C6
        4) If camas, bake underground *á-tamaych-sha*
        5) If *luksh,* make root cakes *áwi?ani-sha sapíl,* initiate sequence
          a) Pound roots *á-tut-sha*
          b) Mix dough *shapátwa-sha*
          c) Form cakes *áwi?ani-sha sapíl*
        6) Dry in sun *áwilaxyawi-sha ichú-pa*
        7) Pack them home *áwishapashap-sha túxna-t*
        8) Put them away in the cellar *á-nich-sha wulchí-pa*
    4. Cook roots *á-shapa?at'i-sha xnít-na*: select means, e. g.,
      a. boil them *á-shapa-lamulayt-sha*
  B. Eat *tk^{w}áta-sha*

---

*Note relationships of goals, activities, and means; of options and sequences; of special selection and identification subplans.

(how does one dig roots), we are likely to receive as answer a description of a sequence of activities. To dig a root requires that one first go root digging *máana-*, on arrival look around for the specific root(s) sought *q'inuq'inú-*, dig them *xni-*,[4] peel them *miik-*, collect them in a bag *yákta-*, pack them back to camp *kʷnáyti-*, wash them *iix-*, pound them *tut-*, dry them *láxyawi-*, cook them *shapá-ʔat'i-*, and finally eat them *tkʷáta-*.[5] Eating is the culmination of the process as well as its motivating goal.

At each step of this sequence one may ask again, how? For example, "How do you 'cook' them?" *míshniki-nam á-shapaʔat'i-xa*? The answers reveal a set of alternative cooking techniques differentially appropriate to various roots. Camas (*Camassia quamash*, liliaceae), for example, must be baked underground *tamáych-*,[6] while *pank'ú (Tauschia hooveri*, umbelliferae) is eaten raw *xapít*. [The cooking step of the sequence is deleted.] The Sahaptin recognition of two distinct varieties of Canby's lomatium (*Lomatium canbyi*, umbelliferae) makes sense when we discover that the first variety is ground, made into dough, then sun-dried as finger cakes *sapíl*, while the other is baked underground. Other ecologically relevant distinctions are revealed by asking "where?" "when?" or "by whom?" the roots are dug.

Asking how? to do something does not always produce a description of a sequence of activities involved in completing the action. At some point the answer will be a slightly annoyed "You just do it." This response suggests that the limits of conscious planning have been reached (or the limits of one's informant's patience). For example, eating ultimately involves a complex sequence of jaw motions, the control of which is largely outside of conscious awareness. Chewing is an atomic activity at the conscious level. Digging likewise involves such atomic physical actions as grasping the digging stick, bending, lifting, and twisting. Such atomic units may be incorporated into a variety of molar activities and are thus not particular to an ethnographic account of such activities. Our ethnoecological description need not proceed beyond this level of detail.

In other situations the question how? may generate a list of alternatives requiring a decision as to which is preferred. For example, "How should one fish?" in the Sahaptin Plan is a question that implies alternative technologies appropriate to the time and place and to the species sought. One fishes by hook-and-line or bone choker; with a spear, dip net, or set net; by weir or trap. To accomplish the task of fishing one must first select an appropriate way to fish. A "hierarchical decision tree" (Gladwin 1980) may be required to describe this segment of the Plan.

As should now be clear, a discussion of folk classification restricted to aspects of perceptual similarity will be woefully incomplete as an account of the Sahaptin Image of their natural environment. The Image includes not only the cultural knowledge of what a plant or animal looks like (which is put to use in identification subplans), but also a representation of the plant or animal in its characteristic cultural contexts. The Sahaptin Image of camas would call to mind not only a collectivity of similar plants but also a scene in which camas plays a central role. We would see in our mind's eye a vernal meadow in summer, full of mature camas, with Indian women actively engaged in uprooting the plants with their digging sticks. In the background of the picture would be other plants and animals characteristic of meadows, ecological associates of camas. We would imagine the underground ovens being prepared. We would be reminded of the firewood, the heating stones, and the various plants used to cover and flavor the baking camas, things that are characteristically part of these activities.

An appropriate data structure for representing this knowledge is an "event" (Agar 1974) or an "episode," as in theories of episodic memory preferred by Shank and Abelson (1977: 17–19), a kind of "schema" (Neisser 1975; Casson 1983) rather than a taxonomy. We would, of course, also recall the camas plant itself, its spike of large blue flowers, its sheathing cluster of leaves, its onionlike bulb pulled fresh from the ground. While a taxonomic structure may be abstracted from such information, such information is also required by the Plan whenever an identification is required to select or enact a Plan segment. We might be reminded of the death camas (*Zigadenus spp.*, liliaceae), a deceptively similar plant. Perceptual similarity is important in this instance because it implies contrasting functional patterns for the two similar items; eat one, carefully avoid the other. Thus similarity and contiguity both play important roles in the Image. Even our plans are reflected in our Image of the environment, as our own activities take place in that environment and are thus incorporated reflexively in the Image.

A cultural Plan is a complex entity, a hierarchical organization of subplans each dominating either a sequence of subsidiary activities or a set of alternatives from which a choice of action must be made (Randall 1977). It is possible to move around in the cultural Plan by systematic questioning, using basic question frames, which are probably linguistic universals. For example, why? moves "the cursor" upward; how? moves it downward through the Plan hierarchy. Each subplan, whether step or alternative, may be expressed as a natural language sentence in which the action or state is indicated by a verbal predicate, the arguments of which include associated actors, objects, implements, and settings indicated by nominal elements marked for case—candidates for status as linguistic universals (Fillmore 1968).

CONCLUSIONS

I have argued for an ethnoecology that unites cognitive anthropology and cultural and evolutionary ecology. I believe this approach answers the most important criticisms that have been raised against each field. Cognitive anthropology's focus on the individual actor who, guided by cultural knowledge, designs a plan for living, is joined with the ecologists' appreciation of the complex web of mutual influence linking individuals and the elements of their natural and social environments. Ecology may also contribute a vision of the encompassing evolutionary processes that govern all life. Cognitive anthropol-

Figure 8.2   Getting the Morning Coffee

ogy contributes a method and conceptual framework for understanding the powerful role of culture in evolution. Culture is seen to be an evolutionary mechanism in its own right, capable of independent replication and subject to selection processes distinct from those governing genetically coded information (Dawkins 1976; Durham 1982; Boyd and Richerson 1985), transformed by the power of human language as a medium of symbolic communication.

I have offered a series of examples to illustrate the application of this view of culture to phenomena of ecological significance. In these examples I have sketched the outline of a theory of culture as a symbolic means for adapting to a changing environment. The theory is closely related to models of human understanding developed in the study of artificial intelligence and in cognitive psychology but is informed by the wider perspective of ethnography. I believe we cannot hope to understand cultural evolution adequately without such a theory of human understanding based in human language use, for that is the locus of the cultural analog of DNA.

The model of culture sketched here is an organization of ideas. The ideas are concatenated in a variety of data structures in memory, both semantic and episodic. Episodic structures, called variously "scripts" or "plans," are stressed here, as they reflect in the Image our experience of significant events as well as the cultural plans that we use to construct our behavior (see Figure 8.2). There is a necessary parallel between the structure of such plans and the structure of sentences in natural language, as human language is the primary means we have of representing to ourselves the reality to which we must adapt.

Detailed and particularistic ethnographic description will be necessary as the basis for generalizations about the effectiveness of cultural practices. The analysis of specific cultural plans should also reveal recurrent patterns of form and content relevant to our understanding of cultural evolutionary processes.

Cultural evolution is ultimately the result of changes in the way individuals choose to pursue the goals set by their cultural Plan, changes that may subsequently alter the goals themselves. Cultural evolution is a process sensitive to nuances of environmental variation continuously reflected in the cultural Image. By such a process our ancestors may have been led to substitute — step-by-step — agricultural strategies for those of hunting and gathering, as Pacific Northwest Indians substituted the white man's potatoes for the native camas and planting of crops for the care of stands of wild plants (Suttles 1951). Likewise, market production superseded subsistence production, and wage labor in cities overcame household production. In sum, I believe our comprehension of the course of human history requires that we first understand cultural adaptation in terms of human individuals engaged in the familiar routines of everyday life.

NOTES

My research on Sahaptin ethnobiology, which has informed much of this discussion, was made possible by grants from the National Science Foundation (BNS 76–16914), the Melville and Elizabeth Jacobs Research Fund (Whatcom Museum Foundation), the Graduate School Research Fund (University of Washington), and the Phillips Fund of the American Philosophical Society. I would like to thank especially my primary Sahaptin consultants, James and Delsie Selam, Sara Quaempts, Elsie Pistolhead, and the late Don Umtuch. I am grateful for comments from Brent Berlin, Morris Freilich, and Eric A. Smith on careful readings of earlier drafts of this chapter. The primary intellectual stimulus for the viewpoint promoted here is the work of Robert Randall. However, interpretive inadequacies are entirely my own. Andie Palmer helped with the graphics.

1. Geertz entertained this analogy briefly in his essay on "Religion as a Cultural System" in *The Interpretation of Cultures*, pp. 92–93, but has not, to my knowledge, capitalized upon it.

2. By "things" I mean to include not only material objects but also events and relationships.

3. Sahaptin is a Penutian language spoken today by several hundred Indians in south central Washington and north central Oregon. My research pertains most directly to the dialects of that language spoken by Columbia River Indians whose ancestral winter villages were located on the Columbia River between Celilo Falls and the Umatilla River.

4. Note the polysemy of *xni-t* used to describe both the action of digging roots and the sequence of activities of which that is the focal segment. It is a nomenclatural pattern with close parallels elsewhere (Agar 1974; Berlin 1976).

5. The verbs are cited in their unmodified stem form. Transitive stems such as these would be inflected to indicate impersonal subject and plural object by adding the prefix *á-* and for continuing action in the present by the suffix *-sha*, thus *á-xni-sha* "you are digging [roots]."

6. The adaptive value of such processing has been demonstrated by Konlande and Robson's nutritional analyses (1972).

REFERENCES

Abelson, Robert P.
1981   "Psychological Status of the Script Concept." *American Psychologist* 36: 715–29.
1976   "Script Processing in Attitude Formation and Decision Making." In *Cognition and Social Behavior*, J. S. Carroll and J. W. Payne, eds. Hillsdale, N. J.: Lawrence Erlbaum.

Agar, Michael
1974   "Talking About Doing: Lexicon and Event." *Language in Society* 3: 83–89.

Basso, Keith
1972   "Ice and Travel among the Ft. Norman Slave: Folk Taxonomies and Cultural Rules." *Language in Society* 1: 31–49.

Berlin, Brent
1978   "Ethnobiological Classification." In *Cognition and Categorization*, E. Rosch and B. Lloyd, eds. Hillsdale, N. J.: Lawrence Erlbaum.
1976   "The Concept of Rank in Ethnobiological Classification: Some Evidence from Aguaruna Folk Botany." *American Ethnologist* 3: 381–99.

Berlin, Brent, Dennis E. Breedlove, and Peter H. Raven
1973   "General Principles of Classification and Nomenclature in Folk Biology." *American Anthropologist* 75: 214–42.

Boulding, Kenneth E.
1956   *The Image: Knowledge in Life and Society.* Ann Arbor: University of Michigan Press.

Boyd, Robert, and Peter J. Richerson
1985.   *Culture and the Evolutionary Process.* Chicago: University of Chicago Press.

Bruner, Jerome S., Jacqueline J. Goodnow, and George A. Austin
1956   *A Study of Thinking.* New York: Wiley.

Casson, Ronald W.
1983   "Schemata in Cognitive Anthropology." *Annual Review of Anthropology* 12: 429–62.

Cavalli-Sforza, Luigi, and Marcus Feldman
1981   *Cultural Transmission and Evolution.* Princeton, N.J.: Princeton University Press.

Chomsky, Noam
1959   "A Review of *Verbal Behavior* by B. F. Skinner." *Language* 35: 26–58.

Cloak, F. T., Jr.
1975   "Is a Cultural Ethology Possible?" *Human Ecology* 3: 161–82.

Dawkins, Richard
1976.   *The Selfish Gene.* Oxford University Press, New York.

Durham, William H.
1982   "Interactions of Genetic and Cultural Evolution: Models and Examples." *Human Ecology* 10: 289–323.
1979   "Toward a Co-Evolutionary Theory of Human Biology and Culture." In *Evolutionary Biology and Human Social Behavior*, N. Chagnon and W. Irons, eds. North Scituate, Mass.: Duxbury.

Fillmore, Charles J.
    1977   "The Case for Case Reopened." In *Syntax and Semantics*. Vol. 8. *Grammatical Relations*, P. Cole and J. Sadock, eds. New York: Academic.
    1968   "The Case for Case." In *Universals in Linguistic Theory*, E. Bach and R. Harms, eds. New York: Holt, Rinehart & Winston.

Fowler, Catherine
    1977   "Ethnoecology." In *Ecological Anthropology*, D. Hardesty, ed. New York: Wiley.

Frake, Charles O.
    1962   "Cultural Ecology and Ethnography." *American Anthropologist* 64: 53–59.

Freilich, Morris
    1980   "Smart-Sex and Proper-Sex: A Paradigm Found." *General Issues in Anthropology* 2: 37–51.

Geertz, Clifford
    1973   *The Interpretation of Cultures*. New York: Basic.

Geoghegan, William H.
    1973   *Natural Information Processing Systems. Monographs of the Language-Behavior Research Laboratory*. Berkeley: University of California.
    1970   "Residential Decision Making among the Eastern Samal." Paper presented to the Symposium on Mathematical Anthropology, 69th Annual Meeting of the American Anthropological Association, San Diego.

Gladwin, Christina H.
    1980   "A Theory of Real Life Choice: Applications to Agricultural Decisions." In *Agricultural Decision Making: Anthropological Contributions to Rural Development*, P. Barlett, ed. New York: Academic.

Goodenough, Ward H.
    1957   "Cultural Anthropology and Linguistics." In *Report of the Seventh Annual Round Table Meeting on Linguistics and Language Study*, P. L. Garvin, ed. Georgetown University Monograph Series on Languages and Linguistics, No. 9. Washington, D.C.

Harris, Marvin
    1979   *Cultural Materialism: The Struggle for a Science of Culture*. New York: Random House.
    1974   "Why a Perfect Knowledge of All the Rules One Must Know to Act Like a Native Cannot Lead to the Knowledge of How Natives Act." *Journal of Anthropological Research* 30: 242–51.

Hunn, Eugene S.
    1982   "The Utilitarian Factor in Folk Biological Classification." *American Anthropologist* 84: 830–47.
    1976   "Toward a Perceptual Model of Folk Biological Classification." *American Ethnologist* 3: 508–24.

Kay, Paul
    1971   "Taxonomy and Semantic Contrast." *Language* 47: 866–87.
    1970   "Some Theoretical Implications of Ethnographic Semantics." In *Current Directions in Anthropology*, Bulletins of the American Anthropological Association 3 (3, part 2).

Keesing, Roger
1974   "Theories of Culture." *Annual Review of Anthropology* 3: 73–98.

Konlande, J. E., and J. R. K. Robson
1972   "The Nutritive Value of Cooked Camas as Consumed by Flathead Indians."
        Ecology of Food and Nutrition 2: 193–95.

Miller, George A., Eugene Galanter, and Karl H. Pribram
1960   *Plans and the Structure of Behavior.* New York: Holt, Rinehart & Winston.

Neisser, Ulrich
1975   *Cognition and Reality: Principles and Implications of Cognitive Psychology.*
        San Francisco: Freeman.

Ortner, Sherry B.
1984   "Theory in Anthropology since the Sixties." *Comparative Studies in Society
        and History* 26: 126–66.

Pike, Kenneth
1956   "Towards a Theory of the Structure of Human Behavior." In *Estudios
        Publicados en Homenaje al Doctor Manuel Gamio.* Mexico, D. F.: Sociedad
        Mexicana de Antropologia.

Pulliam, H. Ronald, and C. Dunford
1980   *Programmed to Learn: An Essay on the Evolution of Culture.* New York:
        Columbia University Press.

Randall, Robert A.
1987   "Plans and Planning in Cross-Cultural Settings." In *Blueprints for Think-
        ing: The Role of Planning in Psychological Development*, S. L. Friedman,
        E. K. Scholnick, and R. R. Cocking, eds. New York: Cambridge University
        Press.

1977   "Change and Variation in Samal Fishing: Making Plans to 'Make a Living' in
        the Southern Philippines." Ph.D. diss. University of California, Berkeley.

1976   "How Tall Is a Taxonomic Tree? Some Evidence for Dwarfism." *American
        Ethnologist* 3: 543–53.

Randall, Robert A., and Eugene S. Hunn
1984   "Do Life Forms Evolve or Do Uses for Life? Some Doubts About Brown's
        Universals Hypotheses." *American Ethnologist* 11: 329–49.

Richerson, Peter J.
1977   "Ecology and Human Ecology: A Comparison of Theories in the Biological
        and Social Sciences." *American Ethnologist* 4: 1–26.

Rosch, Eleanor
1978   "Principles of Categorization." In *Cognition and Categorization*, E. Rosch and
        B. Lloyd, eds. Hillsdale, N.J.: Lawrence Erlbaum.

Ruyle, Eugene E.
1973   "Genetic and Cultural Pools: Some Suggestions for a Unified Theory of
        Biocultural Evolution." *Human Ecology* 1: 201–15.

Schank, Roger
1975   *Conceptual Information Processing.* Amsterdam: North Holland.

Schank, Roger, and Robert Abelson
1977   *Scripts, Plans, Goals, and Understanding.* Hillsdale, N.J.: Lawrence
        Erlbaum.

Silverstein, Michael

1976   "Shifters, Linguistic Categories, and Cultural Description." In *Meaning in Anthropology*, K. Basso and H. Selby, eds. Albuquerque: University of New Mexico Press.

Smith, Eric A.

1984   "Anthropology, Evolutionary Ecology, and the Explanatory Limitations of the Ecosystem Concept." In *The Ecosystem Concept in Anthropology*, E. F. Moran, ed. American Association for the Advancement of Science Selected Symposia Series. Boulder, Colo.: Westview Press.

Sturtevant, William C.

1964   "Studies in Ethnoscience." In *Transcultural Studies in Cognition*, A. K. Romney and R. G. D'Andrade, eds. *American Anthropologist* 66(3, part 2): 99–131.

Suttles, Wayne

1951   "The Early Diffusion of the Potato among the Coast Salish." *Southwestern Journal of Anthropology* 7: 272–88.

PART III

CULTURE AND PRACTICAL ISSUES

If it can be shown that culture directly affects many practical issues, the argument "culture is still relevant" becomes much stronger. This is precisely what we attempt to do in Part III. Although it could be shown that all important aspects of life are in some way related to culture, space limitations permit us to deal only with four issues: suicide, nursing, public policy decisions, and policing.

A bird in the hand, it is commonly believed, is worth two in the bush. This belief can be generalized into: Existence "in hand" (the known life on earth) is worth more than possible existence after death (the unknown life in heaven). Given this perspective, suicide becomes a very enigmatic act (cf. Stack 1987). Yet more enigmatic are acts of suicide which attempt to pass as accidents or unfortunate consequences of attempts to reach some nonsuicidal goal. If the goal really is to take one's own life, why hide or mask the act?

In America, and in other technologically advanced societies, there are many who sit behind a steering wheel and woo death. In some cases those who try to mask their own suicide kill innocent bystanders. A better understanding of masked suicide, clearly, has much practical value.

Why do people take their own lives? Why do they sometimes mask this act? In what manner are suicidal acts masked? These and related issues are analyzed in Karin Andriolo's chapter, "Masked Suicide and Culture." Suicide, an important sociological topic — at least since the classic study of Durkheim (1951) — is here shown to be an equally important cultural topic.

The relevance of culture to understanding health has long been known (Kiev 1964; Lebra 1976; Rack 1982). And those who so believe are not just social scientists. Dr. Jerome Frank wrote over two decades ago:

> [T]he physician must be more than a skilled technician if he is to help many of his patients. The importance of cultural and spiritual factors in disease and healing is seen clearly in the chronically ill. . . . To rehabilitate him, the physician must not

> only treat his body but inspire his hopes, mobilize his environment on his behalf, and actively help him resume a useful place in society. (1964: ix)

More recently Leon Eisenberg and Arthur Kleinman present a more general statement concerning the value of social science for health practices:

> As physicians, we believe that the biomedical sciences have made. . . important contributions to better health. At the same time we are no less firmly persuaded that a comprehensive understanding of health and illness, an understanding that is necessary for effective preventive and therapeutic measures, requires equal attention to the social and cultural determinants of the health status of human populations. (1981: ix)

Like other health professionals, nurses also appreciate the importance of understanding the culture of individuals seeking health care. Sharleen Simpson, a nurse and an anthropologist, carefully and thoughtfully spells out why culture is important for nursing. Nurses working in communities with culturally diverse populations find themselves enmeshed in three culturally related problems. First, in dealing with patients of another culture there will always be problems of communication. Second, such patients will have a variety of different beliefs about illness and health, so that beyond purely linguistic problems of communication, there will be belief-linked problems. As anthropologists have long known, "A rose is *not* a rose is *not* a rose." It all depends — on the meanings, the beliefs, and the feelings attached to roses. Finally, a variety of problems exist linked to the costs of health care, and particularly so for immigrants and those living in cultures with high levels of poverty.

Simpson's analysis of how "culture can affect the delivery of health care by nurses" is both enlivened and given much depth by case studies. She provides fascinating insights into the problems and pressures of working with Aymara and Quechua Indians in Bolivia, Mennonites in Central America, Mexican-Americans in East San José, California, and Korean women in United States hospitals. Simpson also describes the unenviable task of mediating between the American public health bureaucracy and a Mexican-American community. Her final statement merits much thought: "We live in a shrinking world. It is important that we understand our neighbors because the health of one affects the health of all."

Yes, the world is shrinking, and the health of one does affect the health of all. Indeed the word health is usefully considered in a very general way. As our neighbors take risks they consider reasonable, and as we do the same, we can jointly inflict disastrous damage on each other. In "The Relevance of Culture to Science and Technology Policy," Steve Rayner tackles the very difficult problem of culture and technological decision making. He argues that the conflicts over science and technology policy are best understood when we take culture into consideration and when culture is conceptualized as a social control system. His argument commences with an exposition of the role of cultural preferences within applied science with respect to policy. A case study follows. Here we are shown how different cultural preferences for fairness and trust shape the acceptability of new nuclear power technologies. This shaping by culture is discussed with respect to utility companies, public-utility commissions, and public-interest groups. Rayner's chapter concludes with some implications of the cultural approach to technological decision making for international environmental issues.

As might be expected, the editor gets to say the "last word." In "Proper Rules, Smart Rules, and Police Discretion," Frank Schubert and I argue that culture is very relevant to important issues in policing. The issue we deal with is "the gap" — the distance between what the law dictates and what the police tend to do. Our argument is, perhaps, somewhat unusual for social scientists. The unstated postulate is that police officers do an important job, often in spite of the law. Policing problems, it is suggested, are usefully considered within a framework I have called "Smart/Proper Analysis" (Freilich 1988). Smart/Proper Analysis (SPA) presents a theory of action based on the human dilemma. The fundamental problem we all face as humans is more complex than "To be or not to be!" The dilemma identified by Shakespeare is actually part of a larger one, a dilemma which at times asks the existential question, but which more often asks a methodological question. What humans most often want to know is not whether to die, but how to live. And their how-to-live question boils down to two major choices. They can live properly and reap the rewards of dignity, social acceptance, and peace of mind. Or they can live smartly and maximize their chances of survival and success. The human dilemma, in short, is — To be proper or to be smart! Following the proper, it should be noted, does not always lead to physical survival. In every culture some people get into situations where, in order to maintain dignity, it is necessary to commit suicide in a proper manner (see chapter 9).

In dealing with the human dilemma police officers, like everybody else, juggle the proper with what they, and the officers they regularly work with, jointly define as the smart. As if juggling two sets of rules does not provide enough of a challenge, police officers, like everybody else must also deal with a third set, "rules of thumb." Decision making, mired in the human dilemma, is actually more agonizing than just selecting one way from two desirable ways. Decision making must now be seen as choosing one out of three types of rules: (1) rules developed and belonging to the whole society, cultural rules which identify proper action; (2) rules developed and belonging to the group one works with, social rules which identify smart action; or (3) rules developed by the person acting, personal rules which identify what works for the actor. An if this is not complex enough, it is necessary to add that decision making has two purposes: to pick a goal for action and to select the means by which to reach the goal picked. Given two purposes for action, goal selection and means selection, and given the possibility of picking from three rule types for each for each purpose, it is possible to identify nine decision-making strategies.

"Proper Rules, Smart Rules and Police Discretion" explains these nine strategies with the aid of nine short cases. It is hypothesized that the strategy police officers use most frequently is *smart means used for proper goals*. This and several related hypotheses direct attention to variables considered critical in decision making: risks taken, protection for assumed risks by peers ("veil of secrecy") and by superiors (the "blind eye response"), and relationships between risks and possible rewards. In short, it is argued that the gap can be shrunk rather than eliminated. Further, culture — considered as principles and rules for proper action — can become an important shrinking agent.

REFERENCES

Durkheim, Émile
    1951   *Suicide*. A. Spalding and G. Simpson, trans. New York: Free Press.
Eisenberg, Leon, and Arthur Kleinman, eds.
    1981   *The Relevance of Social Science for Medicine*. Dordrecht, Holland: D. Reidel.
Frank, Jerome D.
    1964   Foreword to *Magic, Faith and Healing*, Ari Kiev, ed. New York: Free Press.
Freilich, Morris
    1989   "The Smart, the Proper, and Deviance." In *Deviance: Cross-Cultural Perspectives*, Morris Freilich et al., eds. Granby, Mass.: Bergin & Garvey.
Kiev, Ari, ed.
    1964   *Magic, Faith, and Healing: Primitive Psychiatry Today.* New York: Free Press.
Lebra, William, ed.
    1976   *Culture Bound Syndromes: Ethnopsychiatry and Alternate Therapies.* Honolulu: University Press of Hawaii.
Rack, Philip
    1982   *Race, Culture, and Mental Disorder*. London: Tavistock.
Stack, Steven
    1987   "Celebrities and Suicide: A Taxonomy and Analysis, 1948–1983." *American Sociological Review* 52: 401–12.

9

MASKED SUICIDE AND CULTURE

Karin R. Andriolo

Albert Camus began his book on *The Myth of Sisyphos* with the words:

> There is but one truly serious philosophical problem, and that is suicide. Judging whether life is or is not worth living amounts to answering the fundamental question of philosophy. (1955: 3)

In my student days, propelled by these sentences, I read the entire book. Not that I really believed there could be one serious philosophical problem only. Rather, I was intrigued by the ambivalent attribution of dominance in the relation between the writer and the reader of a text, which is hinted at in these lines. On the one hand, they manifest the supreme arrogance of the writer who declares that the question which burns in his mind is, indeed, the question which has precedence over all others and who claims that his book will usher the reader to the very fountainhead of understanding. On the other hand, they also convey the writer's plea that the book he is placing before the reader must occupy a privileged position in the reader's universe, so as to justify the ardor that engendered it.

As I grew older and fonder of mediating oppositions, or bypassing them as it were, Camus's dictum on the centrality of suicide within our understanding of human existence came to spell a concern different from the question whether the significance of a text is borne out by its creation or by its acceptance: Where should we begin when we distill human existence into a text, when we attempt to verbalize its parameters and their interrelations? Or, to state this question in its specifically anthropological form, where do we start to unravel the tapestry of culture into which human existence is woven? Is there a single gateway beyond which the entire landscape of culture lies open before the traveler? Of course not. Too many books have led us toward precious vistas from diverse starting points, each leaving us off at the edge of a wilderness still to be explored. Rather than being achieved from any privileged starting point, the exploration of culture is carried through by tenacity, by not stopping short of yet another turn in the road.

And as I invoke Camus's opening sentences to his study of the absurd at the beginning of my essay on suicide and culture, I do so for the purpose of stating just this modest claim: Suicide can be as good a topic as any other for leading to an understanding of human existence within culture; and the topic of suicide can provide a very good lead, indeed, if we do not lose track either of the complexities of suicide or of those of culture.

Twice suicide has made a grand entry into anthropological research, that is, it was linked to the general question of cultural similarities and differences. Both times it reverted into the ethnographies of particular peoples.

The first cross-cultural exploration of suicide, by Steinmetz (1894), was precipitated by the question whether the act occurs in all human societies or whether, perhaps, primitive man is exempted from the drive toward self-destruction. The question reflected the autumnal glow of the Western dichotomy between the noble savage whose earthy culture does not instill unfulfillable desires and civilized man corrupted by his evolutionary hubris. Steinmetz and, shortly thereafter, Westermarck (1908) confirmed that suicide was not exclusive to civilization and its discontents. These comparative surveys taught us not to project our longing for a state of paradise onto the Primitive. Yet, since they merely enumerated those cultures for which occurrences of suicide had been reported, they taught us little about either culture or suicide.

At about the same time, Durkheim published his pioneering study (1897). If culture was to make a difference, then it was not in the manner of a digital switch between occurrence and nonoccurrence, but with respect to the frequency of suicide. On the basis of statistics from European countries, Durkheim assumed that the frequency within a given society or subgroup thereof is fairly constant. The task was, then, to account for the social rate of suicide and to determine its, presumably, social causes. And here I paraphrase Douglas's excellent condensation of Durkheim's meandering argument.

Individual behavior reflects three orientations toward society: aloofness, submissiveness, and rebelliousness. The balance among these three orientations is a necessary prerequisite for the functioning of every group, and when any of the three orientations is not restrained adequately by the other two, suicidogenetic factors ensue. The quantity of imbalance determines the rate of suicide, and the quality of imbalance — whether a weak social integration increases aloofness, an overly strong social integration amplifies submissiveness, or a lack of control over the individual's passions encourages rebelliousness — determines the type of suicide which will occur, that is, the egoistic, the altruistic, or the anomic type (Douglas 1967: 39–40, 53).

Durkheim's focus on social determinants and the interpretative centrality he ascribed to social integration linked suicide to culture, to a narrow slice of culture, that is. The preoccupation with causes distracted attention from other significant aspects of culture such as the institutions, beliefs, and expectations from which derive motivations for suicide and the scope of its consequences within a community. Furthermore, social integration was ill defined, as many a sociologist has pointed out with the mixture of exasperation and glee that colors our critique of the giants on whose shoulders we stand.

I do not imply that Durkheim should have taken care of all this in his pioneering paradigm. Rather, anthropologists who subsequently applied his thesis to their exotic data were, potentially, in a position to extend the role of cultural factors and to operationalize the concept of social integration by means of analytic models from their own discipline. They did not, but arranged their data safely into his three types.

The very factor which prompted this conservative choice restricted the range of cultural data it could accommodate. Durkheim had based his analysis on suicide statistics. The scientific aura of numerical tabulations enticed anthropologists, whose discipline suffers from a methodological inferiority complex, to straightjacket their findings into statistical correlations. But little was to be gained from trading qualitative breadth for quantitative rigor. Suicide is a rare phenomenon which anthropologists, furthermore, studied in small-scale societies. The fewness of cases skewed the significance of statistical correlations and humbled interpretative ambitions.

Meanwhile, plentiful and substantive data on suicide in specific societies have accumulated. If we are to probe anew the relation between suicide and culture, we should select a research strategy by means of which we can utilize the full range of information inherent in these data. As a first step I suggest a conceptualization of suicide that concurs with a view of culture as a problem-solving system. As Freilich points out in the introduction to this volume, the problem-solving aspect of culture was already implicit in Tylor's approach; it was made explicit in the functional paradigm and passed on to contemporary approaches of both the materialistic and the cognitive kind.

Predominantly, suicide has been perceived as an *event* that takes place within culture. Yet, suicide is also a *phenomenon that exists*, before and after the specific event, *in the cultural imagination*. The occurrence of a suicide triggers in others interpretations, reactions, ways of coming to terms with it that, though latent, were there all along. Whether people judge the act as appropriate, understandable, blundering, or irresponsible, what motives they ascribe to it, how the corpses of suicides are treated, what fate is envisioned for their souls, and whether their relatives have to undergo purifying rituals — all this is drawn from a culturally constructed understanding of the phenomenon. Borrowing Geertz's felicitous phrase, cultures hold models of and for suicide (1966: 7–9).

The constituent elements of these models derive from the dominant associations which the event of suicide evokes in our mind. A death, even that of a stranger out there, reminds us of our own mortality. A death that is self-inflicted, voluntary, and intended raises issues of choice and alternatives. It releases our awareness of life from its taken-for-granted latency, since both the desirability and the sustainability of life have been questioned. The one who chooses to leave the community of others impels them to fear the erosive traction of his example or to reconfirm the values of their communal existence.

Thus, the cultural model places suicide into the context of death versus life and submerges attention to the individual who performs it into concern with the group in whose midst the act is performed. It is a model constructed by society and in the interest of society, a model that functions for those who do *not* commit suicide. From the individual's perspective, suicide is the solution to a problem; from society's perspective, suicide creates a problem that must be solved.

The dialectic between life and death, individual and society, is spelled out in attitudes toward suicide which, I suggest, shall constitute the primary data for this study. Attitude, however, is a term that merits clarification.

I consider it useful to discern two principal aspects of attitudes, in analogy to the familiar distinction of cognitive data into beliefs and values. The first aspect is the culture-specific understanding of suicide. It comprises the cultural beliefs about the nature of suicide, the attempt to define the phenomenon in terms of its causes and effects, motivations and meanings. The second aspect is the culture-specific evaluation of suicide. It represents the moral judgment on suicide that prevails in a culture; it can be divided into a positive evaluation, ranging from sympathy to approval to glorification, and a negative evaluation, ranging from a reaction of embarrassed silence to explicit moral or legal condemnation.

On first view it appears that attitudes are relative, that understandings of suicide constitute diverse combinations of motives, methods, and circumstances which are evaluated differently in different cultures and times. However, I propose that the following correlation between evaluations and understandings applies transculturally. A positive evaluation of suicide is based upon two aspects of its understanding, namely: (1) The cessation of life is not to be the principal purpose of a suicide, rather it is a means for the confirmation of cultural values; and (2) Suicide ought to maintain rather than rupture relations with others, that is, social and/or supernatural relations. If these conditions are not met, if suicide is understood to lack both a transformational and a relational component, it is evaluated negatively.[1]

Let me illustrate the utility of this hypothesis with an example. Traditional Japanese society, until late into the nineteenth century, held an overall positive evaluation of suicide which varied in degree, however, depending upon the particular type of suicide performed. Most honorable was *seppuku*, self-disembowelment and subsequent beheading by an attendant. It was followed, in descending order of prestige, by the love-pact suicide (*shinju*), the suicide of an impoverished family (*oyako shinju*), and, finally the lonely self-killing of an individual tired of living (*jisatsu*).[2] This evaluation is based on a number of factors which constitute the Japanese interpretation of suicide, that is, the culture-specific understanding of its causes and consequences and the expectations governing its execution.

Suicide relates to the framework of Buddhist thought, which denies the status of ultimate reality to the things of this world and to the consciousness of the self and which advocates a detachment from life and a calm acceptance of death as a gateway to the merger of oneness with allness.[3] Thus, suicide is a means of transformation; the life that it rejects is nothing that ought to be dear to anyone or lived out with fervor, as it is merely suffering and illusion.

While such philosophical notions influence the overall positive evaluation of suicide, its gradation is based upon a concern with social relations. All suicides except *jisatsu*, ranked lowest, stress in their very performance different kinds of relations.

Seppuku emerged in the context of the feudal system and was designed specifically for nobles and warriors. The various motives were: following a master into death, communicating criticism to a superior, expressing indignation about a superior, sacrificing one's life for others, and, finally, expiating a wrongdoing, in which aspect it also functioned as a form of execution that allowed nobles and samurai to preserve their honor.[4]

Thus, all forms of *seppuku* were statements of loyalty, critique, or atonement, addressed to a superior, be he dead or alive, just or in the wrong. In a hierarchy that demanded rigorous subordination, such statements were permissible only because fatal. Death was the price for communicating strong statements to those above, while preserving the honor of both the superior and the inferior. The men, or the women, who committed *seppuku* did not walk out of the system; they confirmed by this very act the feudal order and its rectitude and maintained their relations within it.

Relations, albeit of a different kind, were also central to the love-pact suicide. Its literary prototype presented a young merchant or artisan and his lover, who were prevented from marriage and decided to unite in death. Love-pact suicide, its occurrence as well as its literary appeal, espoused the values of an urban middle class which, to a certain degree, attempted to distinguish itself from the warrior nobility. For the middle class, dignity rested with the ability to be true to one's emotion rather than to one's honor, to be loyal to one's beloved, rather than to the system. The urban and rural poor stressed yet another bond — that within the nuclear family — in their decision to kill themselves and their children when economic pressure threatened familial unity.

The implications of the Japanese data are culture specific as well as transcultural, dependent upon the degree of abstraction employed in their formulation. Culture specific is the notion that suicides are ranked, as are the social classes whose members perform them. Paraphrased for cross-cultural applicability, this means that social status frequently plays a role in attitudes toward suicide, that social status may limit access to the more prestigious forms of suicide.

Culture specific are the philosophical ideas and the social norms that filter into the interpretation of suicide, the Buddhist view on death as transformation, and the hierarchy of relations stressed by the different types of suicide. Yet, transculturally pertinent is the specific correspondence between the evaluative and the interpretative components of attitudes, namely, that between a positive evaluation and a transformational-relational interpretation.

We expect that a society will hold a positive evaluation of suicide only when it considers death to be a means for the achievement of cultural values, rather than to be a goal in itself and when it assumes that the suicidal act maintains rather than severs social and/or supernatural relations. Were suicide understood to be an escape into death, and its consequences to constitute a rupture of the individual's ties with the community and with divine law, it would imply a criticism of society which failed the needs of the individual. Such criticism society is not prepared to accept, since it leaves the survivors with a diffuse sense of guilt and with the fear that, one day, society may fail them as well. A negative evaluation is given to suicides who are deemed a rupture and an escape, thus neutralizing the potential guilt and fear by labeling the suicidal individual as deviant and his criticism as invalid and self-incriminating. The endorsement and the rejection of suicide and their respective corresponding sets of interpretative components are alternative strategies by means of which societies shield themselves from the repercussions of threatening events.

The analysis of the Japanese data reiterated the focal points of my approach to suicide, namely, its social problematic the solution to which is spelled out in attitudes; they stress the supremacy of cultural values and the continuity of social relations by means of a specific correspondence between their evaluative and their interpretative components. Of course, the proposed hypothesis on this correspondence and on its function requires corroboration by means of comparative data. I have attempted this elsewhere.[5] In this chapter the thesis merely provides the context for the analysis of a specific type of suicide which I shall introduce presently while returning to two issues raised by the Japanese example.

Earlier in this chapter I referred to suicide as a death that is self-inflicted, voluntary, and intended. This conforms with the standard definition which differentiates suicide from other forms of death.[6] However, among the variants of *seppuku* I also listed an honorable form of execution. Clearly, voluntarism is lacking there, as it is in other cases in which the authoritative decree that the victim is to perform his own execution is presented as a right befitting his status. Curiously enough, the hemlock which Socrates drank, its mandatory aspect notwithstanding, became the eponym of the American society for voluntary euthanasia. And not every Hindu widow who performed the rite of *sati* threw herself into the flames of her husband's funeral pyre free of any moral or physical coercion.

Neither are we wanting in examples of behavior that is commonly classified as suicide yet does not conform to one of the other two characteristics mentioned. In the event of self-sacrifice or excessive risk taking, the intention to die is questionable, and death may be sought by the hands of others rather than by one's own.

Of course, we could trim with a formalistic shear the amorphous borderline of the phenomenon; we could distinguish between true and marginal suicides and relax in the view of classificatory neatness.

Or we could take up the challenge of an ambivalent reality and consider it telling in two ways. For the insider who lives by cultural models, their ambivalence may be functional, that is, they allow for situational flexibility. For the outsider who analyzes these models, their amorphous margins may throw a contrasting light on their central connotations.

My chief focus here is on a marginal form of suicide in which death is voluntary and intended, yet not self-inflicted, and which is institutionalized in several cultures. Why is this form of suicide institutionalized? What specific purpose does it serve in the context of a problem-solving view on attitudes toward suicide? And while my general thesis on attitudes relates to cultural domain of cognition, this marginal form of suicide will allow me to trace the connection between cognitive and sociostructural factors, which was hinted at in the Japanese example, namely, social status may limit access to certain forms of suicide.

MASKED SUICIDE: THE DEATH OF A WARRIOR

One morning, Fusiwe, the headman of a Yanomamö village, finds his tobacco garden destroyed. It is willful destruction, done by Rashawe, the headman of another village, to provoke Fusiwe into rage and fight.

The Yanomamö live in the Amazonian area of Venezuela. In clearings in the dense rain forest they plant manioc as their main staple. They live in villages which average eighty people. Each family, most commonly a man with two or three wives and their children, inhabits a small hut. The huts are arranged in a circle and are connected by a continuous roof. Their fronts are open and face a large, empty center space, which accommodates the social life of the villagers as well as their guests who are hosted with generous quantities of food and beer brewed from manioc. The formation of intervillage alliances is the long-range purpose of such invitations which also allow men to display their most festive attire, their physical prowess in combative games, and the superiority of their gender. Toward the outside, the circle of huts is protected by a sturdy wall, since warfare among villages is a regular occurrence in Yanomamö life (Chagnon 1968: 25).

Fusiwe had been headman for a long time. His qualities as a man and as a leader were duly recognized by others. He had demonstrated his fierceness, the paramount virtue expected of Yanomamö men, in the past. Now, he could afford to temper his familial and political conduct by an unusual degree of tolerance and diplomacy. In a society in which male supremacy and female repression feed upon each other, the women in Fusiwe's family were frequently listened to, rather than disregarded or beaten. In a society bent on the escalation of violence, Fusiwe performed the headman's moderating function with great sagacity and steered his group successfully through the shifting alliances with other villages.

At other times, Fusiwe would have responded to the provocative destruction of his tobacco garden with diplomacy rather than with militancy. This time, he takes up the challenge angrily and seeks immediate and violent retaliation. He approaches Rashawe's village at dawn to ambush the culprit or a member of his family. A young man comes along the path. He is dear to Fusiwe in whose household he had lived for several years as a prospective son-in-law, in case a girl would be born to Fusiwe. The girl was never born, and, regretfully, the young man left to seek his bride elsewhere. Yet, the young man is also a relative of

Rashawe. Thus, Fusiwe kills him. For a Yanomamö, this course of action is within the expected. For Fusiwe, it is out of line with his character, yet it may relate to the dulled and brooding disposition that has engulfed him of late.

Expecting Rashawe's counter attack, Fusiwe, his family, and his followers leave their village to seek shelter with allies. Sadness, guilt, and the inevitability of his own death tighten around Fusiwe. His companions hurry along the path and leave behind the doomed man, who slows down to meet his fate. They are seen by a woman who informs Rashawe. When Fusiwe rises from his hammock at dawn, he is surrounded by enemy warriors. With proud words and exalted gestures, he attacks and dies in a rain of arrows.

This testimony to the life and death of Fusiwe, which was told by his wife, never mentions the word "suicide."[7] Yet, Fusiwe's actions bespeak the will to die, to kill, and to be killed which constitute the critical components in Karl Menninger's definition of suicide.[8]

It is known from warrior societies that men frequently do not commit suicide by means of self-killing. Rather, they will court death in battle when they are tired of living. Michael Harner reports about the Jívaro of Ecuador who, like the Yanomamö, base their subsistence on horticulture and entrap their lives in fighting and in the anticipation of death:

> In view of the emotional intensity of the feuding, it is not surprising that when a man "no longer wants to live," he does not commit suicide in the ordinary sense, but rather suddenly starts leading assassination raids against the men who are his enemies, insisting on taking the principal risks, such as being the first to charge into the enemy's house. Sooner or later, of course, he will himself be killed, which apparently surprises no one, since his self-destructive bent is seen as evidence that he no longer possesses an *arutam* soul. That this kind of "suicide" appeals to Jívaro men is indicated by the fact that while cases of it are fairly well known, not a single one could be found of self-inflicted suicide by a male. (1972: 181)

The suicide of the warrior in battle was sought by the Jívaro and the Yanomamö in a nonceremonialized manner and without advertising the fatal intention by means of patterned signals. Other societies, like the Indians of the North American plains, exhibited a similar behavior, yet several of them had developed a complex cultural frame that structured such male suicidal actions.

The breeding of horses, the hunt for the buffalo, and warfare were central to the life of Crow Indians. Their social organization provided strong group identifications for individuals—the tribe, the camp, the matrilineal descent group, the military society. Relatively open for individual achievement was the acquisition of status. A man gained his reputation on the basis of skills, mature conduct, and bravery. The destiny revealed to him in the vision quest determined the military society he would belong to and the status he could aspire to. Yet the council of elders had an interpretive control over the signification of his vision and could clip or rechannel his aspirations (Lowie 1935).

A man who was tired of living, because of grief over loved ones who had been killed, because circumstances had thwarted his wishes for achievement, because a sense of impotence made him unable to regain his tainted honor, would proclaim himself a Crazy-Dog-Wishing-to-Die. He would state his intention to members of his family who, at first, tried to discourage him. If he persisted in his resolve, he would communicate this to the entire camp by donning certain paraphernalia, by singing specific songs, and by talking "backwards," that is, he would do the opposite of what he was asked to do. Such behavior meant that the Crazy-Dog pledged himself to dash up to the enemy recklessly and to meet his death during the next season of warfare. He enjoyed considerable prestige in his community, the old women would cheer him on lustily, young women would visit him during the night, even married ones, and their husbands did not seem to mind. The story of a Crazy-Dog killed in battle became a glorious memory of the tribe, while one who was not killed after all would become a laughing stock.[9]

The same is evident among other Indians of the Great Plains. "Hello, you are back? You don't look like a ghost," was the mocking comment that stung a Cheyenne warrior, when he returned from a skirmish with the enemy which he had announced flamboyantly to be his last one (Llewellyn and Hoebel 1941: 164). What varied was the degree of institutionalization:

> The suicide pattern of self-sought death at enemy hands was not so strongly institutionalized among the Cheyennes as it has been found to be with the Comanches. . . . This glorious death, rooted as it was in a military culture, was adequate compensation for the most damaged prestige. It could also be sought by those who had suffered no prestige-loss, but who sought more prestige (or notoriety) and were willing to go over Niagara in a barrel to get it. (Ibid.: 162)[10]

The form of suicide described so far for the Yanomamö, the Jívaro, and the Plains Indians, I call "masked" suicide, and define as follows:

> An individual arranges for a high chance to have himself killed while performing an act which is culturally approved, even highly esteemed; the individual's behavior is guided by a cultural model which synchronizes his actions with the responses of others and which communicates his intention to die, while reinterpreting it as the cost of bravery and as clearly distinct from events of self-killing.[11]

The act of arranging for one's death at the hands of others has been called "indirect" or "vicarious" suicide; the latter is the term used by Devereux (1961: 371). Introducing yet another term is meant to draw attention to two characteristics which are not necessarily included in the broader category of indirect suicide. Masked suicide is patterned and institutionalized rather than individually designed. Moreover, the suicidal intent is eclipsed or camouflaged by the performance of culturally valued rather than deviant behavior.

One case of indirect suicide, in which a person attempts to manipulate someone else into killing him, while behaving in a manner which is idiosyncratic and deviant, took place in the Cajun region in southwestern Louisiana. A man had threatened suicide, and a state trooper responded to the family's call for help. However, the man now threatened the state trooper with his gun, thus effecting his retreat. Subsequently, the man went to the hospital emergency room, taking his gun along; on the way he shot and injured the driver of a passing car. Once in the emergency room, the man had the state trooper summoned again. His gun in reach—not loaded, as it turned out later—he ambivalently tried to provoke the state trooper into shooting him. The incident ended there, as an indirect suicide attempt, since the state trooper's strategy in entering the emergency room prevented the man from reaching for his gun and the state trooper from shooting him in self-defense (Waelde 1984: 12–13).

While the behavior of this man may be akin, on psychological grounds, to that of Fusiwe or of a Crazy-Dog, its cultural implications differ along the line which separates masked suicide from indirect suicide in general. This is not to say that cultural factors are irrelevant in this case. The macho attitude, which is reported as typical for the Cajun, may well have prompted the aggressive circularity with which the man employed his gun, so as to resolve the ambivalence of his death wish in the simultaneous presentation of submissive force and defiant passivity. However, while his actions were fed from the reservoir of cultural impulses, they combined bits and pieces in a manner which is clearly idiosyncratic, pathetic, and deviant in his own culture.

In contrast, the self-reflexive aggression of a Crazy-Dog follows a cultural scenario which integrates his performance with the shared repertory and guarantees applause by billing his self-centered motives as the consequence of altruism. Masked suicide is a cultural rather than an individual strategy for opting out of this life. Yet, why do some cultures provide such an option?

THE FUNCTIONALITY OF MASKED SUICIDE

In my introductory remarks I suggested that the accepting and the rejecting attitudes toward suicide fulfill the same cognitive function for society, insofar as they both stress the values of life and community. While the benefits of attitudes accrue to those who do not kill themselves, the cost is borne by those who do. This cost is alienation. The positive strategy alienates individuals from their suicides, which they have to perform in accordance with a cultural scenario. The negative strategy alienates individuals from society, which dismisses them as deviant.

Alienation from the individualistic design of one's actions is a fact of life-in-culture, a concomitant of maintaining the precarious balance between self and others. It is part of the price we all pay for our social existence, perhaps for good reasons and with a certain equality. In contrast, the label of deviance spells surplus alienation, a burden imposed on the minds of suicidal persons and, frequently, on the social status of their families. Masked suicide is an attempt to mitigate this surplus alienation.

I propose that the institutionalization of masked suicide is to be found in societies that evaluate self-killing negatively and that also provide the opportunity for death-seeking bravery or aggressive self-sacrifice. The latter requires the existence of a militaristic complex, that is, the frequent occurrence and the ideological centrality of warfare and fighting and the definition of male roles and achievements in terms of a warrior ethos. In this case, a suicide that is all but classified as such, that is accomplished as a side effect — however ardently pursued it might be — of actions highly esteemed by society, satisfies both parties involved. The suicidal individual is allowed an honorable retreat, while social values are confirmed rather than repudiated by the camouflaging of the act.

Data from the Philippines demonstrate the proposed connection between the disapproval of self-killing, the warrior ethos, and the recasting of the death wish into a heroic idiom. In the sixteenth century, Islam rapidly expanded over the islands of Southeast Asia, replacing Hindu-Buddhism and various native religions. It was so firmly entrenched in the southern Philippines that it resisted effectively the subsequent expansion of Spanish rule (Kiefer 1972: 3). The Spanish referred to the Muslim tribes summarily as "Moros." The *Quran* strictly prohibits suicide, and an individual committing it has to expect the punishment of hell and social rejection since the act implies betrayal of the religious faith and brings disgrace upon the family. Yet, if a man wished to end his life because he had been shamed, had marital or other difficulties, he could "go *juramentado*." This meant he swore an oath that he would go to a place frequented by Christians and would kill as many as possible in the always realistic hope that he would be killed himself (Ewing 1955: 148–49). His preparations were highly standardized and ritualized. Thomas Kiefer reports on the Tausung, the major ethnic group on the Sulu Archipelago, located between Borneo and Mindanao:

> A person who decided to commit suicide was required to ask permission of the headman, his close kinsmen, and sometimes the sultan. He was given all the rituals of final burial (washing, prayers, purification) while he was still alive; the body would not be recovered and it was necessary to insure that it was prepared to enter paradise. The hair was shaved, the eyebrows plucked, and the penis bound in an upright position in order to insure that he would remain upright and not fall. Special magic would be learned in order to make the person brave. On the morning of the appointed day he would make his way to a Christian settlement (usually Jolo town or Zamboanga), gain entrance to the market, and begin killing with his *kris*. Killing was quite selective: Moslems were excluded if known, and women and children were sometimes spared. The goal was to kill Christian males, preferably soldiers. Since the person was in a complete frenzy of rage, it was sometimes possible for him to dispatch several persons before being brought down. The conduct of ritual suicide was based on the belief . . . that an innocent death brings religious merit to the victim. Since all Christians (particularly the Spanish) were defined as evil, any death at their hands was by definition an innocent death and hence religiously meritorious. The purpose of ritual suicide was not so much to kill Christians as to be killed by them, thus insuring an immediate entrance into paradise. The person who was victimized was snatched up after death by a white horse and conveyed immediately to heaven where his pleasures were multiplied sevenfold, without having first to go to hell. (1972: 133)

An individual's personal plight was thus enveloped in the Islamic concept of the *jihad*, the holy war against nonbelievers, which the Moros had come to emphasize particularly strongly, given their persisting resistance to a "militant

Christian missionary zeal" (Kiefer 1972: 132). This effected a reinterpretation of suicide as being a splendid sacrifice in the line of religious and ethnic duty.

Militant martyrdom has a long history in Islamic cultures and allows for masked suicide in two different ways, providing either a cover for, or a reinterpretation of, self-killing. That Islam promises imminent otherworldly rewards to a fighter killed by the enemy and thus promotes self-sacrificing strategies (as received recent notoriety in Khomeini's Iran and in "suicidal" missions of terrorist squads) is not to be equated with suicide; however, it can provide, in certain cases, a cover for individual suicidal behavior whose self-centered motivations remain hidden. On the other hand, we find institutions like the *juramentado*, which borrow the pattern of militant martyrdom to cloak an overt act of suicide, thus purging it of the disgraceful connotations of self-killing. An example of the former are the Assassins, an example of the latter is Amok.

The Assassins were a small but important Shi'ite sect which flourished from the early twelfth to the mid-thirteenth century in Iran and in Syria. The division between Shi'ites and Sunni is rooted in a disagreement over the descent of the rightful rulers of Islamic societies, and the Assassins terrorized the Sunni establishment by killing selectively some of its leaders. They became known and eponymous in Europe through the horror stories told by the Crusaders. When their struggle against the Sunni failed, their followers gradually changed into a peaceful, law-abiding group. Later, they became know as Isma'ilis, whose religious head is Aga Khan (Lewis 1985). At the height of their terrorist activities, they employed an uncompromising pursuit of martyrdom in the service of their homicidal effectiveness:

> Their emissaries—with negligible exceptions—made no attempt to escape, but died in the accomplishment of their mission. This was indeed part of the mission, and added greatly to the terror which they struck. (Ibid.: 8)

Amok occurs in Malaya, and several scholars have stressed its explicit suicidal connotations.[12] Amok — supposedly the war cry of Malayan pirates (Gimlette and Thompson 1939: 3) — is a murderous frenzy in which a person, always a mature or old man, attacks indiscriminately with a *kris*, until he is beaten down or killed. Ethnopsychiatrists have identified it as "an acute homicidal form of mania" (Kiev 1972: 86). It is triggered by real or imaginary insults, and a sequence of phases builds up to a state of automatism, amnesia, and sudden outbursts of screaming and violent attacks, followed by exhaustion, return of consciousness, and depression (Ibid.: 87).

This violent suicidal reaction to a psychotic crisis is shaped by cultural expectations:

> The unfolding of the drama leaves nothing to chance. Each stage is strictly regulated so that the unfortunate person has nothing to invent: it is sufficient for him to slip into a ready-made cultural pattern. (Baechler 1970: 376)

The popular understanding attributes to Amok the connotations of a ritual — drivenness, inevitability, sacrifice — and considers it with awe.

THE RESTRICTEDNESS OF MASKED SUICIDE

Warfare plays a central role in the three societies from which I originally derived the concept of masked suicide — the Yanomamö, the Jívaro, and the Plains Indians. Ample and detailed data on attitudes toward self-killing are available for the Jívaro and the Plains Indians only. They support our assumption that masked suicide frees individuals from the onus of self-killing. However, they also highlight the inherent restrictedness of this solution.

Among the Jívaro, masked suicide is less ritualized than among the Moros, and neither is their disapproval of "ordinary" suicide as strongly negative. However, the Jívaro clearly distinguish between a warrior's respected resolve to seek death at the hands of the enemy (as noted earlier by Michael Harner) and self-killing by means of poison or, less frequently, by hanging or the use of firearms.[13] Such self-killings arouse sadness, yet their occurrence does not surprise; they are viewed in the light of extenuating circumstances, yet also with a certain contempt. What for the purpose of classification may be labeled a mildly negative evaluation is really a complex layering of judgment and apology, of empathy and condescension, of a sensitivity to restrictive conditions and an arrogant attribution of weakness, with a good bit of ambivalence thrown in. Michael Brown's formulation that among the Jívaro self-killing "is considered a feminine — indeed an effeminate — form of behavior" (1982: 7) helps to sort out the layers of connotations.

Suicides other than masked ones are considered feminine for several reasons. The rate of female suicides is strikingly higher than that of men, and poisoning and hanging are the only means for its execution obtainable by women.[14] The structural position of women allows them fewer alternatives than are available to men for extricating themselves from disagreeable situations (Brown 1986: 324). Since the Jívaro also value strong and prompt emotional reactions, suicide seems a course of action pressed upon women who are caught in the bind between the demand for action and the scarcity of viable ones. The Jívaro response to a woman's suicide expresses their awareness of the structural trap and their willingness to lodge the blame in it. Typically, the kinsmen of a woman who has killed herself

> angrily demanded an explanation from her husband—and they may also seek compensation or exact retribution through a vengeance killing. (Brown 1882: 7)

> A bilingual *maestro* (teacher) turned down an offer of a girl as spouse. Whereupon she took her own life. The teacher was to blame, it was argued, and consequently accused of murder. He was indeed arrested and had to stay in jail for a long time. (Siverts: 6)

While several factors, encapsulated in the descriptive adjective "feminine," constitute a neutral, situation-reflective layer in the Jívaro understanding of suicide, the derogatory variation "effeminate" exposes a second layer of meaning. In a culture that attributes superiority to the male ethos, actions which are typical of women are also typecast as actions which evidence women's inferiority. "Most men seemed content to state that women kill themselves 'because the don't think well' " reports Michael Brown (1982: 13). " 'It does not matter how you treat your wife,' one bewildered man told me. 'Women now kill themselves for no reason' " (Brown 1986: 326). Consequently, "Only young distressed men, who are not yet hunters/warriors, may commit suicide" (Siverts: 31), an expectation which, indeed, is borne out by data on male suicides.

This highlights an important characteristic of masked suicide. It is an institution that functions, primarily, in the context of warfare and fighting and is, by design, exclusive to men. Women's space to maneuver is restricted. To them is left an exit that causes disdain and shame; even if it were to arouse empathy, it is still less prestigious than that open to men.

The choice women are prohibited from making may or may not amount to much. As in other transcultural surveys, we are mapping a range. At its lower end, as among the Jívaro, male suicides are merely spared the pitying shrug reserved for women whose social place and natural endowment, supposedly, predispose them to actions that are commonly expected, yet pathetic. At the opposite end, as in Islamic cultures, female suicides have to anticipate that, in the world they leave behind, shame and disdain will ravage their memory, and in the world they go to, hell will scorch their soul — a fate that is evaded by men who play their game cleverly.

Somewhere in between is the lot of women who committed suicide among the Indians of the Great Plains. The ethnographic record discourages tidy generalizations. Surely, intertribal diversity accounts for a certain range of attitudes toward suicide, the telescoping of which is also offset by diverging reports on the same tribe. For example, the Cheyenne believed that the souls of suicides would not find rest in the afterlife (Hartmann 1973: 137). While the allotment of postmortem punishment usually implies a condemnation of self-killing, we also encounter the more permissive view that "if a Cheyenne chose to take his life, he must have good reason to do so" (Dizmang 1967: 8), and the case studies presented by Llewellyn and Hoebel indicate a motive-based differentiation, according to which some suicides were considered justifiable, others wasteful, unnecessary, and distressing (1941: 316).

I suspect that the seeming incongruity between an unconditionally rejecting view and one tempered by weighing the circumstances of particular cases is not so much a matter of culture change or of embarrassing ethnographic contradictions. Rather, the two ways in which suicide data are elicited may account for this discrepancy. In societies that evaluate suicide negatively, yet not extremely so, informants will describe the general attitude accordingly. However, when they discuss particular cases they are familiar with, they will tend to highlight extenuating circumstances, justifications, empathy with the victim, as is implied, for example, in George Devereux's data on the Mohave (1961: 308–9) and in William Fenton's on the Iroquois (1941: 86). We may thus assume that the overall evaluation of suicide among the Indians of the Great Plains was within the negative range, as it is summarized by Alan Klein, who also contributes further data on the plight of women:

While suicide existed among both sexes, only among the men do we find the acceptable form—a battle-induced form of warrior suicide (Grinnell 1892: 216; Denig 1930: 522). Observers and students of the Plains indicate that suicide in the unacceptable form was punished postmortem regardless of gender; but some point out that while it was considered an abomination, it was far worse an abomination when the subject was a woman. Henry the Younger claimed that while Blackfoot men who took their own lives were punished in the hereafter, the woman guilty of the same offense ". . . is regarded as the most heinous criminal, and never arrives at the Elysian fields; she disappears and is never heard of again" (Henry and Thompson 1898: 529). Or, consider Bradbury's observation on the subject of Dakota suicide; he commented that women committing suicide are condemned to drag the tree from which they hanged themselves around with them forever. He went on to state that rather than cease their actions in the face of such strong sanctions, they "always suspended themselves to as small a tree as possible to sustain their weight" (Bradbury 1906). (Klein 1983: 308–9)

While we tend to philosophize that death is the great equalizer, cultural attitudes bespeak a different social reality and frequently limit access to the "nobler" forms of suicide. While sex roles set limits for masked suicide, social stratification places restrictions on other forms of suicide. In Japan, as shown, styles of suicide are ranked as are the classes whose members performed them. Further examples can be added. From the late Upanishads (approximately fourth century B.C.) until well into the nineteenth century, Indian literature differentiated between two types of suicide. Endorsed and even glorified was the religious suicide, while that committed in ordinary despair was condemned without reservations. This distinction was based on three criteria: the motive for the suicide, the method of its execution, and the state of mind in which it was committed. In an acceptable suicide, a person offered his or her life for a sacred or supraindividual cause, be that to achieve enlightenment, to accompany a husband in death (*sati*), to preserve female sexual honor (*jauhar*, the mass suicide, mostly of women, in the case of military defeat), or to enhance the honor and afterworldly gains of one's family. To accomplish this, starvation, burning, drowning, or jumping from a cliff were recommended, and, throughout, a calm detached state of mind ought to have prevailed. Rejected were self-centered escapes from the problems of personal life. One assumed that they were sired by passion, be it love, anger, pride, despair or fear; hanging or the less frequent use of poison or arms were their means.[15]

However, this distinction did not apply to Brahmins, to members of the highest ranking caste, who could kill themselves for reasons that would have disqualified anybody else, yet still boast an honorable suicide. Disease or great misfortune, but also anger and injured pride were motivations permissible for their suicides only. Also practiced was a custom called "sitting *dharana*"; a Brahmin creditor would sit before the door of his debtor and threaten to starve himself (Thakur 1963: 59, 63–65). This seeming exception to the rule of proper mood and motive receives explanation if we consider that a Brahmin, by virtue of his membership in the caste which is the bearer of *dharma*, or universal order, values, and norms (Dumont 1970: 68), is, by definition, in permanent possession of a proper mental state—dispassionate enlightenment and ritual purity—whatever motivates a particular action.

The strongly negative view on suicide which has dominated Christian Europe since the fifth century was justified, for a long time, on religious grounds. The sin against God became in the nineteenth century primarily a disgrace to the family, whose stigmatization could be circumvented, among the well-to-do at least. Their self-inflicted deaths could be disguised as shooting accidents, heart attacks, or accidental overdoses of medication. Less disguisable were the blunt suicides of the poor and of the servants, accomplished by means of hanging or drowning (Fedden 1972: 249). The duel, practiced among members of the military elite in Europe, possibly provided for men of a certain rank the option to present their death wish as the noble pursuit of honor.

Socioeconomic considerations also draw a baseline for the typical modern guise of suicides as car accidents; these spare the family and assure their receipt of life insurance, as is immortalized in Arthur Miller's play, *Death of a Salesman*.

SUMMARY AND CONCLUSIONS

I have attempted to grasp suicide at the point where it is locked into culture, at the point where an individual's departure from life-among-others marshals the defenses of those who must continue an existence, the desirability and protectedness of which has been called into question. Of course, this is but one among many possible approaches to suicide. It was selected, in part, for reason of resource utilization, for tapping the transcultural significance of ethnographic data which bespeak the social meanings of suicide. It was also selected so as to reveal aspects of the cultural management of problem solving.

Thus, I focused on a form of suicide that can be seen as a solution within a solution. Masked suicide amends an imperfect stratagem, yet remains itself partial, incomplete as well as selective. Consequently, it throws into relief both the functionality and the deficiency of institutions, the benefits and the costs of solutions, the cognitive and the social manipulation of valuations.

Attitudes toward suicide exhibit a transcultural logic. A positive or a negative evaluation of the act is possible, yet each respective evaluation is tied to a specific set of interpretative features. While either set protects society from the guilt and fear which the phenomenon of suicide may arouse, they employ contrasting cognitive strategies. The acceptable suicide demands the *renunciation* of social criticism; the unacceptable suicide renounces the *validity* of social criticism. Both strategies accomplish their social ends; however, their individual costs are different. A negative attitude does not prevent the suicide; it merely burdens the suicidal individual with the stigma of social rejection.

The preceding observation opens the path for masked suicide, which is institutionalized in some of the societies that otherwise reject self-killing. If masked suicide is to be seen as a culture-specific amendment to a solution that does not solve the problem entirely, two lines of inquiry must be pursued: How does it accommodate the transcultural logic outlined above? What are its cultural determinants?

Masked suicide conforms to the transcultural logic while manipulating its terms so as to connote their opposite as well. The escape into death and the rupture of relations are never judged acceptable, yet what is acceptable is never defined as escape or rupture. The abstract logic is always preserved, due to the tautological tie between meaning and judgment. If we were to remain in the realm of cognition, there would be no end to puzzling over the wondrous human ability for *not* calling a spade a spade, while insisting on the significance of spadehood.

Data on masked suicide would suggest that the manipulation of cognitive strategies is determined by sociostructural prerogatives. Three contextual features urge this conclusion: masked suicide is institutionalized in warrior societies; it allows men an honorable retreat; and it disregards the needs of women. Warrior societies provide both incentives and means for relabeling the suicide of men. Their ethos places a high premium on men and protects the interests of their valued members. For them is created an exemption from the stigma of self-killing, and battles offer the opportunity of playing the death-defying role to the hilt of seeking it.[16]

Thus, masked suicide exemplifies that, in the pragmatics of problem solving, cognitive parameters are bent into the service of sociostructural interests. It also demonstrates that, in the course of doing so, the original problem becomes redefined. The cognitive distinction between accepted and rejected suicides safeguards the integrity of society. The institutionalization of masked suicide protects the integrity of society's most valued members. While it is feasible to lift the taint from self-killing and to annul the individual costs of the cultural rejection of suicide, somebody is doomed to serve as the foil for such privileged exemptions. While the despair of men crystallizes into the text of heroic legends, women, perhaps, spend the last moments of a shattered life searching for a tree which is strong enough to carry them, yet light enough to be carried by them forever.

NOTES

An earlier version of this chapter has been published as "Indirect Suicide and Social Status," *Crisis* 8(1): 14–29. I wish to thank James L. Brain, Dorothy Ayers Counts, Christine Ward Gailey, Carole Levin, Roger Mesznik, Benjamin E. Pierce, Douglas Raybeck, and Marleigh Grayer Ryan for their valuable comments on earlier drafts of this chapter. I am grateful to Morris Freilich whose constructive critique has helped me to shape the final version.

1. Robert Jay Lifton, in discussing individually and culturally pertinent connotations of suicide, eloquently stresses both the desire for immortality, and the concern with connections:

> It would seem that all cultures have a place for suicide—recognize it as a human option—along with a certain mixture of awe, terror, and prohibition. That is,

suicide is universally viewed both as possible and a threat to a particular group's definition to human connection. So cultures, religions, governments, and political movements permit, or even embrace, certain forms of suicide, designate specific sets of circumstances and ritual that mobilize suicide on behalf of immortalizing principles. (1983: 245)

However diverse the meanings of induced death in various cultural and historical situations, we should not be blinded to the essential feature of all suicide: its violent statement about human connection, broken and maintained. (1983: 239)

2. See Iga and Tatai (1975); Ohara and Reynolds (1970); Harada (1951); Seward (1968).

3. See Conze (1959: 15–25); Saunders (1964: 52–56, 112–13); Suzuke (1958; 8, 21, 61–62).

4. See Iga and Tatai (1975: 259–60); Seward (1968: 32–39).

5. See Andriolo (1983, 1984a, 1984b).

6. The 1972 *Encyclopedia Brittanica* defines suicide as "the act or insistence of voluntary and intentional self-destruction" (vol.21: 383). Virtually the same definition is given by *Webster's Collegiate Dictionary*, by *The American Heritage Dictionary*, by other dictionary entries, and by many texts on suicide. Durkheim, for example, states that "the term suicide is applied to all cases of death resulting directly or indirectly from a positive or negative act of the victim himself, which he knows will produce this result" (1951: 44).

7. Among the wives of Fusiwe was the daughter of a white settler, who, at the age of twelve, was abducted by Yanomamö. This happened in 1937. Helena Valero lived twenty years among her captors, married to three husbands in succession, the second of whom was Fusiwe. She convinced her third husband to return with her to the life of the whites, hoping that her children would receive a fine education. They never did. Initially, Helena Valero's reappearance made the international headlines, which exploited the dramatic story of Beauty and the Beast, of civilization imprisoned by barbarism. Yet civilization soon forgot the daughter restored to its domain and, returning to its regular agenda, never spilled over Helena Valero the cornucopia of benefits which she so ardently had envisioned and embroidered during the time of her captivity. This woman between two worlds, neither of which she ever inhabited as her own, met the Italian missionary-ethnologist Ettore Biocca. To him she recounted her life, which he published as the book *Yanoáma* (Biocca and Valero 1970; for the account of Fusiwe's death see pp. 225–53).

8. "[S]uicide must be regarded as a peculiar kind of death which entails three internal elements: the element of dying, the element of killing, and the element of being killed" (Menninger 1938: 26).

9. Lowie (1913: 194–96; 1922; 1935: 331).

10. See also Denig (1930: 522); Grinnell (1892: 215); Maynard and Twiss (1969: 67).

11. Of course, such actions could be called excessive risk taking with frequently fatal results. Yet, little insight is to be gained from etching a fine line between suicide and risk taking. The latter seems to be a frequent, if latent, factor of suicides. And Raymond Firth (1961) suggests, on the basis of data from Tikopia, that in some cultures, risk taking is a manifest and salient aspect of suicide.

12. See Baechler (1979: 375–77); Ellenberger (1965: 205); Stoll (1904: 110).

13. Data on Jívaro attitudes toward suicide pose the problem of stemming from different periods of time. Masked suicide is an event of the past, however recent, since increasing contact with white civilization has drastically reduced the occurrence of warfare and raids.

Detailed information on attitudes toward self-killing derive from contemporary fieldwork and may or may not represent an unchanged persistence of past attitudes.

The characterization of attitudes which I present here is based upon the research of Michael Brown (1982, 1986), Jeanne Grover (1973), and Henning Siverts (n.d.) among the Aguaruna Jívaro of Peru.

14. The rate of female : male suicides among the Aguaruna Jívaro is 2 : 1, according to the combined samples of Brown and Grover, which consist of 86 cases within a period from the late 1940s to 1981 (Brown 1986: 313), and 9 : 1, according to Sivert's sample, which consists of ten cases that occurred over a four-year period (Siverts: 6).

15. See Thakur (1963: 51–58, 164–68); Rao (1975: 232–33).

16. Warriors also seem to espouse the surpassing, and even the reversal, of ordinary limits. They judge themselves by a more demanding code, and the suicide-into-sacrifice reversal has its counterpart in turning executions into suicides. Such self-executions were requested from disgraced *samurai* and also occurred in European history; the notorious Colonel Redl, who, prior to World War I, delivered the strategic plans of the Austrian army to Russian intelligence, was expected to shoot himself dutifully.

REFERENCES

Andriolo, Karin
    1984a   "Selbstmord als Krise der Gemeinschaft," in *psychosozial 23: Der Spiegel des Fremden*. Hans-Jürgen Wirth, ed. Reinbek bei Hamburg: Rowohlt.

    1984b   "Accepted and Deviant Suicides," paper presented at the conference on "Deviance in a Cross-Cultural Context," held at the University of Waterloo, Ontario, Canada, June 2–5.

    1983   "The Social Appropriation of Suicide," paper presented at the 23rd Annual Meeting of the Northeastern Anthropological Association.

Baechler, Jean
    1979   *Suicides*. Barry Cooper, trans. New York: Basic.

Biocca, Ettore, and Helena Valero
    1970   *Yanoáma*. Dennis Rhodes, trans. New York: Dutton.

Bradbury, John
    1906   "Bradbury's Travels in the Anterior of America." In *Early Western Travels*. vol. 6. R. G. Thwaites, ed. Cleveland: Arthur Clark.

Brown, Michael
    1986   "Power, Gender, and the Social Meaning of Aguaruna Suicide." *Man* [N.S.] 21: 311–28.

    1982   "The Dark Side of Progress: Suicide Among the Alto Mayo Aguaruna," paper presented at the 44th International Congress of Americanists, Manchester, England.

Camus, Albert
    1955   *The Myth of Sisyphos*. Justin O'Brien, trans. New York: Random House.

Chagnon, Napoleon
    1968   *Yanomamö. The Fierce People*. New York: Holt, Rinehart & Winston.

Conze, Edward
    1959   *Buddhism: Its Essence and Development*. New York: Harper & Row.

Denig, Edwin
  1930   "Indian Tribes of the Upper Missouri." In *Annual Report of the Bureau of American Ethnology*, Bulletin no. 61, J. N. B. Hewitt, ed. Washington, D.C.
Devereux, Georges
  1961   *Mohave Ethnopsychiatry and Suicide: The Psychiatric Knowledge and the Psychic Disturbances of an Indian Tribe. Washington D.C.: Smithsonian Institution.*
Dizmang, L. H.
  1967   "Suicide among the Cheyenne Indians." *Bulletin of Suicidology* (July): 8–11.
Douglas, Jack
  1967   *The Social Meanings of Suicide*. Princeton, N.J.: Princeton University Press.
Dumont, Louis
  1970   *Homo Hierarchicus: An Essay on the Caste System*. Chicago: University of Chicago Press.
Durkheim, Émile
  1897   *Le Suicide*. Paris: Presses Universitaires de France. (*Suicide*. A. Spaulding and G. Simpson, trans. New York: Free Press, 1951.)
Ellenberger, H.
  1965   "Der Selbstmord im Lichte der Ethno-Psychiatrie," in *Selbstvernichtung*. Charles Zwingmann, ed. Frankfurt: Akademische Verlagsgesellschaft.
Ewing, J. F.
  1955   "Juramentado: Institutionalized Suicide among the Moros of the Philippines." *Anthropological Quarterly* 28(4): 148–55.
Fedden, Henry
  1972   *Suicide: A Social and Historical Study*. New York: Benjamin Blom [orig. pub. London: Peter Davis, 1938].
Fenton, William
  1941   "Iroquois Suicide: A Study in the Stability of a Culture Pattern." In *Smithsonian Institution Bureau of American Ethnology Bulletin No. 128*. Anthropological Papers, No. 14: 79–137.
Firth, Raymond
  1961   "Suicide and Risk Taking In Tikopia Society." *Psychiatry* 24(1): 1–17.
Geertz, Clifford
  1966   "Religion as a Cultural System." In *Anthropological Approaches to the Study of Religion*. Michael Banton, ed. New York: Praeger.
Gimlette, J. D., and H. W. Thomson
  1939   *A Dictionary of Malayan Medicine*. London: Oxford University Press.
Grinnell, George
  1892   "Early Blackfoot History." *American Anthropologist* [old series] 5(2): 153–64.
Grover, Jeanne
  1973   *Aguaruna Suicides*. Información de Campo, No. 15a. Dallas, Tex.: Summer Institute of Linguistics. Microfiche.
Harada, Tasuku
  1951   "Japanese Suicide." In *Encyclopedia of Religion and Ethics. vol. II. James Hastings, ed. New York: Scribner's*.
Harner, Michael
  1972   *The Jívaro*. Garden City, N.Y.: Doubleday.

Hartmann, Horst
1973   *Die Plains- und Prärieindianer Nordamerikas.* Berlin: Museum für Völkerkunde.

Henry (The Younger), Alexander, and David Thompson
1898   *New Light on the History of the Greater Northwest.* 2nd vol. Elliot Coves, ed. Minneapolis: Ross & Haines.

Iga, Mamoru, and Kichinosuke Tatai
1975   "Characteristics of Suicides and Attitudes Toward Suicide in Japan." In *Suicides in Different Cultures*, Norman Farberow, ed. Baltimore: University Park Press.

Kiefer, Thomas
1972   *The Tausung: Violence and Law in a Philippine Moslem Society.* New York: Holt, Rinehart & Winston.

Kiev, Ari
1972   *Transcultural Psychiatry.* New York: Macmillan.

Klein, Alan
1983   "The Plains Truth: The Impact of Colonialism on Indian Women." *Dialectical Anthropology* 7(4): 299–313.

Lewis, Bernard
1985   "The Shi'a." *The New York Review of Books* 32(13): 7–10.

Lifton, Robert Jay
1983   *The Broken Connection: On Death and the Continuity of Life.* New York: Basic.

Llewellyn, K. N., and E. Adamson Hoebel
1941   *The Cheyenne Way.* Norman, Okla.: University of Oklahoma Press.

Lowie, Robert
1935   *The Crow Indians.* New York: Farrar & Rinehart.
1922   "Takes-the-Pipe, A Crow Warrior." In *American Indian Life*. Elsie Clews Parsons, ed. New York: Huebsch.
1913   "Military Societies of the Crow Indians." *Anthropological Papers of the American Museum of Natural History*, vol. x, pt. III. New York.

Malinowski, Bronislaw
1926   *Crime and Custom in Savage Society.* London: Kegan Paul.

Maynard, E., and G. Twiss
1969   "'That Those People May Live,' Conditions among the Oglala Sioux of the Pine Ridge Service Unit." Pine Ridge, S.D.: Aberdeen Area Indian Health Service.

Menninger, Karl
1938   *Man Against Himself.* New York: Harcourt, Brace.

Ohara, K., and D. Reynolds
1970   "Love-Pact Suicide." *Omega* 1(2): 159–66.

Rao, Venkoba
1975   "Suicide in India." In *Suicide in Different Cultures*. Norman Farberow, ed. Baltimore: University Park Press.

Saunders, Dale
1964   *Buddhism in Japan.* Philadelphia: University of Pennsylvania Press.

Seward, J.
   1968   *Hari-kiri, Japanese Ritual Suicide*. Rutland, Vt.: Charles Tuttle.
Siverts, Henning
   (n.d.)   "Broken Hearts and Pots: Suicide and Patterns of Signification among the
            Aguaruna Jívaro of Alto Marañón, Peru" Unpublished manuscript. Univer-
            sity of Bergen, Norway.
Steinmetz, S. R.
   1894   "Suicide among Primitive Peoples. *American Anthropologist* 7: 53–60.
Stoll, O.
   1904   *Suggestion und Hyponotismus in der Völkerpsychologie*. Leipzig.
Suzuki, Daisetz Teitaro
   1958   *Zen und die Kultur Japans*. Otto Fischer, trans. Hamburg: Rowohlt.
Thakur, Upendra
   1963   *The History of Suicide in India*. Delhi: Munshi Ram Manoharlal.
Waelde, Lynn
   1984   "Social Meanings of Suicide and Community Networking in a Cajun Parish,"
            paper presented at the 17th Annual Meeting of the American Association of
            Sociology, Anchorage, Alaska.
Westermarck, Edward
   1908   "Suicide, a Chapter in Comparative Ethics." *Sociological Review* 1: 12–33.

10

NURSING AND CULTURE AT THE END OF THE TWENTIETH CENTURY

Sharleen H. Simpson

Although the impact of culture on health has been emphasized by health professionals only since the middle 1950s and early 1960s, it has become an extremely important concept to nurses. In fact, as early as 1937, the National League of Nursing (NLN) recommended that nursing students take at least ten semester hours in the social sciences, and in 1977 the NLN mandated the inclusion of cultural content in nursing curricula (Dougherty and Tripp-Reimer 1985). Nursing is concerned with "the diagnoses and treatment of *human responses* to actual or potential health problems," in contrast to medicine which places its emphasis on disease (American Nurses Association 1980: Dougherty and Tripp-Reimer 1985: Kleinman 1982). Nursing mediates between the model of illness and the model of disease, using the biomedical model when situations are life threatening and the illness model when clients experience life changes which accompany many diseases (Dougherty and Tripp-Reimer 1985). It is only logical, then, that the concept of culture is important to nursing as a discipline.

Any discussion of nursing and culture should take note of Madeleine Leininger's 1967 article, "The Culture Concept and Its Relevance to Nursing." As a pioneer nurse anthropologist, she based her ideas on predictions of a world made smaller by better communication, faster travel, increased foreign trade, and international tension. At that time she predicted that nurses would be called upon to deal more and more with peoples of other cultures, at home and abroad. Now, some twenty years later, that has come to pass. If anything, the experts of that time underestimated the extent of the international migration which has occurred and which has been responsible for bringing nurses everywhere in contact with people of cultures very different from their own.

Added to this, the expanded role of the nurse at the end of the twentieth century means that more and more nurses are responsible for direct management of patient health through a growing system of primary health care throughout the world, particularly among those institutions serving the poor.

Since the poor all over the world are usually not a homogeneous group, but rather a heterogeneous amalgamation of many tributary cultures, nurses are continually faced with the problem of effective health care delivery in a multi-cultural situation.

In 1967, referring to the work of Paul (1955), Saunders (1954), and Spicer (1952), Leininger noted the importance of health care workers, including nurses, understanding the culture of their clients in order to function effectively.

> Nursing can no longer be perceived in the traditional sense of an activity based solely upon knowledge of man's physical and emotional needs. Nursing theory and practice must take into account man's cultural and social behavior so that the nurse's mode of thinking and interacting with individuals will reflect new and penetrating views about behavior in health and illness. Understanding the culture of an individual seeking health care is just as important for effective health care as is knowledge of the physiological and psychological aspects of an individual's illness. (1967: 28)

Has the situation changed today? Is the concept of culture still relevant for nurses? In answer to the latter question, it seems obvious that the concept of culture is even more important than in years past. The following discussion will attempt to answer the first question, as well as to elaborate on the second, by presenting some case studies as illustrations.

A very comprehensive review of cross-cultural nursing research by Tripp-Reimer and Dougherty (1985) indicates that there has been a wide variety of studies done by nurses which describe characteristics of minority cultures, particularly in the decade between 1970 and 1980. Typical of these are works on Paiute Indians (Brink 1971a, 1971b), Salish Indians (Horn 1977), rural blacks (Dougherty 1978), Appalachians (Tripp-Reimer 1980), and Mormons (Peay 1977) in this country and various groups abroad (Brink 1982; Kendall 1977; Leininger 1977; and Sohier 1976).

On the practical side, the nature of the clientele with which most nurses work also dictates that understanding and knowledge of culture should be of paramount importance, particularly in this decade. Cultural plurality has always been a fact of life in the United States. The idea of the great melting pot was probably generated by optimistic bureaucrats. Instead there have always been pockets of people who have maintained their traditional cultural identities, e.g., Polish people in the Midwest, Scandinavian people in Minnesota and Wisconsin, Italians in New York and Boston, Chinese in San Francisco, and Mexican-Americans in Texas, California, and Arizona, to name a few. This is even more true today than it was many years ago.

In recent years, various world events have created new highs in the numbers of people migrating from one country to another. Wars, natural disasters, and economic crises have combined to produce a steady stream of people from poor Third World countries who are seeking refuge or a better life in the United States. In states like New York, Florida, and California, health care workers are now called upon to deal with people of less understood cultural backgrounds such as Vietnamese, Cambodian, Haitian, Guatemalan, Korean, and Laotian.

As a matter of fact, we now supposedly have the third largest Spanish-speaking population in the world. According to news reports during the 1984 Olympics held in Los Angeles, although the athletes came from approximately 140 countries, there were people from each of these countries already living in that city. A colleague of mine recently moved to south Florida where she found herself confronted with patients from six different cultures in the space of an 8-hour shift in the labor and delivery unit of one large urban hospital.

These culturally diverse populations present tremendous problems for the delivery of health care, usually because of three main problem areas:

(1) Poor communication: language barriers
(2) Differing beliefs about health and illness
(3) Economics: new arrivals and minority groups tend to be at the low end of the economic scale.

Confronting these problem areas requires a knowledge and understanding of culture and its many facets.

Given the milieu in which many nurses now function, the concept of culture assumes a new importance. It is really an abstract term which is used as a shorthand for a whole group of related traits and ideas which are passed from one generation to another and which fit together to guide the behavior of people. Although it is important to avoid stereotyping when dealing with large numbers of people and large amounts of data, it is helpful to be able to categorize people who think and behave similarly. With the large amounts of new data that are constantly emerging and the constant changes in technology that professionals in nursing and medicine must assimilate to be able to function, it is very helpful to know that if a client is Chinese, Haitian, or Cuban, she will probably react in certain ways. Even though each person still must be treated as an individual, it is useful to view the client within the norms of her own culture, because this at least gives us a starting point from which variations can be later determined.

Following are some examples of problems encountered by nurses working in cross-cultural situations and, in some cases, the solutions which were devised to cope with these problems. These examples are not presented as definitive works but as illustrations of how the concept of culture can affect the delivery of health care by nurses.

Case No. 1. Introducing Change Across Cultural Boundaries: The Dilemma of the Peace Corps Nurse.

Although nurses during World War II and the Korean conflict came in contact with and worked with peoples of other cultures, and missionary organizations have long provided an opportunity for small groups of dedicated nurses to work among people of many ethnic backgrounds, the advent of the United States Peace Corps in 1961 offered the first major opportunity for many nurses from the mainstream of American culture to work in health care programs all over the world and with peoples of different cultural backgrounds. This organization, in keeping with its grass-roots approach, actually encouraged nurses to learn about the culture of their clients and how to tailor programs effectively to meet the differing needs of these many and varied groups. This is not to disregard those nurses who worked on Indian reservations and with health departments serving large ethnic populations in the United States. The Peace Corps orientation, however, included sensitization training about local cultures and customs and an expectation that the volunteer would participate as much as possible in the local culture. Unfortunately, for most Peace Corps nurses and other volunteers as well, even with the orientation, most of the knowledge about how to function in these cultures had to be learned through trial-and-error.

My first experience taking care of people of another culture occurred when I was a Peace Corps Volunteer in Bolivia. I was stationed at a clinic in a sugar mill town in eastern Bolivia. I was sent there with a fellow volunteer, who had a sociology/social work background. The day after we arrived we went on a tour of the clinic and promptly decided it was filthy. With true American zeal, we determined that our first job was to scrub the clinic from top to bottom. Much to our surprise, this action was not appreciated. We succeeded in making everyone from the doctor to the cleaning lady upset. Obviously, their ideas of what was clean were different from ours. And who among us would enjoy having some foreigners come in and criticize our system, our place of work, or anything about our lives, even if we knew the criticism was justified. Ironically, at the end of this session, the place really didn't look much different anyway. As it turned out, most of the people working there had little or no knowledge of the germ theory and could see no reason for our behavior, since the place was neat; it just had grubby walls and windows.

My days in that clinic were a real learning experience. We had about six inpatient beds and a small surgery which was used for emergency procedures such as appendectomies, cesarean sections, and suturing of lacerations. Our six beds would be occupied at various times by workers from the mill or their family members. Most of the mill workers were Aymara and Quechua Indians who had come down from the altiplano to settle in the area. One day I was taking care of an Aymara woman who had had a cesarean section and needed to get up to the bathroom. I helped her get up, and we laboriously made our way to the bathroom, which was relatively new and contained the pride and joy of the clinic – two new flush toilets. When we finally got there, I was left with my mouth hanging open as the little woman got up and stood on top of the toilet seat and then proceeded to squat, no easy task in her condition. I later learned that people either used the outdoors or latrines which consisted of a hole in the ground and two foot rests. As a Bolivian acquaintance said, when questioned about it, "We are a nation of squatters." People felt that they couldn't carry out the usual body functions if they couldn't squat. Obviously, the flush toilet had a totally different meaning and function in Bolivia.

Technology, whether it be simple flush toilets or sophisticated electronic equipment, is the product of culture. People also tend to perceive technology in terms of their own cultural experiences. A nurse in the United States today cannot function without a good understanding of the high-tech atmosphere of the modern hospital. The effect this technology may have on someone from another culture can be unexpected. One Korean woman who was a patient in the labor and delivery unit of a large hospital didn't move the whole time she was in labor because she thought the belts holding the ultrasound fetal heart rate monitor on her abdomen were seat belts like those in cars and airplanes which would prevent her moving (Lee 1986). No one had thought to explain to her how she could move and how the machine worked.

Effective nursing care of clients really demands an understanding of them and the context in which they function. This point has never been illustrated so dramatically to me as it was near the end of my Peace Corps stint when I was asked to come into the provincial capital and work with the municipal hospital in upgrading its nursing staff. To understand the problems I faced, it is first necessary to know a bit of background. At the time I was in Bolivia there were only one or two trained nurses in the whole eastern part of the country. The main training school was in La Paz on the altiplano. By law, every graduate of medicine and nursing had to do an *año de provincia* or year of service in the hinterlands after graduation. Generally these nurses and doctors were sent out on their own, having come from schools which were very theoretical and which offered little practical application, and left with no support or back-up. As you may imagine, the experience was usually horrendous. The result was that almost everyone who went through this program came out determined never to work in rural areas. Thus, most of the people recruited to care for patients were local people with little or no training and varying degrees of education. They started by sweeping floors and washing walls and graduated to giving shots. This was the motley group I was supposed to provide with inservice training.

I came into this situation with a great deal of energy and high expectations, not quite realizing the wide range of variation that existed. My first project was to begin a system of charting. In good American fashion, I believed that anything worth doing needed to be written down or "documented." I was aghast when I discovered that the hospital kept no charts on anyone. The doctor in charge of the hospital kept a large book in his office in which all patients were noted, along with their diagnosis and the outcome of the case. I thought that this was a very crude and backward way of doing things.

The director of the hospital agreed to let me try a charting system on one ward as a pilot program. In retrospect, I have to believe that these people were very tolerant of a *gringa* who must have been perceived as very naive and strange. We did get a charting system set up on that ward, however. Unfortunately, there were a number of problems which developed. First, the doctors didn't want to write in a chart which would then be available for other people to read. Doctors in Bolivia were accustomed to keeping all their diagnoses very private. There was no concept of the patient's right to have information. Second, many of the nursing personnel who were supposed to be writing in the chart could not read or write well enough to do so. So much for the charting system.

At the same time that the little incident with the charting was occurring, I had also instituted a different method of delivering medications. In the hospital at that time the nursing personnel did not keep everyone's medications and then pass them out at specified hours, as is the custom in the United States. Instead, each patient and/or his family was in charge of taking the appropriate medications. These were left at the bedside. I, of course, thought that this was atrocious and determined to change it. As it turned out, putting all the medications for each patient in a central location and letting the nurses pass them out was a big mistake. Because of the generally poor preparation of the nursing personnel and because there were no regular schedules for anything, it was literally impossible to guarantee that each patient's medications would be given out correctly. These went back to the bedside very soon. After all, no one had as much interest in making sure the patient got his medicine as did the patient himself. As a matter of fact, I have observed with interest that similar systems involving patient control of medications are being set up in some United States hospitals today.

These examples clearly illustrate the clash between the United States/biomedical cultural model, into which I had been socialized, and the Bolivian/traditional system of my clients. Interestingly enough, when I revisited my old haunts five years later, my program was judged to have been a success, but not for the reasons I would have thought. As part of the project, I had gotten the hospital to give each employee a new uniform. This uniform, plus the organization of employees which took place to carry out the inservice education classes, was still remembered and considered to be important. For me it had merely been incidental to the main focus of the program.

Case No. 2. Finding Linkage Areas Between Two Cultures

In my work, I have found that those practices most likely to be adopted are those which have an affinity with the cultural context into which they are being introduced and which have some practical value for the person expected to adopt them. Anna, a nurse who worked with a Mennonite group in Central America, reported an experience which illustrates this concept very nicely.

One of the major problems among children in the tropics is dermatitis, which is aggravated by the hot, humid climate and poor sanitary conditions. The best treatment for this condition is relatively simple and consists of nothing more than bathing the child in soap and water every day. However, Anna had noticed that in the rural clinics they were having trouble getting rid of the dermatitis, even though the treatment was cheap and accessible to everyone. Upon investigation, she discovered that people were very disappointed when, after going to the clinic, they were told to take their child home and give him a bath every day. This treatment did not meet their cultural expectations; they had apparently wanted something more dramatic and ritualistic — an injection, at least. (Shots have been adopted very well in many traditional cultures, probably because of their magico-mystical aura.) The staff puzzled over what to do for quite a while, then Anna finally hit upon an idea. She prepared a number of small bottles with sterile water containing green food coloring. When a child came in with dermatitis, the mother was given a bottle of this mixture and told to prepare a bath each day to which 10 drops of the green liquid was to be added. She was then told to bathe the child in that special water and soap. This approach was very successful. Anna had discovered an excellent way to make the treatment advocated by scientific medicine more compatible with traditional beliefs, thus ensuring its success.

Case No. 3. Traditional Beliefs vs. Socioeconomic Obstacles

In practice, the beliefs of individuals may have less impact on their behavior with respect to adoption of health practices than do other aspects of their culture, e.g., socioeconomic status and family structure.

At one time, I worked with Mexican-American families in East San José, California. A colleague and I conducted a small research project which looked at "cooperative" and "noncooperative" Mexican-American mothers whose children were attending well-baby clinic. Cooperative was defined as coming regularly to the clinic and complying with instructions. Noncooperative, of course, was the opposite. The hypothesis was that mothers who held more traditional health beliefs were less likely to be cooperative, and vice versa. Imagine our surprise when we found that there was no significant difference between the two groups in terms of their beliefs. Whether or not mothers came to the well-baby clinic depended more on whether they had transportation, babysitters for other children, and someone to translate for them if they couldn't speak English than whether they maintained traditional beliefs. All of these are much easier problems to tackle than trying to change traditional beliefs. At the time, however, we thought we must have done something wrong; other studies have since shown that use of scientific medical systems does not mean the client has abandoned all traditional beliefs. People, especially the poor, are above all, pragmatic. They tend to try to use the best of both worlds, either simultaneously or serially (Solien de Gonzalez 1966; Scott 1975; Press 1978).

Case No. 4. The Nurse, Caught in the Clash Between the Public Health Bureaucracy and Traditional Cultural Values

Mainstream culture influences the organization and delivery of health care, just as the traditional healing systems of various ethnic groups are influenced by their individual cultures. Sometimes, in order to assure the adequate and effective delivery of health care to these groups, nurses in the dominant system must be prepared to break out of the accepted pattern. This is a particularly important concept for nurses, since they frequently serve as the liaison between the client and the rest of the system.

While I was working in the Mexican-American community in East San José, my case load included a young Mexican-American couple with two children. The younger child, Miguel, had a congenital heart defect which, with open heart surgery, could be corrected, allowing him to live a normal life. Miguel's mother took him regularly to the well-baby clinic, but when they tried to set up a consultation at Stanford Children's Hospital, she would not come. Health department nurses were getting very concerned, since valuable time was passing, threatening to put the boy past the optimum time for having the surgery. Since I had recently come back from Bolivia and spoke fluent Spanish, they asked me to follow this case as a special project. The mother was from old Mexico and did not speak English.

At this point, I should mention that U.S. Public Health Departments have always had fairly rigid hours, e.g., 8–5 P.M., Monday through Friday, which usually limits the nurses' ability to get to know the whole family, particularly husbands and fathers. When I made my first visit to Miguel's home, I discovered that the problem was that Miguel's father was the one who made all decisions about health care and most other matters, in traditional Mexican fashion. However, Miguel's mother, with her complete lack of English, was the one to whom all the explanations about Miguel's care had been made. She was unable to explain the problem to him. I decided to start visiting them after 5 P.M. so that I could talk to the family as a whole. On my next visit, I came later and over coffee explained Miguel's situation to his father, who contrary to the impressions of health department personnel, was a very concerned man. We spent a number of visits talking about the risks and the advantages of Miguel having the surgery. Within three weeks, they had made an appointment for the initial evaluation. I accompanied them at their request for this visit, but did not translate, since the father could speak fairly well. I was mostly moral support. Miguel eventually had a successful surgery.

At the time, the fact that I visited this family after hours was frowned upon. In fact, the idea that all health problems can be taken care of between the hours of 8 and 5 during the week still seems to be a prevalent notion in the biomedical system.

Case No. 5. Communicating Across Language Barriers

A Korean nurse and student of mine was studying Korean women's experiences during childbirth in United Stated hospitals (Lee 1986). During the course of her investigation it was not unusual for her to find, after talking with a Korean woman who had been hospitalized for the birth of her child or for some complication related to it (e.g., placenta previa), that the woman had no idea what was going on or what she should do and why. She decided to talk to the doctors and nurses to find out why they hadn't been explaining things to these women. Much to her surprise, they were shocked when she raised the question. They had been giving explanations using the women's husbands as translators. Most of these women had come with their husbands who were working on Ph.D.s or master's degrees, so the husband was a better speaker of English and thus was considered a good translator. What they didn't realize was that, because of the nature of Korean culture, most of these men were uncomfortable talking to their wives about matters related to female anatomy and bodily functions. The result was that they were giving their wives very edited versions of the explanations provided by the nurses and doctors, usually with most of the pertinent details lacking.

This problem was solved by trying to make sure a female interpreter was available and by providing written explanations in English. Most of the women were high school and college graduates in Korea and knew how to read English. Their verbal English was what was lacking. Later they could read over the materials with a dictionary or get other friends to help translate so they would know what was happening to them.

This last problem demonstrates that being able to speak a language and being able to translate from one language to another are two very different skills. An untrained translator can actually create problems. The nurse needs some basic knowledge about the culture of her client in order to use a translator effectively. This knowledge will help her to know if factors such as using husbands or children are inappropriate in terms of cultural norms.

Another aspect of this communication problem has to do with nonverbal cues. Although Korean culture does not permit emotions to be expressed in the face, these women had discovered that American's faces were very expressive. Therefore they always looked closely at the faces of the Americans for clues about what was being said, illustrating the importance of nonverbal communication, although perhaps in a reverse fashion.

The experience of another student of mine further emphasizes the need for nurses to improve communication across cultures and language barriers. She went to make a home visit at the home of one of her Haitian patients, after helping her during the labor and delivery of her baby. When the student arrived she found, to her horror, that the Haitian woman got hysterical and started to run away. As it turned out, the only American people the Haitians ever saw were bill collectors, coming to repossess various items when people got behind with their payments. The Haitian woman, therefore, thought that the student had come to take the baby back because they hadn't paid their bill. This was a rude awakening for the nurse, who had thought that the limited communication they had shared in the hospital would be enough for the Haitian woman to regard her as a friend. When she was finally able to come back with a translator, she managed to straighten things out and establish a friendship with her former patient.

CONCLUSION

The words written by Leininger in that 1967 article summing up the importance of the concept of culture for nurses are probably even more relevant today:

> [T]he nurse needs to understand the *why* of human behavior from a cultural viewpoint and to deal with behavior that is culturally conditioned. [T]he nurse must realize how culture beliefs regarding health and illness are learned by specific cultural agents and become as pervasive and important to individuals as the clothes they wear and the food they eat. In sum, culture is a universal and a significant

concept tightly interwoven into the life of man and continually pervades his thinking, actions, feelings, and particularly his health state. (p. 37)

We live in a shrinking world. It is imperative that we understand our neighbors, because the health of one affects the health of all. We as nurses can no longer hope our good intentions will automatically be communicated across cultural barriers; we must make sure that they are. We must learn about and appreciate the cultural heritage of the people we care for to deliver adequate health services in these modern times.

REFERENCES

American Nurses Association
    1980   Nursing—A Social Policy Statement. Kansas City, Mo.: American Nurses Association.

Brink, P. J.
    1982   "Traditional Birth Attendants among the Annang of Nigeria: Current Practices and Proposed Programs." *Social Science and Medicine* 16: 1883–92.
    1971a   "Paviotso Child Training: Notes." *The Indian Historian* 4: 47–50.
    1971b   "Some Aspects of Change in Northern Paiute Childrearing Practices." In *Great Basin Anthropological Conference 1970: Selected Papers.* C. Aikens, ed. *University of Oregon Anthropological Papers*, no. 1: 167–75.

Dougherty, M. C.
    1978   *Becoming a Woman in Rural Black Culture.* New York: Holt, Rinehart & Winston.

Dougherty, M. C., and T. Tripp-Reimer
    1985   "The Interface of Nursing and Anthropology." *Annual Review of Anthropology* 14: 219–41.

Horn, B. M.
    1977   "Transcultural Nursing and Childrearing of the Muckleshoot People." In *Transcultural Nursing Care of Infants and Children: Proceedings of the First Transcultural Nursing Conference.* M. Leininger, ed. Salt Lake City: University of Utah College of Nursing.

Kendall, K.
    1977   "Maternal and Child Nursing in an Iranian Village." In *Transcultural Nursing Care of Infants and Children: Proceedings from the First Transcultural Nursing Conference.* M. Leininger, ed. Salt Lake City: University of Utah College of Nursing.

Kleinman, A. M.
    1982   "Clinically Applied Anthropology on a Psychiatric Consultation—Liaison Service." In *Clinically Applied Anthropology: Anthropologists in Health Science Settings.* N. J. Chrisman, ed. Boston: Reidel.

Lee, W. S.
    1986   "Korean Women's Perceptions of Childbearing Experiences in the United States." Master's thesis. College of Nursing, University of Florida, Gainesville.

Leininger, M.
    1977   "The Gadsup of New Guinea and Early Child-Caring Behaviors with Nursing Care Implications." In *Transcultural Nursing Care of Infants and Children:*

Proceedings form the First Transcultural Nursing Conference. M. Leininger, ed. Salt Lake City: University of Utah College of Nursing.

1967   "The Culture Concept and Its Relevance to Nursing." *Journal of Nursing Education* 6: 27–37.

Paul, B. D., ed.
1955   *Health, Culture and Community: Case Studies of Public Reactions to Health Programs.* New York: Russell Sage Foundation.

Peay, D.
1977   "Some Cultural Values of Mormons and their Implications for Health Care of the Elderly." In *Transcultural Nursing Care of Infants and Children: Proceedings from the First Transcultural Nursing Conference.* M. Leininger, ed. Salt Lake City: University of Utah College of Nursing.

Press, I.
1978   "Urban Folk Medicine: A Functional Overview." *American Anthropologist* 80: 71–84.

Saunders, L.
1954   *Cultural Difference and Medical Care: The Case of the Spanish-Speaking People of the Southwest.* New York: Russell Sage Foundation.

Scott, C. S.
1975   "Competing Health Care Systems in an Inner-City Area." *Human Organization* 34: 108–10.

Sohier, R.
1976   "Gaining Awareness of Cultural Difference: A Case Example." In *Health Care Dimensions.* vol. 3. *Transcultural Health Care Issues and Conditions.* M. Leininger, ed. Philadelphia: F. A. Davis.

Solien de Gonzalez, N. L.
1966   "Health Behavior in Cross-Cultural Perspective: A Guatemalan Example." *Human Organization* 25: 122–25.

Spicer, E. H., ed.
1952   *Human Problems in Technological Change.* New York: Russell Sage Foundation.

Tripp-Reimer, T.
1980   "Appalachian Health Care: From Research to Practice." In *Transcultural Nursing Care: Teaching, Practice and Research, Proceedings from the Fifth National Transcultural Nursing Conference.* M. Leininger, ed. Salt Lake City: University of Utah College of Nursing.

Tripp-Reimer, T., and M. C. Dougherty
1985   "Cross-Cultural Nursing Research" *Annual Review of Nursing Research* 3: 77–104.

11

THE RELEVANCE OF CULTURE TO SCIENCE AND TECHNOLOGY POLICY

Steve Rayner

My thesis in the following pages is that the concept of culture is particularly relevant to science and technology policy in complex modern societies. In particular, I argue that the "social accountability" view of culture as a social control system (Geertz 1973; Douglas 1980) holds the key to many of the strident societal conflicts over technology choices that have beset the world's leading industrial democracies. The argument proceeds through an exposition of the role of cultural preferences in the production and evaluation of scientific knowledge, to a case study that illustrates how diverse cultural preferences for fairness and trust shape the acceptability of new nuclear power technologies to utility companies, public utility commissions, and public interest groups. Finally, I consider some of the implications of this approach for international disputes concerning global technology impacts, such as anthropogenic climate change.

CULTURE AS SOCIAL ACCOUNTING

The social accountability approach conceptualizes culture as a set of plans, instructions, and rules or, less purposively, a means of social accounting. Culture thus provides the framework by which we justify our actions to others and call them to account to us for theirs. This concept of culture starts from the assumption that much of human thought is basically both social and public. As Ryle (1949) has suggested, thinking does not take place in the head, but all around us. We do not think with a private metaphysical mind, but with words, pictures, gestures, actions, and both natural and manufactured objects. Indeed, we assign symbolic meaning so as to impose some sort of order and coherence on the stream of events. In so doing, we sift and filter our sensations of the world; some perceptions are admitted, some rejected, and others combined or broken down.

If we did not filter experiences in this way or make use of public symbols for organizing perceptions and communicating them to others, then we would likely be overwhelmed by the variety of possible interpretations that could be assigned to events. We would have to abandon intellect and discourse and thereby be forced, like the lower animals, to rely on instinct. Mankind would be reduced, as Geertz (1973) has observed, to mental basket cases.

The filtering of sensory input and the use of symbols in thought are public processes, aspects of the cultural control mechanisms. Individual decisions are made according to a shared structuring of consciousness that is readily observable — in the organization of markets, in the layout of houses, in the adoption of dress codes, and, indeed, everywhere in the realm of public behavior.

CULTURE AND PUBLIC POLICY

Public policy in complex societies is largely concerned with the dynamic interaction of a number of cultures that share the same location in time and space. There are stark contrasts, such as agrarian and rural communities within developing societies, bourgeois and proletarian life-styles coexisting in industrial nations, and black and white social networks juxtaposed in neighborhoods of modern cities. In such dynamic settings, culture is much more than an artifact produced by a given set of people: it is the common way that a community of persons makes sense of the world. Understanding the culture of a constituency or institution tells us how its members define themselves in relation to members of other communities and how they define their standing among themselves (Gross and Rayner 1985).

From this standpoint, the cultural interpretation of the acceptability of a technology revolves around different perceptions of what constitutes the technology as a social and cultural system, rather than on a simple evaluation of costs and benefits. This applies not only to the major contingencies of public policy debates, but also to more mundane choices such as whether to subscribe to cable television or purchase a video recorder.

CULTURE AND TECHNOLOGICAL RISK

Consider the issue of potential hazards of technology. The cultural theory of technology choice provides a challenging contrast to the approaches advocated in sciences other than anthropology. For example, rational-decision theorists in economics and political science argue that individuals decide to adopt a technology according to the utility principle; they first weigh its potential costs and benefits and then pursue the course of action that they think will maximize the advantages that will accrue.

A widely recognized problem with the utility principle, particularly at the formalized level of cost-benefit analysis, is its awkwardness in explaining a choice between qualitatively different costs and benefits. For one example, how can the aesthetic, historical, and spiritual costs of demolishing an ancient church be weighed against the economic benefits which a new airport might bring (Self 1975)? Or, how can the certainty of statistical loss of life through an industrial process be balanced against the loss of employment which outlawing the process might bring? These are not just hypothetical questions; they have been the focus of major public policy debates in Britain and the United States during the last ten years. Although many ingenious attempts have been made to balance radically different evaluations (Merkhofer 1986; Peelle 1987), none has succeeded in reconciling disagreements about values in the world of real policy making.

When people deviate from the optimum cost-benefit solution by rejecting a technology — or, at the opposite extreme, by reckless pursuit of it — the rational-decision theorists can fall back on only one explanation: those concerned have failed, through ignorance, false consciousness, quirkiness, or even willful malice, to make a correct assessment of costs and benefits. The concept of culture, on the other hand, offers a much richer range of explanation of why people choose options that some experts deem contrary to their best interests. The maximization of anticipated utilities is only a second step. It must be preceded by the ranking of diverse utilities, which is primarily a phenomenon of culture, not of economics.

CULTURAL RELATIVISM VERSUS NAIVE REALISM

Douglas and Wildavsky's *Risk and Culture* (1982) called the attention of risk analysts to the argument that risks are defined and perceived differently by people in different cultural contexts. Hence, in complex societies, as in the contemporary United States, considerable disagreement is expected between the members of various constituencies regarding what constitutes a technological risk, as well as how such risks should be managed.

Douglas and Wildavsky's viewpoint has met with a mixed reception in scientific and technical circles as well as among policy makers who depend on the guidance of scientific experts. Some individuals reject the concept of cultural relativism in risk analysis because they fear that the view of scientific truth as relativistic, that is to say context dependent, precludes a systematic cross-cultural consensus about the natural order that is independent of cultural viewpoint. Since, for example, the Japanese and the Americans agree on the number of protons in the nucleus beryllium, we are told that relativism is either scientifically trivial, in that it refers to kinds of knowledge that are not significant to science, or it is simply false. These critics fail to recognize that the social and cultural contexts sustain a category of human activity called "science" and influence decisions made within science about how to organize the various activities that constitute the scientific enterprise (Agassi 1984).

This naive-realist view of science provides the rationale for the National Academy of Science report (1983) that recommends dividing risk analysis into separate stages in which facts are first established and later evaluated for their social implications. Ironically, this viewpoint is cherished equally by the academic champions of both capital and labor. Big business executives seem to fear that acceptance of relativism may strengthen the legal actions of community and labor activists, who currently have to prove probable cause of injury according to quite stringent scientific and legal criteria. Cultural relativism sometimes is viewed in such circles as opening the door to successful lawsuits for an endless list of imagined harms. Labor and community leaders, on the other hand, seem to fear that relativism will allow industry to reject liability claims on the basis that risk is a subjective notion, having no objective existence in nature, and therefore does not justify expensive compensatory or corrective action (Kaprow 1985). The error, in both camps, is to confuse cultural relativism with individual subjectivism and to suppose that differential cultural construction of risk precludes an intersubjective consensus based on empirical feedback from human interaction with an objective universe.

Even those who reject the naive-realist view of science and are sympathetic to the notion that cultural relativism operates within the hallowed confines of science have questioned the usefulness of this insight to the science-for-policy process unless it enables us to do something more practical than appreciate the cultural diversity of perceptions of risk with much the same detachment that we appreciate divergent perceptions of beauty in museums of ethnic art. Determining an appropriate role for the cultural perspective in science and technology is simultaneously a theoretical rational problem of epistemology and a practical empirical problem of usable knowledge (Ravetz 1986). The first problem is to understand the status of culturally generated knowledge in its relation to a world that exists independently of it, but can only be known through it. The second problem is to demonstrate how cultural analysis improves the ability of technology policy makers to resolve conflicts that arise from differing perceptions of a technology and its appropriate management.

CULTURAL RELATIVISM VERSUS PERSONAL SOLIPSISM

The problem of the epistemological status of cultural relativism in scientific knowledge is rooted in the process by which that knowledge is created and the relationship between that process and the particular variety of relativism that is advocated. It is interesting that critics often characterize the relativist position by the extreme argument that knowledge created in one set of social circumstances is entirely self-validating and incommunicable to members of another culture or subculture. On this basis, it is objected, any one person's version of the world has as valid a claim to be scientific truth as any other, and any ludicrous proposition is believable (Agassi 1984).

However, this final solipsism is actually the very antithesis of cultural, as opposed to individual, relativism. Cultural relativism emphasizes that the validity of public knowledge depends on the relation of knowledge to the context of its creation through social activities such as science, technology, religion, and even magic. By denying the possibility of directly comparing knowledge to nature, except through the culturally created categories of human thought, we emphatically are not denying the existence of any basis for validating public knowledge, including scientific knowledge. On the contrary, we argue that public knowledge must always be evaluated as part of the social system, laboratory, workshop, community, or sect that creates and sustains it (Douglas 1978). The socially determined rules for establishing claims to knowledge, as well as testing and evaluating such claims, therefore, become part of that knowledge, as do the rules that interdict certain kinds of inquiry (Ravetz 1986). The point is that public knowledge can only be evaluated as a whole system, a process of production and use, and not as an artifact to be compared to nature's pattern (Bloor 1976).

CULTURAL CONSTRUCTION AND NATURAL FEEDBACK

To reduce this argument to the personal solipsism that critics ascribe to us is a travesty of the cultural relativist position. However, such a reductionism enables the naive realists to attack cultural relativism on yet another front. Accepting solipsism would oblige cultural relativists to deny that knowledge created in different contexts may refer to the same thing. Yet it is clear that at least some culturally created concepts may refer to phenomena that exist independently of the concepts, but may be knowable only through one or another version of them. Culturally created categories and modes of reasoning are not the only constraints on human knowledge. Much of human knowledge is obtained through experience with forces that would continue to exist in the absence of human agency (Barnes 1974; Bloor 1976). Practical experience is interpreted through cultural categories, but, in some useful sense, the object of such experience may be said to exist independently of those categories. Such forces may, therefore, be described as natural or ecological feedback into the knowledge process.

Natural feedback into the knowledge process is always subjected to the conceptual massaging imposed by existing categories of thought. The combination of natural feedback with cultural constraints on the organization of information forms a total knowledge system, parts of which may be determined by either cultural or ecological constraints at different times and places. Both types of constraint are always present in the knowledge process and profoundly shape our most fundamental ordering concepts such as space and time (Bloch 1977; Rayner 1982). Traditional empiricism has tended to reify the feedback process, according the artifactual status of objective knowledge to the information it provides, while seeking to separate the culturally determined components of knowledge and reducing them to the status of subjective values. The convenience of the fact/value dichotomy clearly is attractive to exponents of science for policy who seek clear and simple solutions to complex problems (Cohen 1985). Alas, it does grievous violence to our ability to find real solutions which must be sought in an understanding of actual social conflicts over the deployment of technology.

Despite arguments by some cultural relativists (Wittgenstein 1953), the transferability of knowledge from one cultural constituency to another is not precluded by a cultural relativist approach. Such a transfer, however, inevitably would transform the recipient culture and in some way, trivial or significant, alter the social relations within it. In these cases, the interesting question for the technology policy maker is not whether different sociocultural systems can converge on common definitions of technological problems at some useful level. Modern world history has demonstrated indisputably that convergence is possible, though often difficult. Rather he should start by asking what is at stake for those involved in developing a cross-cultural consensus, and how is a particular knowledge process able to accommodate change?

THREE KINDS OF SCIENCE

Fortunately, the philosophy of science already has produced a model of the production of scientific knowledge that enables us to address these questions. Funtowicz and Ravetz (1985) have described a model of three kinds of science predicated by two variables, "systems uncertainty" and "decision stakes." Whereas systems uncertainty refers to the elements of inexactness, uncertainty, and ignorance encountered in all technical studies, decision stakes is a measure of the costs and benefits to interested parties of the various policy options (see Figure 11.1).

Low systems uncertainty and low decision stakes describe situations in which data bases are large and reliable and the technical community generally agrees on appropriate methods of investigation. Funtowicz and Ravetz call this "applied science." I prefer the term "consensual science" because the adjective "applied" is commonly used to describe scientific activities designed to produce information for practical, technical purposes, even where decision stakes and systems uncertainty are higher. The consensus referred to here is achieved, in part, by the low decision stakes. Controversies about scientific facts are unlikely to be heated here, where the symbolic loads that such facts carry are either clearly established or unimportant. Knowledge is likely to have a very strong component of ecological feedback based on long-term practical interaction between the sociocultural systems represented here and the nonhuman universe. Within consensual science the variations in perspective on risk emphasized by cultural relativism are likely to be minor.

When both systems uncertainty and decision stakes are considerable, Funtowicz and Ravetz define a different style of activity, the "clinical" mode of technical consultancy. This kind of activity requires professional expertise in the use of quantitative tools supplemented explicitly by experienced qualitative judgment. Exercising this judgment increases the decision stakes for the consulting scientist and begins to bring to the fore differences of interpretation rooted in competing institutional, educational, or disciplinary cultures. There is some kind of unstable balance or alternation of determination between ecological feedback and cultural constraints on the knowledge process throughout this kind of activity.

Figure 11.1. Three Kinds of Science

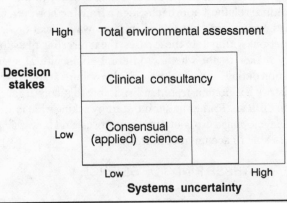

SOURCE: Based on S. O. Funtowicz and J. R. Ravetz, "Three Types of Risk Assessment: A Methodological Analysis," in Risk Analysis in the Private Sector; C. Whipple and V. Covello, eds. New York: Plenum.

Finally, when decision stakes and systems uncertainty are very high, Funtowicz and Ravetz present us with a scientific style they term "total environmental assessment." This kind of activity is permeated by qualitative judgments and value commitments. Inquiry, even into technical questions, often takes the form of a dialogue in an advocacy or even an adversary mode. Although only a few risk assessments fall into the category of total environmental assessments, they are often the ones of greatest political significance. As the authors of this typology note, total environmental assessment provides the most plausible opportunity for the application of a cultural-relativist perspective, for here the social constraints on the knowledge process are clearly dominant over natural feedback.

Given the compatibility of this framework with the version of cultural relativism that I have described, it is unfortunate that Funtowicz and Ravetz present their model as a critique of cultural relativism, which they disparagingly term "social reductionism." Although not naive realists themselves, they share the realists' concern that recognizing the cultural construction of risk will lead to social irresponsibility in facing threats to life and limb arising out of technology and the environment. I have argued already that this concern is misplaced except insofar as any theory can be abused by the unscrupulous. However, Funtowicz and Ravetz describe their model as a solution to "the difficulty created by the contradiction between the ideal of public-knowledge science and the characteristics of the problems encountered in risk assessment, without falling into sectarian relativism or social reductionism" (p. 227).

Rather than being an antidote to cultural relativism, the distinction of three kinds of science more properly defines those instances where the role of cultural variation in knowledge is, respectively, trivial, integral, and dominant as we move from consensual science through clinical consultancy to total environmental assessment. The role of ecological feedback varies inversely to that of cultural constraints through the same progression.

SCIENCE AND TRANS-SCIENCE

There are certain parallels between the three kinds of science just described and Weinberg's (1972) distinction between science and trans-science. It is instructive to note these in passing, partly to clarify the Funtowicz-Ravetz model and partly to enable me to emphasize that although natural feedback and cultural constraint may dominate opposite ends of the knowledge spectrum, neither element will ever be entirely absent.

Initially Weinberg distinguishes trans-scientific questions as those which attempt to deal with social problems through the procedures of science, yet cannot be answered by science. In other words, these are the culturally determined questions, as distinct from the questions that can be answered by manipulating information determined by ecological sources that Weinberg therefore calls scientific. To his great credit, Weinberg recognizes the fuzziness of the boundary between these two types of activity. Science is maintained by critical judgment by peers — clearly a social activity. Only those with the proper credentials are allowed to participate in the scientific subculture, but propriety has little to do with whether a question can be answered by science in principle. Further into his argument, Weinberg seems to say that science is consensual knowledge arrived at through criticism, while trans-science is preconsensual criticism, beset by uncertainty, that may or may not, at some future point, converge on an agreed solution. Or, in cultural-relativist terms, in trans-science cultural variation is dominant, and science is where cross-cultural consensus about knowledge has been achieved and confirmed by natural feedback.

HOW CULTURE CAN INFORM POLICY DECISIONS

Having indicated what I take to be a defensible epistemological justification for cultural relativism in science and technology for policy making, we are left with the question of how these general observations about the cultural foundations of human knowledge can be operationalized for societal technology choice, risk analysis, and management. Indeed, to assert that, in the absence of consensus, different perceptions of technology and its attendant risks are just different, rather than right or wrong, does not appear to simplify the problems facing a policy maker attempting to satisfy diverse constituencies. If each constituency has a unique way of looking at the world, are there not so many cultures that the array of possible interpretations is as vast operationally as if we were dealing with the solipsistic worldviews of individuals? Happily, this is not the case. Anthropologists have devised a variety of classificatory schemes that reduce the range of cultural variation to a useful number of culture types.

One such approach is to consider four ideal-typical kinds of social organization found in the socioeconomic literature, each of which generates its own characteristic view of the world, variously referred to as a "cosmology" or "cultural bias" (Douglas 1978). In turn, it has been suggested that characteristic attributes of cultural bias, particularly, preferred aesthetics, principles of social justice, and perceived economic interests, lead members of each type of constituency to choose particular principles for obtaining public consent to a technology policy and for the distribution of liabilities arising from that policy (Rayner 1984).

It should be borne in mind that each of these four types of social structure has been generated deductively as an ideal type (Weber 1947). No real constituency could be expected to fit one of these descriptions in every respect. The value of such a typology is as a heuristic guide to clear thought about what is really similar and what is significantly different about a variety of social units. The typology is applicable to the problem of liabilities arising from potentially hazardous technologies because the social organization of each type of system makes its members sensitive to different aspects of the problem and leads them to favor characteristically different decision strategies. Therefore, the preferred spread of liabilities and benefits from technologies varies among the four different constituencies (Rayner 1984).

The first type of social organization is an entrepreneurial or market individualism, where restrictions on social behavior arising from rules or prior claims of others are kept to a minimum, giving rise to a competitive way of life. In contrast, a hierarchical or bureaucratic social environment exists where formal institutions make increasing demands of incorporation and regulation. Control is vested in formal systems of accountability. Often opposed to both competitive individualism and bureaucratic hierarchy is a third type, the collectivist egalitarian constituency such as that which is maintained within many religious sects, revolutionary political groups, and some segments of the antinuclear energy movement. Finally, there is the constituency of atomized, often alienated, individuals. In competitive organizations there are people who, having no goods or services to exchange, get driven out of the market. In hierarchical systems there are people who are excluded from the established institutions of representation. Very often, these are people who have the fewest or the least socially valued skills in a wider social arena; they tend to be the most vulnerable members of any social system.

Because entrepreneurial organizations strive for success in the marketplace, their decisions likely will be shaped by a preference for market mechanisms to spread costs and liabilities. Also, they are apt to determine consent to risk according to the notion that people will pay for the level of safety they are willing to accept. Trust is vested in successful individuals to manage risk, whether it is technological (e.g., Red Adair) or economic (e.g., Lee Iaccoca).

On the other hand, the driving force of bureaucratic organizations is system maintenance. Accordingly, they prefer to apportion liabilities in a way that is seen as least disruptive to the stability of the institution. Consent is assumed to be given by all who acknowledge the institution's legitimacy, even though individual members may dislike particular decisions. Long-established institutions that have stood the test of time, such as the British Factory Inspectorate, are trusted by this constituency.

Egalitarian groups aim to create a new social order and will favor a strict-liability principle that makes the guilty pay for the consequences of their own activities. Explicitly rejecting revealed and assumed consent, egalitarians favor expressive mechanisms for determining explicit consent. Consequently, they trust participatory democracy, such as town meetings, not markets or bureaucracies.

There is less to be said about the preferences of stratified individuals. They tend not to articulate any distinctive theory of distribution or consent. When it comes to issues of trust and confidence, these people tend to rely for protection on nonhuman agencies such as luck, providence, or, in some cases, the spirit world. Generally, atomized individuals are not decision makers themselves since most of the options for societal choice are monopolized by the other three cultural types. Their consent seldom, if ever, is sought by any means, and they constantly bear the costs of other people's errors.

From the contrasts among the four institutional cultures engaged in controversies over technological risk, it is clear that scientists and policy makers within each type of sociocultural framework may have great difficulty understanding the fears and objections of others. Particularly, given the variation in the desired spread of costs, each constituency is likely to encounter problems in designing a liability package for technological risk that satisfies another constituency whose cultural bias is different.

A PILOT STUDY: NEW NUCLEAR TECHNOLOGIES

In 1985, Oak Ridge National Laboratory (Tennessee) conducted a pilot study exploring the cultural hypothesis of technology choice in the context of the market acceptability of new nuclear power reactor technologies within the A.D. 2000–2010 time period. Our analysis of technology acceptance was part of a larger program of evaluating these reactors on engineering, economic, and regulatory criteria (Trauger et al. 1986). The new reactors included, for example, the PIUS and the modular high-temperature gas-cooled reactor, both of which embody "passive safety" features. In essence, this means that they require constant human intervention to maintain a chain reaction. Any deviation from operating specifications will cause the reactor to close down, not through the the intervention of operators or automatic safety systems, but through the action of nature. This is the opposite of the operating principle of existing reactors which require intervention in order to shut off a chain reaction once it is in progress.

Two aspects of this technology-acceptance problem made it a good candidate for an approach based on the cultural hypothesis. First, experiences with current generation nuclear technologies suggest strongly that the viability of the future concepts will not depend solely upon their technical plausibility and projected economic feasibility. If these experiences have taught us anything, it is that large public and private expenditures on research, demonstration, and manufacture of new reactors cannot be justified on technical criteria alone. Second, nuclear power has been engulfed in a long list of social and technical issues that are likely to haunt any concept associated with the nuclear family. The absence of operational experience in the new reactor technologies, even in pilot plants, places the issues associated with this technology choice firmly in the realm of Funtowicz and Ravetz's total environmental assessment. Like the current generation of nuclear technology, future concepts will be objects of social conflicts. To determine the likely acceptance of these technologies, we need to understand the conflicts, their implications, and possible resolutions.

The cultural approach to technology choice highlights the social issues of trust and equity. Consequently, our study focused on questions about the differences in preferred principles used to obtain consent from societal constituencies affected by the risks, distributing the liabilities, and justifying trust in the relevant institutions. For the purposes of this pilot study, we limited the scope of our analysis to three constituencies: the electric utilities, state public utility commissions (PUCs), and public interest groups critical of nuclear power.

Interviews were conducted with a cross-section of electric systems planning personnel and executives of seven utilities. Most utility executives and staff feel that they have been burned by nuclear power because of increasing regulatory burdens and/or soaring construction costs. Direct questions about present intentions to order future reactors almost invariably elicit a negative response. We, therefore, decided that the best way to project what the electric systems planners might recommend in the year 2010 is to look at each utility's decision-making process for ordering new generating capacity rather than to conduct an attitude survey of the present incumbents of systems-planning departments. We investigated the criteria used to select new capacity, the types of employees participating in capacity decisions, the data sources and modeling techniques applied, and the alternatives considered in a particular utility's process of capacity choice. The underlying premise of the method is that the process of decision making ultimately influences how each utility values alternative technologies. If the process differs among utilities, presumably their preferred choices also will differ.

Although this part of the research established the criteria that each utility would generally prefer to use in decisions to build power plants, our present focus is on the potential social conflicts arising from these decisions. The sources of conflict, in this case, are grounded in the constraints that PUCs and interest groups exercise on utility decision making. The channels through which these conflicts are routed are the regulatory and legal processes established for such purposes as power plant construction approval, technology licensing, and determination of electricity rates.

One approach to examining the cultural hypothesis is to observe the public display of the arguments about risk from each constituency and then relate the arguments to specific preferences regarding the trust and equity issues. However, it is often difficult to extract a meaningful relationship because risk arguments are framed carefully so as to be successful in the particular public forum in which they are made.

We sought to avoid these analytical problems by conducting direct interviews with members of the PUCs and public staffs about their roles in the utility's decision to build a new power plant. The PUC's role in the marketplace is generally to approve the need, site, technological option, and apportionment of financial responsibilities for building a plant. Because of these regulatory powers, state PUCs effectively hold a potential veto over the commercialization of any nuclear technology.

Public interest groups were selected for study because of their ability to place major hurdles in the way of nuclear licensing activities. The role of these groups in relation to the construction and operation of nuclear plants was analyzed through focus-group discussion which were held in each state.

DIFFERENT CONSTITUENCIES, DIFFERENT RISKS

Analysis of the focus-group discussions and the interviews with utility and PUC staffs indicated that the predominant concerns about risks were fundamentally different in each constituency. For the utilities, the risk arising from the decision is investment risk, i.e., the risk that the costs of plants will not be recovered fully from ratepayers. This is not to say that utilities are not concerned with health and safety risks; however, they view safety as part of the technical design which is licensed by federal regulators. Both the utilities and the PUCs implicitly trust that the engineers already have done their part in designing the plant, that the designers would not allow their plans to leave the drawing board without determining that the plant is safe enough. State PUCs, therefore, focus on economic risks that might arise because of unanticipated costs, utilities failing to perform as expected, or demand failing to grow at a rate that warrants new capacity.

Contrasting PUCs and public interest groups reveals that these constituencies focus on different issues. These differences suggest implicit agendas of interest that make it difficult for each constituency to understand the concerns of the other. The different ways of conceptualizing problems are indicated in three critical regulatory concerns: the need for the plant, who will pay for it, and how it will be managed.

According to the PUCs, need for the plant is primarily a forecasting problem that simply requires the utility to present adequate data and justification that the power will be needed when the plant becomes operational. Many PUCs also have become involved in judging whether the utility has selected the correct technological option to meet the demand forecast. If they are to use the forum provided by licensing procedures, public interest groups are constrained to contest the issues on these terms. However, the more important philosophical question for them is the need to secure consent of the parties affected by construction and operation of a nuclear plant. Rather than delegating responsibility to regulatory bodies to decide if the plant is needed, public interest groups prefer to decide, perhaps by popular referendum, if people want the plant.

The second important regulatory concern is who pays the costs of the plant. PUCs view this concern as primarily a financing one frequently with some overtones of equity intervening in the decision. If the utility can demonstrate that its construction costs were reasonably incurred and not the result of poor management, then costs of the plant will be allowed in the rate base and consumers will pay for the plant. If some construction costs are found by the PUC to be unwarranted, then the normal procedure is to pass those costs along to stockholders rather than ratepayers.

In contrast to the PUCs, public interest groups tend to view concerns associated with costs of the plant in broader ethical terms. While they address the issue of paying for the plant on the PUCs' terms because the regulatory process requires it, they would prefer to focus on the more basic issues of who bears the various safety, economic, and managerial costs resulting from the plant, who enjoys the benefits, and how the costs and benefits can be shared equitably. Health and safety risks present a particular problem for the public interest groups because when such risks become costs, they cannot be spread evenly. Actual, as opposed to statistical, death or disability must fall on individuals.

The third important regulatory concern is that of management in the nuclear enterprise. PUCs focus on issues associated with management "prudency." Prudent management is commonly defined as the process that would lead to decisions that a reasonable utility manager would make in light of the circumstances then existing and known to the manager, or that reasonably could have been known (Cantor 1986). Management prudency admittedly lends itself to vagueness and regulatory expansiveness. It has evolved in recent years into a catchall category of issues that facilitates greater regulatory intervention into utility management. PUCs frequently appear to approach management prudency issues from technical bases in the sense that technical problems may have been created or made worse by mismanagement.

Public interest groups conceive the management concern to be not merely a judgment of the utility's qualifications but also a question of the regulators' qualifications. Ultimately, public interest groups doubt whether nuclear technology can, indeed, be managed safely. They demonstrate a strong consensus that the technology is simply too complex to oversee and that nothing can be done to alter this inherent flaw. Their view of the regulators is that such agencies are too sympathetic to the industry and so not to be trusted.

Thus, in respect to the concern of managing the nuclear enterprise, PUCs tend to view the issues in narrower terms that allow regulators to address specific management problems, frequently in technical contexts. Public interest groups expand the scope of management beyond the utilities to include any institutions that are responsible for nuclear technology. They distrust these institutions because regulators and the technology itself are perceived to be parts of the nuclear problem.

These results support the propositions regarding implicit agendas of the cultural model of institutional risk management shown in Table 11.1 (Rayner and Cantor

Table 11.1   Summary of Preferred Principles of Consent, Liability, and Trust According to Type of Constituency

	Competitive/ Market	Bureaucratic/ Hierarchical	Egalitarian	Atomized Individual
Liability	Loss spreading	Redistributive	Strict-fault system	No special principles elaborated for liability or consent
Consent	Implicit; revealed preference	Hypothetical	Explicit; expressed preference	
Trust	Successful individuals (Red Adair, Lee Iaccoca)	Long-established formal organizations (AMA, USCG)	Participatory information (town meetings, affinity groups)	Nonhuman forces (nature, luck, spirits)
Justification	Consequentialist	Contractualism	Rights based	No consistent justification
Goal	Market success	System maintenance	New social order	Survival

1987). Process is the domain of the regulators, whose objective is the adherence to that process, regardless of the outcome it produces. This objective suggests an implicit agenda for system maintenance. On the other hand, public interest groups are concerned with an outcome that is consistent with their antinuclear goals. Adherence to process is irrelevant. Their concerns are broad and directed at policy questions for which regulatory environments are not well suited. Their implicit agenda calls for a new social and political order that would make the current distribution of resources more equitable. Indeed, public interest groups, in a very real sense, are fighting legislative battles in regulatory proceedings.

In short, the approach of each of the constituencies in our pilot study corresponded quite well to one or another of the packages of consent liability and trust principles predicted by the cultural hypothesis. PUCs are clearly adopting bureaucratic values, particularly with respect to hypothetical consent and the institutional redistribution of liabilities, provided that certain standards of prudency are observed by the utility. The utilities are happy for the market for electric power to stand as a surrogate for societal consent and prefer to spread losses among consumers rather than stockholders. The public interest groups express clear preferences for direct participation in decision making and favor stockholder responsibility for managerial decisions. The utilities trust good managers to make decisions, PUCs trust the process, and the public interest groups trust only the explicit collective will of the people.

All three constituencies portray themselves as the champions of those stratified individuals who are excluded, in practice, from participation in the debate. This fourth category provides the ideological legitimation for the activities of the utilities (public service), the PUCs (representative democratic regulation), and the public interest groups (participatory democratic control). The stratified individualists themselves played no part in our experiment because the issues of technology selection for 2010 are too general and too far into the future to capture their attention. As Gross and Rayner (1985) point out, this constituency only coalesces for political activity when members' interests are threatened directly at the local level. We would expect the NIMBY (not in my back yard) response from these people at a particular site were construction of a new reactor under immediate consideration, but we would anticipate less concern about overall societal decision making.

Our example illustrates that the problem of finding a risk-management solution to satisfy all constituencies would be a difficult one. However, both greater understanding of the liability issues and the processes of policy debates could be enhanced by this kind of approach. Further research into the trust and equity aspects of risk can benefit from using the cultural approach for other examples of societal technology choice and risk management. Of particular urgency is the problem of cross-national problems of environmental management, where the balance of institutional cultures in each country facing a common hazard may lead a nation to favor solutions that are incompatible with those preferred by its neighbors.

CULTURE AND THE GLOBAL MANAGEMENT OF COMMON RESOURCES

The reactor fire at Chernobyl highlighted a problem of practical urgency for all nations—managing common technological hazards and common resources across national boundaries in the absence of global government. In addition to radiological catastrophe, the greenhouse effect, acid rain, desertification, ground water quality, pesticide pollution, and environmental consequences of oceanic exploitation are prominent samples from the catalog of transnational technological problems.

Success in grappling with these problems will depend upon the ability of decision makers in each of the affected countries to understand the cultural preferences of the others and to recognize that their own favored solution may be incompatible with other decision-making and regulatory traditions. This is no small challenge given the difficulties of creating a common discursive framework that we have seen in the small-scale example of our case study, in which all participants at least share a common national culture.

In approaching transnational problems of technology acceptance, it is useful to distinguish between horizontal and vertical dimensions of social affiliation. The horizontal dimension includes people across societies who by their stated positions and actions within their own countries share the same interests and hold the same stakes in a technology dispute as, for example, a prodevelopment entrepreneur, antiproject protester, scientific/technical advisor, or government regulator. The vertical dimension includes inhabitants of a particular country or society, irrespective of their particular stance on issues and profession of interest.

For some purposes, horizontally affiliated populations will be quite similar in their actions and beliefs and will be more likely to communicate successfully with each other than with those with whom they simply share a common national heritage. At least at one level, antinuclear protesters in the United States are much like those in West Germany and the United Kingdom, and they have a common basis on which to act. Likewise, personnel in the nuclear industry in the United States are much like their counterparts in the Federal Republic of Germany and the United Kingdom.

This viewpoint was adopted by researchers at the International Institute for Applied Systems Analysis (IIASA) in Laxenburg, Austria, to help explain the rigid positions taken by international participants at their seminars on energy futures in the late 1970s (Thompson 1984). Although participants, invited from the United States and Western Europe, were requested to consider various energy futures in an objective, speculative, and open fashion, the participants remained locked into positions essentially paralleling those in energy controversies across Europe and the United States. They fell into rival camps, each expressing a different package of preferences, each apparently guided by a different worldview.

There are those who, while strongly opposed to nuclear energy, felt that there were marked limits to economic growth and endorsed both a quest for small scale energy technologies and political decentralization. Other participants subscribed to a quite opposite package of views and preferences; they were progrowth, pronuclear, and favored large-scale and centrally managed development. Members of each camp were linked by their views of problems and solutions rather than by the country from which they came. Thompson identified these as kinds of rival energy tribes whose membership crossed national boundaries.

Certainly in the energy controversies of the 1970s protesters in many different countries sought to build international networks. They listened to some of the same traveling evangelists, for example, the well-known advocate of soft-energy paths, Amory Lovins. Similarly, energy industry executives and their public relations specialists collaborated in both formal and informal associations, such as the Atomic Industrial Forum, to counter protest and to lobby for their projects. More generally, it has been argued elsewhere that in the world system of the '70s and '80s, multinational corporations constitute a kind of global social class, with more loyalty to their corporation than to their country (Barnet and Mueller 1974).

Similarly, it has been claimed that social movements have become multinational entities, with global concerns (Willetts 1982). In any event, a good case can be made for the proposition that the constituencies in technology decision making and disputes are quite similar in structure and function across societies. In other words, we can expect to find technological disputes in various countries characterized by issues similar to those that we found in our nuclear pilot study.

However, the relative size and structure of governmental, legal, regulatory, corporate, and public interest institutions clearly vary from country to country.

No matter how much the various constituencies in a process of technology decision making and dispute are shaped by their particular adaptive strategies and tasks, they are also operating in and from a larger cultural context. They are products of their larger society and its culture—what Goodenough (1971) calls a "public culture." In our terms, British corporations may be more bureaucratic than American, which are strongly influenced by decentralized and egalitarian forms of organization. Centralized bureaucracies may be more powerful and acceptable to the French than to the Americans. Certainly, until recently the entrepreneurial spirit has not been publicly admired in cultural hierarchies like the Soviet Union. However, America too has its ossified bureaucracies, and egalitarian champions trumpet their causes in Europe while Soviet and Chinese leaders attempt to harness entrepreneurial talents to their cause. It is the particular mixture of institutional cultures that gives each country its characteristic cultural flavor, a particular preference for the German, British, French, or American way of doing things.

Existing research on the topic of national differences in institutional arrangements for making technological decisions is somewhat fragmented. Some comparative studies have been made on national debates over certain technologies. For example, Nelkin and Pollack (1981) have compared French and German controversies over nuclear energy. Sweden and the United States have been compared with regard to air quality (Lindquist 1980) and occupational safety and health policies (Kelman 1981). An IIASA study of liquified natural gas siting in Europe and the United States (Kunreuther et al. 1982) focuses on different institutional arrangements for managing technology.

Many of these studies tend to emphasize contrasts between the essentially cooperative approach to technology acceptance in Europe and the more confrontational approach that predominates in the United States. As Jasanoff (1986) points out, the cultural determination of scientific issues has played a relatively small part in these studies. Their emphasis has been on the demands of interest groups and the responsiveness of political and legal institutions to rival claims about technology.

But my argument is that scientific and technological knowledge about new technologies is dominated by cultural interpretations. Indeed, Jasanoff (1986) brilliantly illustrates that information about established technologies, such as formaldehyde use, is interpreted differently by scientific advisory committees in different countries. In particular, she has argued (Brickman, Jasanoff, and Ilgen 1985) that the decentralization of decision making in the United States both increases demand for scientific details of technological hazards and engenders competition between different explanations. Hence, the more intensive public debate in the United States about technological regulation than in France, Britain, or the Federal Republic of Germany.

The implications of such studies for the global management of common resources are daunting. However, international research programs, such as

IIASA's International Biosphere Program (Clark and Munn 1986) and the developing Global Environmental Decision Making Program at Oak Ridge National Laboratory, are beginning to address both the technical and cultural aspects of international science and technology policy. The relevance of culture for such studies surely must receive increasing recognition.

NOTE

This chapter has been authored by a contractor of the U.S. Government under contract No. DE–AC05–840R21400. Accordingly, the U.S. Government retains a nonexclusive, royalty-free license to publish or reproduce the published form of this contribution, or allow others to do so, for U.S. Government purposes.

The case study described in this chapter was conducted by the author in collaboration with economist Robin Cantor and political scientist Bob Braid of Oak Ridge National Laboratory. In the course of this study, many insights were obtained that enriched the basic anthropological framework. Without the contributions of these colleagues, this chapter would not have been possible.

REFERENCES

Agassi, Joseph
    1984   "The Cheapening of Science." *Inquiry* 27: 167–72.

Barnes, Barry
    1974   *Scientific Knowledge and Sociological Theory*. London: Routledge & Kegan Paul.

Barnet, Richard, and Ronald Mueller
    1974   *Global Reach*. New York: Simon & Schuster.

Berkeley, George
    1710   *A Treatise Concerning the Principles of Human Understanding*. Dublin: Rhames & Pepyat.

Bloch, Morris
    1977   "The Past and the Present in the Present." *Man* [NS] 12: 278–93.

Bloor, David
    1976   *Knowledge and Social Imagery*. London: Routledge & Kegan Paul.

Brickman, R., S. Jasanoff, and T. Ilgen
    1985   *Controlling Chemicals: The Politics of Regulation in Europe and the United States*. Ithaca: Cornell University Press.

Cantor, Robin
    1986   "Prudency Hearings and Management Audits." Unpublished manuscript.

Clark, William C., and Robert Munn, eds.
    1986   *Sustainable Development of the Biosphere*. New York: Cambridge University Press.

Cohen, Bernard
    1985   "Criteria for Technology Acceptability." *Risk Analysis* 5: 1–3.

Douglas, Mary
  1986   "Institutionalized Public Memory." In *The Social Fabric*, J. F. Short, Jr., ed. Beverly Hills: Sage.
  1980   *Evans-Pritchard*. Brighton, Eng.: Harvester Press.
  1978   *Cultural Bias*. London: Royal Anthropological Institute.

Douglas, Mary, and Aaron Wildavsky
  1982   *Risk and Culture*. Berkeley: University of California Press.

Funtowicz, S. O., and J. R. Ravetz
  1985   "Three Types of Risk Assessment: A Methodological Analysis." In *Risk Analysis in the Private Sector*, C. Whipple and V. Covello, eds. New York: Plenum.

Geertz, Clifford
  1973   *The Interpretation of Culture*. New York: Basic Books.

Goodenough, Ward
  1971   *Culture, Language, and Society*. Reading Mass.: Addison-Wesley.

Gross, J. L., and S. Rayner
  1985   *Measuring Culture*. New York: Columbia University Press.

Jasanoff, Sheila
  1986   *Risk Management and Political Culture*. New York: Russell Sage Foundation.

Jaulin, R.
  1971   "Ethnocide: The Theory and Practice of Cultural Murder." *The Ecologist* 1: 12–15.

Kaprow, Miriam Lee
  1985   "Manufacturing Danger: Fear and Pollution in Industrial Society." *American Anthropologist* 87: 357–64.

Kelman, Stephen
  1981   *Regulating America, Regulating Sweden: A Comparative Analysis of Occupational Safety and Health Policy*. Cambridge: MIT Press.

Kunreuther, H., J. Linneroth, and R. Starnes, eds.
  1982   *Liquified Energy Gases Facility Siting: International Comparisons*. Laxenburg, Austria: International Institute for Applied Systems Analysis.

Lindquist, Lennart
  1980   *The Hare and the Tortoise: Clean Air Policies in the United States and Sweden*. Ann Arbor: University of Michigan Press.

Merkhofer, Miley
  1986   *Decision Science and Social Risk Management*. Dordrecht: Reidel.

National Academy of Science
  1983   *Risk Assessment in the Federal Government: Managing the Process*. Washington, D. C.: National Academy Press.

Nelkin, Dorothy, and Michael Pollack
  1981   *The Atom Besieged*. Cambridge: MIT Press.

Peelle, Elizabeth
  1987   "Innovative Process and Inventive Solutions: A Case Study of Local Public Acceptance of a Proposed Nuclear Waste Packaging and Storage Facility." In René Dubos Institute for Environmental Management, *Symposium on Land-Use Management*. New York: Praeger.

Rapoport, A.
   1977   *Human Aspects of Urban Form*. Oxford: Pergamon Press.
Ravetz, Jerome
   1986   "Usable Knowledge, Usable Ignorance: Incomplete Knowledge with Policy
           Implications." In *Sustainable Development of the Biosphere*, W. C. Clark and
           R. Munn, eds. New York: Cambridge University Press.
Rawls, John
   1971   *A Theory of Justice*. Cambridge: Belknap Press of Harvard University Press.
Rayner, Steve
   1984   "Disagreeing About Risk: The Institutional Cultures of Risk Management
           and Planning for Future Generations." In *Risk Analysis, Institutions, and
           Public Policy*, S. Hadden, ed. Port Washington, N. Y.: Associated Faculty
           Press.
   1982   "The Perception of Time and Space in Egalitarian Sects: A Millenarian
           Cosmology." In *Essays in the Sociology of Perception*, Mary Douglas, ed.
           London: Routledge & Kegan Paul.
Rayner, Steve, and Robin Cantor
   1987   "How Fair Is Safe Enough? The Cultural Approach to Societal Technology
           Choice." *Risk Analysis* 7(1): 3–9.
Ryle, Gilbert
   1949   *The Concept of Mind*. London: Hutchinson.
Self, Peter
   1975   *The Econocrats and the Policy Process: The Politics and Philosophy of Cost-
           Benefit Analysis*. London: Macmillan.
Thompson, Michael
   1984   "Among the Energy Tribes: A Cultural Framework for the Analysis and
           Design of Energy Policy." *Policy Sciences* 17: 321–39.
Trauger, Donald B., et al.
   1986   "Nuclear Power Options Viability Study." vol. III. ORNL/TM–9780/V3, Oak
           Ridge National Laboratory, Oak Ridge, Tenn.
Weber, Max
   1947   *The Theory of Economic and Social Organization*. New York: Free Press.
Weinberg, Alvin
   1972   "Science and Trans-Science." *Minerva* 10: 209–22.
Willetts, Peter
   1982   *Pressure Groups in the Global System*. New York: St. Martin's.
Wittgenstein, Ludwig
   1953   *Philosophical Investigations*. Oxford: Blackwell.

12

PROPER RULES, SMART RULES, AND POLICE DISCRETION

Morris Freilich and Frank A. Schubert

Anthropology gained much momentum in theory when "culture" was defined as standards.[1] Standards is part of a family of concepts whose head member is *rules*. Standards, therefore, is usefully replaced by the more general concept rules. Rules has for long attracted much interest and discussion by philosophers. Anthropology can mine the philosophical wisdom lodged in rules by linking culture to rules. Digging in this philosophical treasure for over two decades, Freilich has come up with a theory of action called "Smart/Proper Analysis." Smart/Proper Analysis (SPA) is here presented as a tool for rethinking discussions about police discretion.[2]

SPA sits on an axiom formulated in "the spirit of Marx" (cf. Giddens 1976). SPA's axiom is: Human life is built on conflict and mired in a major dilemma. The conflict is not between classes but within the individual. The dilemma is not which mode of production to promote but which form of philosophy to follow. Metaphorically presented, the human conflict is which camp to join. Camp P promotes "properness," a philosophy which respects history, tradition, and ancestors. Camp S promotes "smartness," a philosophy which respects problems of survival, the pursuit of success, and the love of power. The messages received from each camp are convincing. But each camp demands loyalty. It is understandable, therefore, that humans actually stand in the middle of a tug-of-war.

The human conflict creates mental anguish. Which camp will provide the "good life?" Why is it not possible to join both camps? Questions such as these plague all human minds and create that general condition of nervousness sometimes called "neurosis." Neurosis, psychiatry to the contrary, seems to be a normal condition of normal humans. Neurosis is normal because it is created by the major dilemma which all humans face.

The Human Dilemma appears under many masks. It is gently described to children in "Beauty and the Beast." It is linked to science in "Dr. Jekyll and Mr.

Hyde." And it is given a mystifying, dreamlike form in *Steppenwolf*. Following Smart/Proper Analysis (Freilich 1980), the Human Dilemma is to be forced to choose between *dignity* and *sanity* (on the one hand) and *success* and *power* (on the other). A major dilemma, by any name, will hurt the same. The hurt, the mental anguish, along with the comforts that humans invent, give human life that "sweet and sour" flavor we all experience.

SPA's axiom — the Human Condition = Psychological Conflict + Philosophical Dilemma — presents a general picture of human existence. It helps explain strategies of escape, such as drugs, drama, and games. And it makes better sense of such linguistic forms as sarcasm, irony, and unsolvable riddles (*koans*). This general picture of existence is operationalized for anthropological research by five key propositions. First, culture consists of principles and rules which guide proper action. Second, a culture is a guidance system for proper action which belongs to a society. Third, each culture competes for guidance with two other guidance systems: smart rules and private rules. Fourth, smart rules belong to social units, such as work groups, clans, clubs, and cliques. Fifth, private rules (generally called "habits") belong to individuals.

The five key propositions of Smart/Proper Analysis, formally tied together, create a model for decision making. This model, Smart and Proper Strategies, along with the rest of the theoretical technology of SPA, has been used for a number of projects. It has been used to develop a method for myth analysis, to present a novel perspective on warfare, and to rethink theories of deviance (Freilich 1975, 1983, in press). This theoretical technology is also being used in the study of police discretion (Freilich and Schubert 1983, 1984). In this chapter SPA will be used to reexamine a problem — "the gap" — which plagues policing.

THE POLICE DILEMMA AND THE GAP

The gap — the "distance" which exists between (1) the police role as formally spelled out by the law and (2) the police role as actually practiced — is not easily understood *well*. To facilitate the fullest understanding, we introduce the gap with three propositions. First, in societies such as the United States — societies which proudly pronounce that they operate by the rule of law — police activities must be regulated. Second, the more police activities are regulated, the less effective is the policing system. Third, the quality of social life is enhanced when the policing system is effective. These propositions, carefully read, lead to a sad conclusion: The Human Dilemma is alive and well, right in the middle of the law-enforcing process.

From the inception of the town watch to modern times, considerable efforts have been made to regulate police activities. In the United States these regulatory efforts have consisted largely of such formal writings as constitutions, statutes, judicial opinions, agency rules, and policy statements. These formal writings are based, in part, on philosophical assumptions concerning optimal social conditions and relationships. They represent a reaffirmation of ideals and values passed on to us as "traditions" (Shils 1981). They give social institutions political legitimacy, and they give people who live by them pride, purpose, and (some level of) predictability (Freilich 1978). While these formulations tend to reflect lofty societal ideals, they minimally consider the needs of those who are policing our streets (Dougherty 1964; H. Goldstein 1977; Kamisar 1965).

Constitutional provisions tend to be vague and imprecise, making them subject to widely fluctuating interpretations. The Constitutional provisions of the Bill of Rights, for example, have permitted a host of practices in the past which would be impermissible today.[3] Statutes are similarly deficient. Frequently, they mandate a full enforcement role for the police which is impractical if not impossible to implement (Moran and Cooper 1983).[4] At the same time they fail to define the extent to which police officers are expected to perform the multitude of social service functions which constitute the majority of "police work."[5] Police departmental rules and policies, to the extent that they exist, rarely clarify constitutional and statutory deficiencies. Moreover, few departments expose police officers to all the laws and regulations they should know.

Police officers who patrol the streets are forced to juggle both the law (as they know and understand it) and practical considerations. As street practitioners these police officers must adapt to work conditions, to environments which they define as filled with "assholes" (Van Maanan 1978). Therefore, they evaluate the rules and use them to the extent that, experientially, they are known to be effective, safe, and in the officer's best interest (Brown 1981; Aaronson, Dienes, and Musheno 1984). The few meaningful guidelines that do exist tend to lack a concern with practical issues such as workmanship, the pride in the specialized skills of the experienced officer (Bittner 1983). In sum, from the perspective of the police officer, it is often necessary to substitute the rules derived from experience for the rule of law (Milner 1971).

Substituting the use of discretion for a rigid enforcement of the law solves some policing problems. However, this solution creates new problems, both for the street practitioners and for the general public. For street practitioners discretion often means making arbitrary decisions without either adequate training or enough street experience to act prudently. It means having to balance street wisdom with perceptions of what superior officers would formally approve and what the public would accept. Most police officers learn to use street wisdom and learn, simultaneously, how to appear to be operating within the law.

Discretionary decisions by police officers confuse the general public. Depending on who does the research and on what questions are asked, the results obtained are different. According to some sources (U. S. Commission on Civil Rights 1979; Muir 1977; Takagi 1974) discretionary decisions, generally, are seen as ill-advised. However, the 1975 National Crime Survey (NCS) reported that police performance was seen as good or average by 74 percent of black respondents and 84 percent of white respondents. And this NCS report is consistent with the results of a study conducted by the National Opinion Research Center in 1966.[6]

Irrespective of whose perspective is taken, the relatively uncontrolled use of police discretion creates a system which is antithetical to democratic values, a system which has been aptly termed "justice without trial" (Skolnick 1966). Even the harshest critic of police behavior, to be objective, must recognize that policing includes a dilemma. The policing dilemma in its simplest terms is *law or order*: either to follow rigidly the rules and accept ineffective policing or to use arbitrary discretionary powers in the service of order (Skolnick 1966). By often selecting order over law, police officers find themselves charged with creating a gap.

The gap problem has been noticed by many. Reactions to it can be characterized as empirical, legalistic, empathetic, or policy oriented/analytical. Empirical writings have documented the existence of the gap in various regions of the country and at various levels of police work. Legalistic studies have suggested that it could be greatly reduced by improving the statutes. Empathetic writers have sought to explain the gap from a police officer's perspective. Policy-oriented analysts have proposed solutions which primarily place the responsibility for gap shrinking on police administrators.[7]

To date none of these perspectives has had much impact, either on police behavior or on the law. According to Brown this failure is understandable. He believes society has yet to grapple with the problem from a realistic perspective. As he puts it:

> No one should entertain any illusions about the outcome of any efforts at reform. Police work inevitably entails the arbitrary use of power: brutality, corruption, the violation of individual rights, and the penchant to take the law into one's own hands, to use it as a tool to right wrongs and attain "justice." (1981: 304)

If one follows Brown (and Bittner 1970: 52–62), reform efforts will continue to fail as long as they move in the direction of more law. What are actually needed, according to this point-of-view, are reforms geared to enlarging rather than stunting the patrol officer's capacity to exercise judgment. Whether this can be accomplished within a democratic framework is a major and unanswered question.

The gap problem, we suggest, is more complex than it appears to be. Therefore, it needs to be studied in general terms. A general approach to the gap must, of necessity, be a theoretical approach. And, as noted, the theoretical approach we will use is Smart/Proper Analysis. SPA forces us to keep focusing on the Human Dilemma: to follow proper rules (and enjoy dignity) or to follow smart rules (and maximize the probabilities of success).

The Human Dilemma interferes with the work of police officers essentially in much the same way it interferes with other members of the work force. It keeps police on edge, struggling with two strategies, neither of which is totally satisfactory. Should they put all their energies toward examining the task in hand? Sometimes the task is dangerous, and their lives are really at stake. A lack of concentration can here have very serious results. Can they really worry about the law at such times? But if they forget the law, the consequences again will be serious. There may be administrative, civil, or criminal charges to face; the possibility of the loss of a job and a dismal future. Clearly, although essentially, the Human Dilemma is much the same for police as it is for others, its consequences are different. Police work includes taking and risking life and limb. Moreover, police officers serve as role models for dealing with the law. If police officers are seen breaking the law or even juggling it, respect for the law is lowered.

Here, Smart/Proper Analysis provides three contributions to gap handling. First, as noted, SPA thinking suggests that if we look carefully at any work force – bankers, judges, professors, taxi drivers – we will find a gap. Each faces the Human Dilemma. Each must juggle practical and effective strategies along with traditional and legal strategies. The police, therefore, cannot be chastized as the only group that creates a gap. Second, SPA provides an emotion-free language which is likely to promote rational discussion. Such rational discourse is likely to restrain us from branding police officers as power-hungry street judges. Such discourse will also help us to avoid hero worship – giving the police officer a halo and labels, such as fearless defender of the law. Finally, SPA thinking can steer us away from popular but useless modes of handling the police gap. These useless modes seem to be based on two principles of American culture: (1) Life is a zero-sum game – more simply, there are always "losers" and "winners" – and (2) Every problem is solvable. The police gap, following SPA, is a problem which is not solvable. Problems like the gap are encased in a dilemma (here the Human Dilemma). And dilemma-linked problems push us in the direction of one of the dilemma's "horns." As we go for one horn (as we embrace the law), we are gored by the other horn (ineffective policing). Should we grab this latter horn, the former will get us. The classic solution to all dilemmas is to try to slip between the horns. In less metaphorical language the solution is to look for some middle ground, some kind of compromise. The search for a compromise does not lead to losers and winners; it leads to partners. The partners do not rid us of the gap; they do not solve the problem. Rather, the partners develop ways of shrinking the gap.

WORKING WITH SMART/PROPER ANALYSIS (SPA)

Following SPA, formal writings created to control police behaviors are termed proper rules and principles. Police officers who avoid or evade these rules and principles are considered as deviants, actors who deviate from the proper. Deviants, contrary to public opinion, sometimes make positive contributions to the success and vitality of organizations. Deviants, as Albert Cohen has noted (1965: 6–11), sometimes identify patterns of behavior which are more effective or practical than those based on organizational norms. Such deviant behavior sometimes is copied by actors who have important positions in the organization. As other actors join the bandwagon, a new rule slowly develops. In SPA language this new rule is called a "smart rule."

The new rule, defined as smart, will differ in quality from proper rules (see below). However, the smart rule will still function as a rule, a guide-to-action given power by an "ought." The power of the ought ("You ought to do it this way because.... ") will lead the smart rule to create a pattern of behavior. Such a pattern will represent actions which more effectively reach organizational goals.

The analysis presented is plausible. However, a critical question remains unanswered: What empirical support exists for this type of thinking? In actuality, substantial empirical support exists for the two propositions which sit behind this analysis. 1. *Deviant behavior is often patterned.* 2. *Rules or norms lie behind such deviant patterns.* Moreover, the empirical support for these propositions comes from research among peoples who live in very different societies. Patterns of deviant behavior have been discovered among the Polynesians, the Purum of Eastern Manipur, navy personnel in the United States, the Apache, the employees in a Soviet firm, the staff of a public employment agency in the United States, tribal people in New Guinea, Trobriand Islanders, African-Americans in American ghettos, the Mehinaku of Central Brazil, Americans at all social levels, Trinidadian peasants, and the rich and powerful in the United States.[8]

In considering these (and related) data, a number of scholars have come to the obvious conclusion. Patterns of behavior are the result of norms or rules for action. Since patterns of deviance exist, there must be a second, normative system. This second system has been given many names by scholars working in several disciplines. It has been called "established modes of not conforming to custom" (Firth 1939), "customary ways of not conforming to culture" (Slotkin 1950), "pragmatic rules" (Bailey 1968), "practical rules" (Bailey 1968; Good 1981), and "emerging norms" (Drabek 1968). For an elaboration and a comparison, see Figure 12.1. It appears reasonable to conclude, therefore, that all social systems have a second set of rules, a set here referred to as smart rules.

Smart rules, it must be noted, actually consist of n-subsets. Each subset consists of smart rules which belong to a specific social unit. As members of a social unit (say, a work group) interact, they share information. Shared information which members of social units find interesting or consider valuable gets discussed and analyzed. Is John a reliable reporter? Or does he tend to exaggerate in order to make a point? Are Bill's lucky breaks due more to experience than luck? Is it really possible to cut corners the way Sally does and still get good results? Talk such as this is often put down as gossip. Actually it has important functions (Spacks 1983). Such talk is part of a process: Information is shared for fun and profit. Shared information leads to generalizations. Generalizations become smart rules. The generalizations which become smart rules are put into phrases that sound something like: Under Conditions C, if there is Problem Q, you ought to do Y. It is noteworthy that the ought ("You ought to....") that is linked to a smart rule is simple to explain.

Take, for example, a smart rule which belongs to those who teach in universities: You ought to publish a lot! Should a novice ask "Why ought I to publish a lot?" a simple answer exists that all experienced university teachers know. "Publish or perish" — keep publishing or risk losing your job. Similarly, all smart rules have a simple answer to the "Why ought I?" question. Indeed, the *easily explained ought* is a distinguishing characteristic of smart rules. In contrast the

Figure 12.1 **Two Informational Systems Comparable as Contrasts between the Proper and the Smart**

	Proper	Smart
Bailey (1968)	Normative rules	Pragmatic rules
Bittner (1983)	Legal criteria	Workmanship criteria
Bourdieu (1979)	Formal rules	Habitus
Coser et al. (1983)	Official norms	Counter norms
Dexter (1981)	The desirable	The marketable
Diamond (1972)	Culture	Social signals
Drabek (1968)	Established norms	Emergent norms
Durkheim (1953)	Value judgments	Judgments of reality
Hall (1969)	Formal	Informal
Hocart (1970)	Cultural	Practical
Howard (1963)	Normative decisions	Strategic decisions
Hunn (1982)	Formal	Practical significance
Hymes (1970)	Social	Empirical
Kant (1966)	Categorical imperatives	Hypothetical imperatives
Kroeber (1952, 1957)	Value culture	Reality culture
Leach (1954, 1961)	Ritual formal structure	Practical informal structure
Marcuse (1964)	Truth value	Exchange value
Page (1946–47)	Formal system	Informal system
Rawls (1955)	Rules of a "practice"	Rules as experience summaries
Redfield (1953)	Moral rules	Rules of expedience
Reisman (1979)	Myth systems	Operational codes
Santayana (1955)	Judgments of value	Judgments intellectual
Searle (1964)	Institutionalized rules	Regulatory rules
Shils (1971)	"Traditional" traditions	Rational, empirical traditions
Stoddard (1968)	Formalized norms	Reference group norms
Turk (1969)	Cultural norms	Social norms
Weber (1947)	*Wertrational*	*Zweckrational*

ought linked to proper rules is very difficult to explain. The *difficult-to-explain ought* creates serious problems for proper rules, as we shall see.

The statement, "smart rules exist," is now a proposition that must be considered as true beyond a reasonable doubt. A society, clearly now, has at least two types of rules monitoring action. Smart rules, in charge of survival and pushing for success, stand in opposition to proper rules. Proper rules, assigned the general and difficult-to-explain purpose of creating and maintaining properness, might appear as a weak opponent to the easily understood smart rules. After all, survival is the first goal of life, and the joys of success and power are easy to sell. But proper rules have an ally—a system of principles. And the allies, *principles and proper rules*, provide some powerful arguments against the lure of the smart. Let us, but briefly, examine the ways principles and proper rules work together.

Principles and Proper Rules

Proper rules have been given many names (see Figure 12.1). One of these names, "tradition," points to the fact that proper rules are old and valuable. Proper rules come out of the past, as a shared heritage. This inheritance, given by a set of ancestors to the members of a society, is too complex to be presented as just proper rules. Rules do their best work in directing action. Their explanatory power is weak. The nagging question behind each rule is "Why ought that to be done?" And the shared heritage or tradition includes answers to this question. These answers are lodged in a system which Ronald Dworkin (1967) has called "principles."

Principles provide general orientations to situations. They identify the logic of events, they explain forms and give meanings to all proper happenings. We learn principles, often, without really knowing that we are learning anything. They come to us (among other ways) in myths, proverbs, jokes, and metaphors. Consider some ways that metaphors-as-principles orient our reality in American society. We believe, following Lakoff and Johnson (1980) that: (1) Argument is war. ("She *demolished* my argument by *attacking* my examples." (2) Time is money. ("My time is *expensive*. Did you *spend* much time there?") (3) Happy is up. Sad is down. ("My spirits *rose*, but later I got depressed. Now I feel *down*.") These and other metaphors concretize processes and feelings. Various phenomena become interrelated, linked by a common logic. For example, "*Time is money* entails that time is a *limited resource*, which entails that time is a *valuable commodity*." (Lakoff and Johnson 1980: 9)

In the legal sphere, principles make such abstract concepts as justice more understandable. In American society, and following Dworkin (1967), justice includes the legal principle:

> No one shall be permitted to profit by his own fraud, or to take advantage of his own wrong, or to found a claim on his own iniquity, or to acquire property by how own crime. (pp. 23–24)

This legal principle, just like any metaphor principle, provides a point-of-view. It contrasts sharply with a legal rule, say, "A will is invalid unless signed by three witnesses" (Dworkin 1967). The rule tells us what to do. Or better, rules tell us what ought to be done. They assume that we understand the rules from knowing the principles. A further assumption is that the principles explain everything. Now, while principles explain much, there is also much that principles leave unexplained. The unexplained within the rule causes protectors of the proper some difficulties. Invariably someone finds something that is either unexplained or poorly explained and then demands an explanation. Consider the proper (and legal) rule: "One must have three witnesses when making a will." A reasonable question is "Why three witnesses?" "Why not two or four?" The questioner, we can reasonably assume, wants a real explanation, not "Well, that's the law!" The questioner wants to know why three witnesses makes sense. Similarly, a child in American society might want to know why three strikes cause a batter to be "out." Similarly, a Yanomamö youth might ask: "Why ought I to marry a mother's brother's daughter or a father's sister's daughter?" (Both of these suggested mates are "cross-cousins," and cross-cousin marriage is proper among the Yanomamö, cf. Chagnon 1977.)

In short, cultural principles tie proper rules together into a system of meanings and explanations. Yet, as Lakoff and Johnson (1980) show for American culture, the principles are not all consistent with each other. Somehow the system gains some coherence; it fits together, but there are some rough edges. It therefore takes a very knowledgeable and wise "native" to fully explain why given proper rules take the form they do. An average Yanomamo, when questioned about the reason for cross-cousin marriage, probably first will flounder and then fabricate an answer. The fabrication is likely to take the form of similar fabrications often heard in American society: "This is our way of doing things; we have always done it this way."

Now, clearly, such an answer is a fabrication. It is hard to imagine any rule which has always been in force and which has always met with compliance. Should the one asking the question be daring enough to suggest that the answer is not true, he may be punished or left with a vague answer. The latter is likely to take the form of: "This is what we do, and this is what you ought to do, because it is right!" Given the difficulty of making total sense of many proper rules and given pressure to do so from questioners, fabrications (it must be assumed) are often used as answers. Fabrications only rarely are foolproof. Hence proper rules can easily be attacked by statements such as: "These rules really make no sense!" or "These rules are given support by a pack of lies!"

Proper rules, as noted, have as their major "enemy" sets of smart rules. In addition, proper rules must contend with a minor irritation. Most humans seem to have their own rules for handling given situations. In the language of the street we note this fact by saying people have "habits." In philosophy, personal or private rules have been called "rules-of-thumb" and "summary rules" (cf. Rawls 1955; Diggs 1964). Following Smart/Proper Analysis, a person who avoids both the proper rules of the total society and the smart rules of his or her social units will be described as using private rules.

Those who often use private rules for serious occasions assume a high level of risk. The risks assumed are greater if these private rules are used to identify goals (rather than means). A goal, the planned end result of an activity, is generally more visible than the means used to achieve it. A visible achievement of an end which is not proper (not acceptable to the members of the society) and is not smart (not acceptable to members of important social units) must (surely) tend to create problems for its planner.

THE FORMAL MODEL: SMART AND PROPER STRATEGIES (SAPS)

Smart and Proper Strategies (SAPS) links three types of rules (proper, smart, and private) with two functions of rules, to identify goals and to describe means. SAPS, therefore, uses six elements to discuss decisions: proper means, proper goals, smart means, smart goals, private means, private goals. Each of these elements, shown in Figure 12.2, is discussed below.

Figure 12.2 SAPS: Smart and Proper Strategies

GOALS

	Cultural (shared) P	Social (shared) S	Private (not shared) Z
Proper p	pP 1	pS 2	pZ 3
Smart s	sP 4	sS 5	sZ 6
Private z	zP 7	zS 8	zZ 9

MEANS (row label for the table)

KEY: P = proper, that which is culturally shared
S = smart, that which is socially shared
Z = a personal strategy
The first letter refers to means; the second
letter refers to goals. Example: sP = smart
means for proper goals.

Proper Means and Proper Goals

These elements are more generally referred to as customary, traditional, institutionalized, formal, correct, and lawful. These are means and goals which are either specified by the law or are consistent with the law. Both proper means and proper goals tend to lack input from experiences in the streets. Lacking street wisdom, proper means tend to hamper more than help police work. The law is rarely written with the police officer in mind. The police officer as both de facto interpreter of the law and the person charged with maintaining order is likely (often) to circumvent proper means in order to reach proper goals.

Smart Means and Smart Goals

These elements are developed by members of a social unit. Police officers who work together and who otherwise interact — in bars, in clubs — share experiences of the streets. Members of an information-sharing unit (ISU) discuss and analyze these shared experiences and come up with generalizations. These generalizations are often most useful to the society as a whole when they specify what smart means to use. These generalizations are likely to be harmful to the society as a whole when they create new goals — goals which are smart.

Smart means which are actually successful seem to move across information-sharing units; they move from ISU to ISU. Such widely used smart means include:

Like how a pusher delivered horse in a metal capsule stuck up his ass [suggesting places to search]. Or how to check inside the boot of a guy you're frisking, some of these dudes carry blades in there. Or how to puncture the taillight of a car you're following, so the rear end shows one red light and one white and is easier to spot. Or how an undercover cop should wear mirrored sunglasses, so that he can stop to polish them and use the glasses like a rearview mirror.[9]

Smart means, whether widely used or used by just one information-sharing unit, all have the same quality. They are used because it is believed that these means are really effective. But, whether these means are actually effective is an empirical question. After all, a given group could be wrong for many reasons: its data could be inaccurate; it might be too emotionally involved to come to correct conclusions (see below, Case 4.2). Further, even if smart means are actually effective, it is sometimes questionable whether they are desirable. For example, a group could develop actually effective smart means to take payoffs from mobsters. The group has a technique which guarantees (1) that the payoffs always get paid and (2) that those receiving bribes never get caught. Most readers will probably agree that this actually effective smart means is undesirable. It is undesirable because the goal is generally considered both immoral and illegal.

Private Means and Private Goals

Private means are personal strategies based on personal experiences. The use of private means represents a rejection of both proper means and smart means. Those who use private means become double deviants; hence they are likely to be punished by two types of punishing agents. Take, for example, Officer Q, who uses private means in dealing with S cases. Q is likely to incur the wrath of his superiors for not using proper means. Additionally, Q is likely to be shunned by his peers for not using smart means. Moreover, Q's ability to hide his deviant behavior (from both superiors and the general public) is weakened, because his peer group is not likely to help him hide his deviations from the proper when its strategies (smart means) have also been rejected. Put otherwise, like other professionals, police officers "run interference for each other" when smart means are used in place of proper means. However, those who replace proper means with private means make themselves marginal members of the work group. What reason would the group have to protect its marginals?

Those who pursue private goals are in much the same position as those who use private means. They too are double deviants. They too are likely to be punished by two punishing agents — superiors and peers. And they too are not likely to get any protection from the peer group. However, the use of private goals is a more serious offense than the use of private means. As noted, goals are more visible than means. Further, and generally, the use of private goals does more to change the quality of life of the society than the use of private means.

Following Smart/Proper Analysis each type of means discussed — proper, smart, and private — can be mixed or used together with each type of goal discussed: proper, smart, and private. Theoretically, then, nine kinds of mixes or strategies-of-action exist. However, while nine strategies can be identified, it is likely that some strategies are more often used than others. The relative popularity of different strategies for different types of police work is currently unknown by us. And some of our future research will try to nail down this question. Based on impressionistic evidence, we hypothesize that three strategies are most popular. Additionally, we hypothesize that the order of popularity is as follows: (1) most popular is the sP mix or smart means for proper goals; (2) second in popularity is the pP strategy or proper means for proper goals; and (3) the last of the most popular strategies is zP or private means for proper goals. We go on to briefly describe these there "mixes" or strategies of action.

Smart Means for Proper Goals (sP strategy)

We believe that the sP strategy is the one most frequently used by police officers for both empirical and hypothetical reasons. First, as noted, we have impressionistic data that support this belief. Second, we have several general hypotheses (GH) that lead us to the same conclusion.

GH 1: Smart means *tend to be more effective* than proper means.

GH 2: Smart means when used for proper goals create a strong spirit of camaraderie among the police officers who use it. There are here (generally) what are considered by the officers "minor irregularities for noble ends." These irregularities include "cutting through red tape" and "getting the job done that we are paid to do."

GH 3: Smart means used for proper goals are protected by a powerful veil of secrecy. The officers using smart means, obviously, keep them secret. The group as a whole helps to protect each member in the use of smart means. And superiors who happen to discover that smart means are being used for proper goals will tend to rationalize this behavior. Rationalizations used include the American cultural principle: "The ends justify the means."

GH 4: Smart means used for proper goals develop a special kind of invisibility. This invisibility of irregularities that "need to be done" seems to be a function of the blind-eye response. The blind-eye response—not seeing what is best not seen—helps maintain a high level of secrecy for the sP strategy. This high level of secrecy lowers the level of risk of using nonproper means.

In sum, we believe that in using the sP strategy officers increase the probability of effectiveness while incurring a low level of risk.

The popularity of sP, clearly, remains to be tested by research. However, we expect that under certain conditions, where a case is well publicized, the sP strategy will be avoided (see Case 1).

Proper Means Used for Proper Goals (pP strategy)

Those who regularly use the pP strategy are unwilling to risk being caught by unsympathetic superiors. This strategy is not lacking in costs. As previously stated, we believe that smart means tend to be more effective that proper means. Hence police officers who never use smart means will tend to do a poor job, even though all their behavior is lawful. Further, since they belong to a workforce, initially (at least) attempts will be made to have them join other officers in the use of smart means. As they continue to resist such attempts, they will be defined as "outsiders" or unloyal members of the information-sharing unit. It is likely that information shared by this unit will be kept away from these pP strategists. This lonely and ineffective existence is not likely to attract many police officers. We hypothesize, therefore, that there are fewer pP strategists than sP strategists.

Private Means Used for Proper Goals (zP Strategy)

The pursuit of proper goals is a lawful, respectable pursuit. It represents an attempt to increase the level of justice and to improve the quality of life. Police officers motivated by such noble purposes are likely to be irritated by the fact that the proper means given to them by society tend to hamper them in the pursuit of their proper goals. A reasonable move is to switch to means which are likely to be more effective. The move from proper to smart means is therefore very understandable. Why would a police officer reject the means developed by his peer group? After all, we tend to believe that "two heads are better than one." Many heads, therefore, should be many times better than one. Moreover, there is the risk factor. The group tends to protect its members.

The zP strategist is a strange kind of loner, idealistic as to goals and idiosyncratic as to means. The consequences of zP strategies depend on the degree of their success and the kinds of cases. To facilitate future research, let us distinguish some types of zP strategists. The crazy zP is rarely successful. This actor is protected by neither the rules (i.e., proper rules) nor the work group. Further, there is not even the excuse of "Well, G really does a good job. So let's ignore his weird ways." There is no blind-eye protection for the crazy zP. Predictably this actor will soon be on the streets, looking for another job.

The art-ball zP is the police officer who is about as successful as the average officer on the force and continually rejects both proper means and smart means. The motivations of this officer are difficult to fathom. For the strange kick of being different, the art-ball zP becomes a marginal member of the work group. Curiously, higher risks are taken by following private means, yet the rewards are but average.

It is when zP strategists have dramatic success that everyone — superiors, peers, the public — gets very fascinated with their activities. Very successful zPs play the "Dirty Harry" role. Their successes make them public figures. For most of the society they are heroes. Yet, it soon becomes known, they do not use proper means. Protectors of the proper — powerful church leaders, civil rights advocates — scream against the Dirty Harry style: "The Law Must Be Obeyed!" they keep repeating.

What to do with Dirty Harry types is indeed a problem. They seek to rid society of its criminals, and, important as their work is, there is the law — effective or ineffective. Dirty Harry shows up the law for its flaws, attacks given smart rules for their inadequacies, yet yells a religious message: Evil must be rooted out of this land! Little wonder that Dirty Harry movies make millions of dollars. But what should be done with the officers who play Dirty Harry in real life?

It seems clear to us that putting these three types of means (proper, smart, and private) with three types of goals (proper, smart, and private) sheds a new light on policing. We will continue our attempt to demonstrate that fact by providing illustrative examples of the nine strategies identified.

Case 1: Proper Means Used for Proper Goals (coded pP)

It is always a proper goal to find, capture, and bring to trial the perpetrator of a crime. Although police officers have been found to have other reasons for taking persons into custody (Milner 1971), there are special conditions under which police officers are virtually compelled by events into using proper means for proper goals. Such conditions exist when there is a great public outcry to find and convict an offender, as has been the case in the highly publicized "Son of Sam" in New York and the Williams child murders in Atlanta. In cases like these, the use of proper means may not be essential in developing leads and in finding suspects. However, once a suspect is identified, police investigators are likely to use proper means in seeking evidence under a suspect's control and in interrogating suspects. With the top police administrators, the public, and the media all following developments closely, police behavior regarding a suspect becomes subject to intense scrutiny. By strictly limiting themselves to proper means, police investigators give up many effective strategies for gathering evidence. But the use of essentially proper means also increases the likelihood that the offender, once brought to trial, will be convicted.

Case 2: Proper Means Used for Smart Goals (coded pS)

In discussions with detectives, Westly was taught the value of creating good sources of information. As he put it:

> You get them [stool pigeons] by arresting them for minor cases and doing them favors, like charging them with [only] 1 out of 5 [possible] offenses. Prostitutes are especially good [as stool pigeons] because they get around a good deal. (1970: 40)

Westly actually learned three rules which detectives consider smart. First, you must keep adding to your supply of stool pigeons. Second, stool pigeons can be caught by threatening them with serious charges and then offering them deals. Third, prostitutes, since they meet a lot of lawbreakers, make good informers. Creating a team of stool-pigeon prostitutes is considered a smart goal. By pursuing this smart goal with proper means, by breaking no laws in the manner of arrest, the detectives insure themselves against charges of illegal arrest. Prostitutes, lacking legal loopholes in this type of situation, are likely to negotiate with detectives. Put another way, in this situation prostitutes plea bargain on the streets. They assume informer assignments and are rewarded with lesser charges.

Case 3: Proper Means Used for Private Goals (coded pZ)

In the case known as the "Largo Eight" (Lawrence, Mass. *Eagle-Tribune* 1982) detectives handcuffed and brought to jail eight octogenarian penny ante poker players. The arrest generated much negative publicity in the press, and the police department and the community it served suffered considerable ridicule. In this instance, even though the police used proper means, they were used for goals which were neither proper (supported by the general public) nor smart (supported by their peer group). For reasons which are unclear a detective decided to go strictly by the letter of the law and to use this strict interpretation for a minor infringement of the law by the elderly. This case indicates that, at times, a gap exists between what the law says and what the law means, as widely and commonly interpreted. Where such a gap exists, the proper represents the latter—the law as commonly interpreted. The public expects police to go after "real" crime and not elderly, petty gamblers. Citizens are critical of police officers who bring embarrassment and national ridicule on themselves and their community. Gambling is a basic aspect of our free enterprise culture. We admire people who take risks, especially when their risk taking produces large profits. Penny ante gambling is neither admired nor considered wrong. It is an acceptable, time-consuming game, particularly so for the elderly.

Case 4: Smart Means Used for Proper Goals (coded sP)

4.1: When testifying in the courtroom, police officers sometimes fill in the gaps to make the testimony sound right (Rubenstein 1973). Officers know that if they testify in a certain way, a conviction is more likely. Such false testifying in order to convict a "known criminal" is often considered a smart means for a proper goal. The argument is: right-sounding testimony closes loopholes in the law which defense attorneys could use to thwart a conviction and expose police officers to civil liability.

4.2: In *Mincey v. Arizona* (1978), police officers conducted an extensive four-day warrantless search of an apartment in which an undercover officer had been killed during a narcotics raid. The search yielded between 200 and 300 objects which were used by the prosecution to convict Mincey of murder. The United States Supreme Court unanimously reversed the Arizona state courts. The Supreme Court ruled:

> The Fourth Amendment proscribes all unreasonable searches and seizures, and it is a cardinal principle that searches conducted outside the judicial process, without prior approval by a judge or magistrate, are per se unreasonable under the Fourth Amendment—subject only to a few specifically established and well-delineated exceptions. . . . We decline to hold that the seriousness of the offense under investigation itself, a homicide in this case, creates exigent circumstances of the kind that under the Fourth Amendment justify a warrantless search.[10]

The police decision to ignore the warrant-getting route is understandable; a police officer had been killed, and there was much anger, sadness, and frustration among his colleagues. The search provided a wealth of evidence which clearly established the identity of the murderer. However, the search was not effective, since it led to the reversal of the murder conviction. The government's appellate lawyers, called to defend the police before the Supreme Court, failed to persuade even a single justice to support their claim.

Mincey v. Arizona well illustrates the importance of a critical distinction made in Smart/Proper Analysis. Smart means are what some social unit considers smart: what is defined as effective, not what is necessarily effective. Some social units develop some smart means which (in actuality) are very ineffective. In these cases social units somehow come up with wrong conclusions. Perhaps the data they share contain some inaccuracies. Or, as in this case, perhaps the emotional climate is such that rational analysis is absent. To use an illegal search, generally, is to invite a court decision in favor of the alleged criminal.

Case 5: Smart Means Used for Smart Goals (coded sS)

Brown reports the following case history based on his research in California:

> While cruising his beat, a patrolman recognized the brother of a man he had arrested earlier in the year for murder, driving down the street. The time was abut 2:00 a.m. The patrolman decided to stop him to see what he was doing. He was a Mexican-American youth, and a young white girl was in the car with him. He had no identification nor any proof that the car was his. The officer informed the youth that he could be arrested for no identification (see 40302A C.V.C. and Grand Auto Theft), but since he (the patrolman) knew him, he would not be arrested. The youth was released after being given a stern warning. Later the patrolman said that "the kid's problem was that he was just plain dumb" and that one had to "get on him once in a while in order to keep him in line." (1981: 173)

In this case, because there were no facts or circumstances which reasonably connected the youth's driving to any offense, the officer had no lawful right to stop the vehicle—not even for a license and registration check.[11] The means used, therefore, were not proper. But, for the patrolman and his peers, such means were smart because (1) the youth was not expected to know that this was an illegal stopping, (2) the youth had kin links to a murderer, and (3) this was not a normal time to be out for a drive. Having stopped the youth and discovered a lack of identification and no proof of ownership of the vehicle he was driving, an arrest could have been made. Had the arrest been made, the police officer would have been using the *sP* strategy—using a smart means for a proper goal. However, the officer decided to follow a smart goal, as defined by his peers, namely, not to arrest for a petty crime when an arrest might push the rule breaker into bigger felonies in the future, while a nonarrest might be used to teach the youth how to live within the law. Here, as in Case 2, some kind of street plea bargaining was taking place. In essence, the police officer was trying to make a bargain with the youth: "I could arrest you now, but I won't. In return for this favor I want to see you live within the law." It would be valuable to interview many police officers who have made similar bargains and see how they worked out. Two important questions are: Do such bargains tend to help youths avoid a criminal career? Do such bargains tend to send the message "It's good to know a cop; he or she will help you get away with law breaking"?

Case 6: Smart Means Used for Private Goals (coded sZ)

Muir (1977: 71–73), in his study of the Laconia (N. H.) Police Department discussed an "old-time policeman" called Bee Heywood. Heywood's goal was to intimidate and dominate the skid-row inhabitants of his patrol district. His methods involved brutality or the threat of brutality. Heywood's methods were defined as smart by some of his peers. By fighting with savagery and by appearing to be savage, Heywood and like-minded partners believed they could force even a hostile crowd into submission. However, the goal of long-term domination and intimidation was not considered a smart goal. It was a goal which "belonged" to Heywood, one that had more to do with his personality than with the needs of the situation. Using this private goal, Heywood created a garrison state out of his beat. In this environment Heywood had to be preoccupied with the tasks of self-defense. He had to worry constantly about ambush and reprisals. Heywood was on his own; he could count on no community assistance should he run into trouble.

It should be noted that Heywood was pursuing a private goal which runs counter to major principles found in American culture. In situations of this type – where a goal is considered wrong by the larger society – questions concerning means are almost irrelevant. If the means that Heywood's clique defined as smart proved to be really effective, then a garrison state was maintained in a society which is totally against garrison states. If the means defined as smart proved to be ineffective, then, positively, a garrison state would soon disappear, and, negatively, a community would exist lacking in both law and order. It seems safe to conclude that private goals of police officers are likely to be considered undesirable by the public-at-large and by most police officers. Private goals, therefore, merit very careful scrutiny by responsible members of the policing system.

Case 7: Private Means Used for Proper Goals (coded zP)

During an arrest of a factually guilty individual, the investigating officer forged the defendant's name on a Miranda waiver form.[12] It is unknown how often the same officer got away with using this personal means of dealing with lawbreakers. In this case it backfired. After the officer attempted to use the forgery to establish a voluntary and knowing waiver of the defendant's Fifth Amendment rights, the defendant hired a very capable attorney.

The attorney was able to get the state's crime laboratory to analyze the signatures of both the police officer and the defendant and compare them with the one on the waiver form. The report from the crime laboratory concluded that the signature on the waiver probably belonged to the investigating officer. The officer was trying to get a conviction in court of a person he considered to be guilty. The goal was proper. The means, however, was the private means of the arresting officer.

It is our belief that forging a defendant's name will rarely be defined as a smart means by any group of officers. We base this hypothesis on the fact that it is possible to subject writings to analysis by crime laboratory technicians and determine those which are forgeries. Forgeries, once discovered, can result in civil penalties, criminal penalties, and departmental discipline for the forger.

Case 8: Private Means Used for Smart Goals (coded zS)

A police officer (we call him K) pursued a goal of harassing people suspected of drug dealing. K's goal was shared by the officers with whom he worked and interacted; it was a smart goal. At times, however, K used a private means in pursuit of this goal. He sometimes searched the homes of those suspected of being in the drug trade without having obtained a search warrant. During one such search of an apartment (of someone we call "Smith"), K found evidence that Smith was manufacturing a controlled substance. Smith was properly charged, prosecuted, and, after pleading guilty, sentenced to twenty years in prison.

On the advice of his attorney Smith filed a civil suit against K. Smith's claim, that his Fourth Amendment rights were infringed, was upheld by the court. Officer K suffered seriously from this suit. Officer K's department also suffered from the negative publicity which followed this case. And policing as a whole, it is reasonable to assume, got negative publicity.

This case[13] requires a two-act scenario for an accurate description. Act 1 presents Officer K searching without a warrant (using z or private means) to harass a suspected criminal (for an S or smart goal). Act 1 is well coded zS. But Act 1 produces evidence for a new goal. Therefore, Act 1 as a whole must be considered as a means for this new goal. Now zS (together) have become the means for putting criminals in prison. Putting criminals in prison is a proper goal; so what we have here is a complex means, zS, used for a proper goal. Accurately coded, this case is zS-P. Spelled out, this becomes: "Pursuing a smart goal with private means in order to *later* pursue a proper goal."

This case seems to show that Smart and Proper Strategies is more than a way of describing nine strategies of action. SAPS does describe nine strategies. However, each strategy can be considered as an attempt to reach a goal at time t. Each goal achieved at time t can become a means for a later goal at time $t + x$.

Case 9: Private Means Used for Private Goals (coded zZ)

Rubenstein (1973) reports a lecture given to police recruits in Philadelphia. The topic was bribes. The reason for this lecture, we assume, is that some police officers have as a private goal trying to get bribes. This private goal can be pursued in many ways. Some officers use as their private means the threat of giving someone a traffic ticket. We make these assumptions about this private goal (getting bribes) and about this private means (using the power of ticketing) to explain the need of the lecture. If this goal and these means did not exist, the lecture would be unnecessary.

The lecture included the following messages:

Listen, fellas, let me tell you something you should know, since it's gonna come up as soon as you get on the street. We ain't supposed to talk this way, but it's important for you to know. Don't fuck with a motorist. Don't take a note from him. He's not like a prostitute or a numbers writer. If he complains, you are going to be in real trouble. If you pull a guy over for something and he cops a plea about not knowin' the neighborhood, you can go with that. If he offers you a little something for a cup of coffee or lunch, well, that's your business. But don't go out there and pinch him for a note. That's a stupid fuckin' note and there's no sense blowin' a good job for a nickel or dime. You understand me?

SUMMARY AND CONCLUSIONS

Culture has been presented as a guidance system for proper action. This guidance system for properness seems to have two primary units: *principles* which describe, define, and explain that which is proper and *rules* for proper action. Our focus has been on proper rules and their major enemy, smart rules. This conflict between the proper and the smart — between a desire to be good, correct, moral, and aesthetic (on the one hand) and a desire to survive with comfort and power (on the other hand) — seems to form the bedrock of human existence. This bedrock of conflict appears to get more dense the deeper we dig into its foundations.

First, being smart seems to mean two things to most people: using the wisdom of the group (work group, play group) — learning the ropes, using street smarts, discovering the routes around red tape — and using the wisdom gleaned from personal experience. These two kinds of wisdom need to be distinguished, and they are in Smart/Proper Analysis. The group's wisdom is called smart rules and the individual's wisdom private rules.

Second, the nature of this wisdom requires careful thought. Both smart rules and private rules are what people think are effective or desirable in given situations. These rules are defined as useful by their users. Whether they are really (empirically speaking) effective is a question to be answered by research. Whether they are really desirable is a question to be probed from different perspectives: Who are they good for? Does anyone else get harmed by them? These and similar questions require thoughtful consideration.

Third, by describing some rules as proper (i.e., as rules for proper action), there is no necessary implication that such rules are definitely impractical or ineffective. Rather, by describing some rules as proper rules, the implication is whether or not these rules are effective is not the point. Proper rules are not created to be effective. Indeed, when we ask about effectiveness concerning proper rules, the very question seems ludicrous. Is "Three strikes and you're out" effective? Is it effective that in chess "Bishops can only move on diagonals?" No, proper rules are not created to be effective. What, then, are they created for? At this point we are touching on the meaning of human.

Feathers (some say) tell one peacock that another animal that has them is a peacock. Proper action (it could be said) tells one human that another animal who is doing it is a human being. The proper—as it can be interpreted in behavior, speech, sentiment, belief, dress—is defined by a social unit called a "society." The set of definitions provided, essentially, has little to do with being effective, with surviving, obtaining comforts, and achieving power. Yes, there are proper ways of doing all of these things. But their achievement is not the point of proper rules. Proper rules seem to be based on three assumptions. First, humans *need to be proper*. Second, this need can be satisfied by the dictates of a major social unit. Third, creating properness, like cooking, takes time; properness includes an ingredient called "tradition."

Why do we need to live properly? This question is about as easy to answer as: Why do we enjoy art? Indeed, following anthropologist Sir Edmund Leach, because we do enjoy art, we need to live properly. Proper living—living by a culture's dictates—then becomes an attempt to transform beastly living into an art form—into something beautiful.[14] But Beauty needs the knowledge of the Beast. And the Beast has desires for Beauty. So we human beings are stuck with the Human Dilemma.

The Human Dilemma, as conceptualized by Smart/Proper Analysis, becomes transformed from a simple smart or proper to a set of choices. Nine strategies exist to be used. The sP strategy is ranked "first in popularity" due to our beliefs that: (1) the American cultural principle, the end justifies the means, is just as influential in policing as it is in other activities; (2) smart means tend to be more effective than proper means or private means; (3) police officers want their work to be effective; (4) police officers try to minimize the risks of effective action; (5) smart means minimize the risk of effective action; (6) minimal risks attached to smart means are a function of the veil of secrecy that tends to cover them; and (7) when smart means are used for proper ends, the risks are yet further reduced, since such a strategy generates a blind-eye response from superiors.

We place the pP strategy next in popularity because the third (zP) has all the problems already discussed. As noted, even the very effective zP (the Dirty Harry type) has many problems surviving in a job. The zP strategy is based on defining the Good Life as the life of a loner. We do not think many people live by that definition of the good life.

In sum, the analysis presented has restructured the gap problem. An amorphous space—a big black hole—has been changed into living (actually, lived-in) cells. Each cell is a strategy of action which can be investigated. How frequently is a given cell used? Are some cells (say, smart means for proper goals, Cell 4) most frequently used by certain types of police officers? Are there clear relationships between types of personalities and the use of given cells? How, very precisely, does a social unit develop smart rules? What kinds of pressures exist on members of a social unit to follow smart rules? How do smart rules from Social Unit S "travel"? That is, how do they get to be known by members of Social Units P, Q, R, and S? What conditions are actually favorable to a blind-eye response? Have some smart rules actually become proper rules? If so, how did this transformation occur? These and related questions can be systematically investigated. And as data flow in, we suspect, they will force a rethinking of the nature of the law.

If the law is "holy" or perfect, then police officers who (at times) avoid and evade the law are bad people. However, if the law is considered an honest, and understandably imperfect, attempt to do a job, then police officers who (at times) evade or avoid the law may be good people trying to do a good job. Put otherwise, it is reasonable to assume that parts of the law are flawed. The flaws we have in mind related to practical matters rather than abstract issues of justice (cf. Rawls 1973). A growing distrust of police officers seems to have led to many rules which impede rather than aid the goals of policing. Along with Brown, we believe that

> enveloping policemen in a maze of institutional controls without grappling with the grimy realities of police work does not necessarily promote accountability and may only exacerbate matters. (1981: 303)

Smart/Proper Analysis seems to provide better tools to grapple with the grimy realities of police work. Well used, these tools should provide data to help us change the law where it is flawed and change policing where it is flawed. In short, change is needed, but change based on good evidence. In the words of Richard Greene:

> Sure, the legal system needs reform. But a better understanding of how things work is a logical first step. Any good lawyer will tell you that the facts are always more persuasive than rhetoric. (1984: 66)

NOTES

It is a pleasure to acknowledge, with gratitude, the valuable editorial work done by Marilyn Churchill and Ann Gross.

1. Culture as standards "for deciding what is... what can be done... how one feels about it... what to do about... how to go about doing it" (Goodenough 1981) has influenced the work of many cultural anthropologists.

2. Both "Smart/Proper Analysis" and its debt to philosophical writings will be fully explained in Freilich, *Culture in a New Key* (forthcoming). Philosophers, long on logic and short on data, are marvelous associates for anthropologists. Anthropologists, (almost) drowning in data, can use conceptualizations of philosophers to develop more elegant models.

3. Many illustrative cases could be cited, but the following exemplify the changing interpretation of the Constitution: *Wolf v. Colorado*, 338 U. S. 25 (1949); *Mapp v. Ohio*, 367 U. S. 643 (1961); *Miranda v. Arizona*, 384 U. S. 436 (1966).

4. The Ohio Revised Code in Section 737.11 is a typical example: "The police force of a municipal corporation shall preserve the peace, protect persons and property, and obey and enforce all laws of the state and the United States...."

5.   James Q. Wilson (1968) found that only 10.3 percent of the calls in his study of the Syracuse police related to law enforcement. Much of what officers do involves tasks such as finding lost children, directing traffic, managing domestic disputes and landlord-tenant squabbles, and maintaining a visible presence within the community.

6.   The 1975 National Crime Survey is discussed in *U. S., Department of Justice* (1977); the 1966 survey is discussed in *President's Commission on Law Enforcement and Administration of Justice* (1968).

7.   Many of the specific solutions flowing from these perspectives have considered policing on an ad hoc basis, thus ignoring the impact that one rule change may have on the entire matrix of related policing problems (Goldstein 1967b). The few systematic attempts to redefine the police role generally gave been ignored. Indeed, even the prestigious joint proposal of the American Bar Association and the International Association of Chiefs of Police (The Urban Police Function, 1973) has failed to receive legislative endorsement (see also J. Goldstein 1960; Remington and Rosenblum 1960; Davis 1969, 1975). Following Brown (1981), reform efforts fall into several types based, respectively, on the policy-making model, the professional model, the community-control model, and the team-policing model. Each model, according to Brown, has serious flaws.

8.   Each of the research projects noted is summarized, respectively, in the writings of Firth (1939), Das (1945), Page (1946–1947), Opler (1947), Berliner (1952), Blau (1955), Meggit (1964), Malinowski (1966), Liebow (1967), Roberts and Gregor (1971), Stone (1979), Freilich (1980), and D. Wilson (1981).

9.   This quotation comes from an ex-police officer turned novelist, Lawrence Sanders (1978).

10.   *Mincey v. Arizona*, 437 U. S. 385 (1978).

11.   In the case of *Delaware v. Prouse*, 440 U. S. 648 (1979), the Supreme Court by a vote of 8–1 held that random vehicle stops solely to check an operator's license and registration are unreasonable under the Fourth Amendment.

12.   A Miranda waiver form is a document used by police officers in conjunction with custodial police interrogations. The first part of the form consists of the printed Miranda warnings. A signature line follows the warnings. If the person to be interrogated, after reading the warnings, wishes to waive the Miranda protections, the person will be asked to sign the waiver on the signature line. The second part of the form consists of space in which the statement is either handwritten or typed. A signature line is located at the end of the statement.

13.   *Haring v. Prosise*, 462 U. S. 306 (1983).

14.   Leach has written : "Logically, aesthetics and ethics are identical. If we wish to understand the ethical rules of society, it is aesthetics we must study" (1954: 17) (cf. Santayana 1955).

REFERENCES

Aaronson, D. E., C. T. Dienes, and M. C. Musheno
  1984   *Public Policy and Police Discretion*. New York: Clark Boardman.

Allen, B., and D. Bosta
  1981   *Games Criminals Play: How You Can Profit from Knowing Them*. Susanville, Calif.: Rae John.

American Bar Association and the International Association of Chiefs of Police
    1973   *Standards Relating to the Urban Police Function.* Chicago: American Bar
            Association

American Law Institute
    1966   *A Model Code of Pre-Arraignment Procedure.* Philadelphia: American Law
            Institute.

Bailey, F. G.
    1968   Parapolitical Systems. *Local Level Politics.* M. J. Swartz, ed. Chicago: Aldine

Berliner, J. S.
    1952   "The Informal Organization of a Soviet Firm." *The Quarterly Journal of
            Economics* 66: 342–65.

Bittner, E.
    1970   *The Functions of the Police in Modern Society.* Washington D.C.: United
            States Government Printing Office.

    1983   "Legality and Workmanship: Introduction to Control in the Police Organiza-
            tion." In *Control in the Police Organization.* M. Punch, ed. Cambridge, Mass.
            MIT Press.

Blau, P. M.
    1955   *The Dynamics of Bureaucracy.* Chicago: University of Chicago Press.

Bourdieu, Pierre
    1979   *Outline of a Theory of Practice.* Cambridge: Cambridge University Press.

Brown, M. K.
    1981   *Working the Street.* New York: Russell Sage Foundation.

Cavell, Stanley
    1982   *The Claim of Reason.* Oxford: Oxford University Press.

Chagnon, Napoleon A.
    1977   *Yanomamö: The Fierce People.* New York: Holt, Rinehart & Winston.

Clinard, M. B., ed.
    1964   *Anomie and Deviant Behavior.* New York: Free Press of Glencoe.

Cohen, A. K.
    1965   "The Sociology of the Deviant Act: Anomie Theory and Beyond." *American
            Sociological Review* 30: 5–14.

Cole, S.
    1957   "The Growth of Scientific Knowledge: Theories of Deviance as a Case
            Study." In *The Ideal of Social Structure.* L. A. Coser, ed. New York: Harcourt
            Brace Jovanovich.

Coser, Lewis A., et al.
    1983   *Introduction to Sociology.* New York: Harcourt Brace Jovanovich.

Das, T.
    1945   *The Purums.* Calcutta: University of Calcutta Press.

Davis, K. C.
    1975   *Police Discretion.* St. Paul, Minn.: West.

    1974   "An Approach to Legal Control of the Police." *Texas Law Review* 52: 703–25.

    1969   *Discretionary Justice.* Baton Rouge: Louisiana State University Press.

Dexter, L.
    1981   "Marketers, Not Donors." *Society* 18 (6): 58–61.

Diamond, Stanley
    1972   Review of *Man and Culture: A Philosophical Anthropology.* A. W. Levy, ed. *American Anthropologist* 74: 10.

Diggs, B. J.
    1964   "Rules and Utilitarianism." *American Philosophical Quarterly* 1: 32–42.

Dougherty, R.
    1964   "The Case for the Cop." *Harper's Magazine* (April 1964): 129–33.

Drabek, T.
    1968   *Disaster in Aisle 13.* Columbus, Ohio: Disaster Research Center, The Ohio State University.

Durkheim, Émile
    1953   "Value Judgments and Judgments of Reality." In *Sociology and Philosophy,* D. F. Pocock, trans. Glencoe, Ill.: Free Press.

Dworkin, Ronald
    1967   "The Model of Rules." *University of Chicago Law Review* 35: 14–46.

Finckenauer, J.
    1976   "Some Factors in Police Discretion and Decision Making." *Journal of Criminal Justice* 4: 29–46.

Firth, Raymond
    1939   *Primitive Polynesian Economics.* London: Routledge.

Freilich, Morris
    In   "Smart Rules, Proper Rules, and Deviance." In Morris Freilich et al., eds.
    press *Deviance: Cross-Cultural Perspectives.* Granby, Mass.: Bergin & Garvey.

    1983   "Beauty in the Beast." Introduction to *The Pleasures of Anthropology.* M. Freilich, ed. New York: New American Library (Mentor Books).

    1980   "Smart-Sex and Proper-Sex: A Paradigm Found." *Central Issues in Anthropology* 2: 37–51.

    1978   "The Meaning of 'Sociocultural.'" In *The Concept and Dynamic of Culture.* B. Bernardi, ed. The Hague: Mouton.

    1975   "Myth, Method, and Madness." *Current Anthropology* 16: 207–26.

Freilich, Morris, and Frank A. Schubert
    1984   "Boston Police Rules 1850–1890: An Analysis of Smart and Proper." Paper presented at the Annual Meeting of the Academy of Criminal Justice Sciences. Chicago, Ill.

    1983   "Police Discretion: A Matter of Proper and Smart." Paper presented at the Annual Meeting of the Academy of Criminal Justice Sciences. San Antonio, Tex.

Gardiner, J. A.
    1969   *Traffic and the Police: Variations in Law-Enforcement Policy.* Cambridge, Mass: Harvard University Press.

Giddens, Anthony
    1976   *Central Problems in Social Theory: Action, Structure and Contradiction in Social Analysis.* Berkeley: University of California Press.

Goffman, Erving
    1959   *The Presentation of Self in Everyday Life.* New York: Doubleday.

Goldstein, H.
    1977   *Policing a Free Society.* Cambridge, Mass.: Ballinger.

1967a "Administrative Problems in Controlling the Exercise of Police Authority." *Journal of Criminal Law, Criminology and Police Science* 58: 160–72.

1967b "Police Policy Formulation: A Proposal for Improving Police Performance." *Michigan Law Review* 65: 1123–46.

1963 "Police Discretion: The Ideal Versus the Real." *Public Administration Review* 23: 140–8.

Goldstein, J.

1960 "Police Discretion Not to Invoke the Criminal Process." *Yale Law Journal* 69: 543–94.

Goodenough, Ward H.

1981 *Culture, Language and Society.* Menlo Park, Calif.: Benjamin/Cummings.

Green, R.

1984 "Law by the Numbers." *Forbes Magazine* (January): 66.

Hall, E. T.

1969 *The Silent Language.* Greenwich, Conn.: Fawcett.

Hocart, A. M.

1970 *The Life-Giving Myth and Other Essays.* Rodney Needham, ed. London: Methuen.

Howard, A.

1963 "Land, Activity Systems and Decision-Making Models in Rotuma." *Ethnology* 2: 4077–440.

Hunn, Eugene

1982 "The Utilitarian Factor in Folk Biological Classification." *American Anthropologist* 84 (4): 830–47.

Hymes, Dell

1970 "Discovering Oral Performance and Measured Verse in American Indian Narrative." *New Literary History* 20: 431–57.

Jacob, H.

1978 *Justice in America: Courts, Lawyers, and the Judicial Process.* Boston: Little, Brown.

Kamisar, Y.

1965 "When the Cops Were Not Handcuffed." *New York Times* (November 7): 34.

Kant, Immanuel

1966 *The Fundamental Principles of the Metaphysics of Ethics.* O. Manthey-Zorn, trans. and introduction. New York: Appleton-Century Crofts.

Kroeber, Alfred L.

1957 *Style and Civilization.* Ithaca: Cornell University Press.

1952 *The Nature of Culture.* Chicago: University of Chicago Press.

Largo Eight

1982 *Eagle-Tribune* (Lawrence, Mass.), February 8, p. 8.

Leach, Edmund

1961 *Pul Elia: A Village in Ceylon.* Cambridge: Cambridge University Press.

1954 *Political Systems in Highland Burma* London: Bell.

Liebow, Elliot

1967 *Tally's Corner.* Boston: Little, Brown.

Lundman, R. J.
  1974 "Routine Police Arrest Practices: A Commonwealth Perspective." *Social Problems* 22: 128–41.

Malinowski, Bronislaw
  1966 *Crime and Custom in Savage Society*. New York: Humanities.

Marcuse, Herbert
  1964 *One Dimensional Man*. Boston: Beacon.

Merton, Robert K.
  1957 *Social Theory and Social Structure*. Glencoe, Ill.: Free Press.

Meggit, M. J.
  1964 "Male-Female Relations in the Highlands of Australian New Guinea." *American Anthropologist* (special issue): 204–24.

Milner, N.
  1971 "Supreme Court Effectiveness and the Police Organization." *Law and Contemporary Problems* 36: 359–95.

Moran, T., and Cooper, J.
  1983 *Discretion and the Criminal Justice Process*. Port Washington, N. Y.: Associated Faculty Press.

Muir, W. K., Jr.
  1977 *Police: Street-Corner Politicians*. Chicago: University of Chicago Press.

Opler, M.
  1947 "Rules and Practice in Jicarilla Apache Affinal Relatives." *American Anthropologist* 49: 453–62.

Page, C.
  1946–47"Bureaucracy's Other Face." *Social Forces* 25: 89–94.

President's Commission on Law Enforcement and Administration of Justice
  1968 *The Challenge of Crime in a Free Society*. New York: Avon.

Rawls, John
  1973 *A Theory of Justice*. Cambridge, Mass.: Harvard University Press.

  1955 "Two Concepts of Rules." *Philosophical Review* 64: 3–32.

Redfield, Robert
  1953 *The Primitive World and Its Transformation*. Ithaca: Cornell University Press.

Reisman, W. M.
  1979 *Folded Lies: Bribery, Crusades, and Reforms*. New York: Free Press.

Remington, F., and Rosenbloom, W.
  1960 "The Criminal Law and the Legislative Process." *Illinois Law Forum* 60: 481–99.

Roberts, J. M., and Gregor, T.
  1971 "Privacy: A Cultural View." In *Privacy*, J. R. Penno and J. W. Chapman, eds. New York: Atherton.

Rubenstein, J.
  1973 *City Police*. New York: Farrar, Straus & Giroux.

Sanders, Lawrence
  1978 *The Second Deadly Sin*. New York: Putnam.

Santayana, George
  1955 *The Sense of Beauty*. New York: Dover.

Searle, J.
 1964   "How to Derive 'Ought' from 'Is.'" *Philosophical Review* 73: 43–58.
Shils, E.
 1981   *Tradition*. Chicago: University of Chicago Press.
Skolnick, J.
 1955   *Justice Without Trial*. New York: Wiley.
Slotkin, J. S.
 1950   *Social Anthropology*. New York: Macmillan.
Spacks, Patricia Meyer
 1983   "In Praise of Gossip." In *The Pleasures of Anthropology*, M. Freilich, ed. New York: New American Library.
Stoddard, E. R.
 1968   "'The Informal Code' of Police Deviancy: A Group Approach to 'Blue Coat Crime.'" *Journal of Criminal Law, Criminology, and Police Science* 59: 2.
Stone, M.
 1979   "Why Cheating Grows." *U. S. News and World Report* 87: 100.
Takagi, P.
 1974   "A Garrison State in a 'Democratic' Society." *Crime and Social Justice* 1 (Spring-Summer): 27–33.
Turk, A.
 1969   *Criminality and Legal Order*. Chicago: Rand-McNally.
Turner, R. H.
 1970   *Family Interaction*. New York: Wiley.
U. S. Commission on Civil Rights
 1979   *Police Practices and the Preservation of Civil Rights*. Washington, D. C.: U. S. Government Printing Office.
U. S. Department of Justice
 1977   *The Police and Public Opinion*. Washington, D. C.: U. S. Government Printing Office.
Van Maanen, J.
 1978   "The Asshole." In *Policing: A View from the Street*. P. K. Manning and J. Van Maanen, eds. Santa Monica, Calif.: Goodyear.
Weber, M.
 1947   *The Theory of Social and Economic Organization*. New York: Oxford University Press.
West, W. F.
 1983   "Institutionalizing Rationality in Regulatory Administration." *Public Administration Review* (July/August): 326–34.
Westly, W. A.
 1970   *Violence and the Police*. Cambridge, Mass.: MIT Press.
Wilson, D.
 1981   "Fudge Mixed with Politics Leaves a Bad Taste." In *The Meaning of Culture*, M. Freilich, ed. Cambridge, Mass.: Schenkman.
Wilson, James Q.
 1968   *Varieties of Police Behavior*. New York: Atheneum.

CONTRIBUTORS

KARIN R. ANDRIOLO, a professor of anthropology at the State University of New York at New Paltz, earned her Ph.D. at the University of Vienna. She has published widely in U.S. and German anthropological journals.

ROBERT BOYD, an assistant professor of anthropology at UCLA, received a Guggenheim Fellowship in 1988 for research on cultural evolution.

MARY DOUGLAS, who was educated at Oxford University, is presently Visiting Professor at Princeton University. She is the author of *Purity and Danger*, *Natural Symbols*, and *Risk and Culture* (with Aaron Wildavsky).

ROBERT DUNTON is currently studying philosophy at Louisiana State University as an Alumni Fellow.

MORRIS FREILICH, author of *Myth, Method, and Madness* and *The Natural Triad in Kinship and Complex Systems* and editor of *Marginal Natives: Anthropologists at Work*, is professor of anthropology and sociology at Northeastern University.

WARD GOODENOUGH is University Professor of Anthropology at the University of Pennsylvania, where he has taught since 1949.

EUGENE HUNN has conducted fieldwork on Tzeltal Maya in Mexico and Sahaptin Indians on the Columbia River. He teaches at the University of Washington in Seattle.

JUDITH A. PERROLLE, an associate professor of sociology at Northeastern University, is studying the effects of artificial intelligence and computerization on professional and technical work.

STEVE RAYNER, a member of the Research Staff of Oak Ridge National Laboratory, holds a Ph.D. in anthropology from University College, London. His current research addresses problems of global risk management.

MILES RICHARDSON is professor of anthropology at Louisiana State University.

PETER J. RICHERSON is professor of environmental studies and director of the Institute of Ecology at the University of California, Davis.

FRANK A. SCHUBERT, assistant professor of criminal justice at Northeastern University, formerly was a police administrator in Ohio and an assistant district attorney in Wisconsin.

SHARLEEN H. SIMPSON has graduate degrees in both nursing and anthropology and many years of applied experience in these fields. She presently teaches in the graduate program at the University of Florida College of Nursing.

ANTHONY F. C. WALLACE is University Professor of Anthropology at the University of Pennsylvania and the author, most recently, of *Rockdale* and *St. Clair.*

AARON WILDAVSKY is professor of political science and public policy at the University of California, Berkeley, and the author of *Risk and Culture* (with Mary Douglas) and *The Nursing Father: Moses as a Political Leader.*

INDEX

A

Altruism, 40, 134

Anthropological methods, 5, 6, 18–19, 122; comparative, 12–13; ecological, 93, 143; functional, 32, 120; humanistic, 75, 83, 88; interpretive, 11–13. *See also* Cognitive anthropology

Artificial intelligence (AI), 104, 105, 107, 146, 150, 155. *See also* Computers

Aztec sacrifices, interpretations, 16–17

B

Becker, Gary, 40

Biology, evolutionary, 123, 146

Boas, Franz, 5, 8; quoted, 4

Bourdieu, Pierre, 46

C

Cognitive anthropology, 144–46, 147, 154–55

Collective good, 42, 43, 45. *See also* Public good

Communication, 134–35, 189; cultural variations of, 195; and technology, 110–13

Community, 41–42, 44, 55, 64, 199; legitimation of, 48–54. *See also* Models of culture

Computers, 98, 102, 107, 108, 113. *See also* Artificial intelligence; Technology, acceptance of; Tools

Cultural adaptationalism, 10, 143

Cultural change, 4, 100, 105

Cultural evolution, 4, 111–13, 122, 124, 125, 128–29, 137, 156

Cultural ideationalism, 10, 17, 143

Cultural "maps," 11, 147

Cultural materialism, 15, 17, 143. *See also* Marvin Harris

Cultural Plan, 77, 78, 146, 150–54, 156; illustrated, 152, 155; relation to Image, 150–54

Cultural pluralism, 13, 31, 58, 135, 188–89

Cultural relativism, 200–2, 203, 204

Cultural theory, 7, 46–47, 63–65; predictive power of, 72–73, 123, 211

Cultural transmission, 111–13, 121, 122, 144; indirectly biased, 121; unbiased, 127

Culture: defined, 2, 6, 7, 9, 10, 60–61, 76, 93, 121, 145, 199; as evolutionary mechanism, 155; and high culture, 2–3; as human characteristic,